FLOWER TYPES

SPIKE   RACEME   CORYMB   PANICLE   UMBEL   CYME

COROLLA SHAPES

ROTATE   CAMPANULATE   FUNNELFORM   URCEOLATE   SALVERFORM

TREE AND SHRUB SHAPES

LOW TRAILING   ROUND COMPACT   HORIZONTAL SPREADING

ERECT   ARCHING   UPRIGHT

CONE   COLUMN   WEEPING   GLOBE   FASTIGIATE

Consultants
Dr. Laurie Hodges, University of Nebraska Horticulture Department
Mary Irish, Desert Botanical Garden, Phoenix, Arizona
Richard Isaacson, Minnesota Landscape Arboretum
Michael Maltas, Fetzer Organic Garden, Hopland, California
Aviva Toporoff, Chicago Botanic Garden
Janet Whippo, The New York Botanical Garden

Historical Consultant: Frank Anderson, former curator,
The New York Botanical Garden Library
Botany Consultant: Dr. Lucile M. McCook
Enabling Garden Consultant: Eugene Rothert,
Chicago Botanic Garden

vegetable
gardening

Callaway Gardens

By David Chambers
MANAGER, MR. CASON'S VEGETABLE GARDEN

and Lucinda Mays
SENIOR CURATOR, THE VICTORY GARDEN

With Laura C. Martin

Series Editor: Elvin McDonald
Principal Photographer: Sylvia Martin
Preface: Dr. William E. Barrick

Pantheon Books,
Knopf Publishing Group
New York
1994

Acknowledgments
This book was created with the help, expertise, and encouragement of a great many people. We would like to thank all the consultants who contributed so much to it, Laura Martin who helped us write it, and Sylvia Martin who took magnificent photographs. We also owe much to people at Callaway Gardens, including DeeAnna Chase, Magdaline Yanko, Bill Barrick, Susan Hadaway, Tom Brinda, and the vegetable garden Staff–Wiliam Clark, Edward Harris, Jerry Harris, Miriam Callihan, and Russell Allen. We also appreciate the efforts of Susan Ralston, Jennifer Bernstein, Ellen McNeilly, Jennifer Parkinson, Alan Kellock, Chani Yammer, Albert Squillace, Jay Hyams, Eric Marshall, Susan Kilpatrick, Shad Todd, James Giblin, Dale Ferguson, Kathy Sammis, Michelle Stein, and Deena Stein.

Project Director: Lori Stein
Book Design Consultant: Albert Squillace
Editorial Director: Jay Hyams
Associate Art Director: Eric Marshall

 Published in the United States by Pantheon Books, a division of Random House, Inc., New York, and simultaneously in Canada by Random House of Canada Limited, Toronto.

Library of Congress Cataloging-in-Publication Data
Chambers, David (James David)
Vegetable gardening / by David Chambers and Lucinda Mays, with Laura Martin ; preface by Dr. William E. Barrick ' principal photography by Sylvia Martin.–1st ed.
p cm. –(American garden guides)
Includes indexes
ISBN 0-679-41434-7 :
1. Vegetable gardening–United States. 2. Vegetable gardening–Canada. 3. Vegetables–Pictorial works. I. Mays, Lucinda II. Martin, Laura C. III. Title IV. Series.
SB321.C42 1994 93-11360
635'.097–dc20 CIP

Manufactured in Singapore

First edition

9 8 7 6 5 4 3 2 1

contents

'Red Riding Hood' lettuce

Overhead irrigation system

the american garden guides

The network of botanical gardens and arboreta in the United States and Canada constitutes a great treasure chest of knowledge about plants and what they need. Some of the most talented, experienced, and dedicated plantspeople in the world work full-time at these institutions; they are the people who actually grow plants, make gardens, and teach others about the process. They are the gardeners who are responsible for the gardens in which millions of visitors exclaim, "Why won't that plant grow that way for me?"

Over thirty of the most respected and beautiful gardens on the continent are participating in the creation of *The American Garden Guides*. The books in the series originate with manuscripts generated by gardeners in one or several of the gardens. Drawing on their decades of experience, these originating gardeners write down the techniques they use in their own gardens, recommend and describe the plants that grow best for them, and discuss their successes and failures. The manuscripts are then passed to several other participating gardens; in each, the specialist in that area adds recommended plants and other suggestions based on regional differences and different opinions.

The series has three major philosophical points carried throughout:

1) Successful gardens are by nature user-friendly toward the gardener and the environment. We advocate water conservation through the precepts of Xeriscaping and garden health care through Integrated Pest Management (IPM). Simply put, one does not set into motion any garden that is going to require undue irrigation during normal levels of rainfall, nor apply any pesticide or other treatment without first assessing its impact on all other life—plant, animal, and soil.

2) Gardening is an inexact science, learned by observation and by doing. Even the most experienced gardeners often develop markedly dissimilar ways of doing the same thing, or have completely divergent views of what any plant requires in order to thrive. Gardeners are an opinionated lot, and we have encouraged all participants to air and share their differences–and so, to make it clear that everyone who gardens will find his or her own way of dealing with plants. Although it is important to know the rules and the most accepted practices, it is also important to recognize that whatever works in the long run for you is the right way.

3) Part of the fun of gardening lies in finding new plants, not necessarily using over and over the same ones in the same old color schemes. In this book and others in the series, we have purposely included some lesser-known or underused plants, some of them native to our vast and wonderful continent. Wherever we can, we call attention to endangered species and suggest ways to nurture them back to their natural state of plenty.

This volume was originated by the gardeners at Callaway Gardens in Pine Mountain, Georgia. It was reviewed by six other gardeners: Dr. Laurie Hodges of the University of Nebraska Horticulture Department; Mary Irish of Desert Botanical Garden, Phoenix, Arizona; Richard Isaacson of the Minnesota Landscape Arboretum; Michael Maltas, former director of Fetzer Organic Gardens, Hopland, California; Aviva Toporoff of Chicago Botanic Garden; and Janet Whippo of The New York Botanical Garden.

Elvin McDonald
Houston, Texas

director's preface

Vegetable gardening has always been an integral part of the horticultural emphasis of Callaway Gardens. Our founders, Cason and Virginia Callaway, had a lifelong interest in helping the citizens of Georgia gain financial security through farming. Although his roots were entrenched in the textile business, upon retirement in 1935, Cason Callaway began Blue Springs Farms, which ultimately became a model farm illustrating principles of soil erosion, fertilization, and crop diversity. He experimented with many of the crops that are synonymous with the South, such as muscadine grapes, pecans, and blueberries.

Blue Springs Farms clearly demonstrated that farming in Georgia could be profitable, and farmers in the South didn't have to rely solely on agronomic crops like cotton, corn, and soybeans to earn a living. In order to assist farmers, Cason created the Georgia Better Farms program. Through this program, he persuaded 700 Georgia businessmen to contribute $1,000 to assist 100 farmers in Georgia with financing.

Perhaps the most significant aspect of Blue Springs Farm and the Georgia Better Farms program was Cason Callaway's willingness to share his knowledge in order to help farmers improve their agricultural and financial skills. This willingness to help educate his fellow man is clearly evident in "Mr. Cason's Vegetable Garden" which he conceived, although unfortunately it did not open until after his death in 1962. This 7½-acre farm demonstrates that vegetable gardening can be a continuous activity providing recreation and enjoyment for all ages. We are fortunate in Pine Mountain, Georgia, to be able to produce vegetables for almost 9 months a year.

In 1984, a home demonstration garden was installed and serves as the Southern filming site for the PBS series *The Victory Garden* and shows how we Southerners grow everything "from black-eyed peas to collard greens." Cason Callaway would no doubt be pleased to see this garden continue to help educate interested gardeners.

The authors of this book–David Chambers and Lucinda Mays–are well-qualified to share their gardening experience with you. David Chambers, manager of Mr. Cason's Vegetable Garden, has been working in this garden for more than 24 years. Lucinda Mays, curator of the Victory Garden, will no doubt be a familiar face to those who routinely watch *The Victory Garden*. I am confident that this important volume will increase your appreciation and knowledge of vegetable gardening.

Happy gardening,

Dr. William E. Barrick
Executive Director
Callaway Gardens

1   **INTRODUCTION**

People grow vegetables for many different reasons; but for just about everyone, the thrill of seeing the first green leaves spring from the ground is among the most important. *Above:* A young cucumber plant sends up its first leaves.

Preceding pages: Victory Garden South, in Mr. Cason's Vegetable Garden, at Callaway Gardens, Pine Mountain, Georgia.

Few of life's pleasures are equal to the taste of homegrown vegetables still warm from the sun. Though grocery stores and supermarkets are full of beautiful produce throughout the year, few store-bought vegetables can compare to homegrown in taste and sheer pleasure.

Gardening is one of the most popular hobbies in this country, and the millions of Americans who garden do so for a multitude of reasons. Some raise vegetables because they believe theirs taste better than anything they could find for sale. Others are concerned about the use and misuse of pesticides and other chemicals; by growing their own, they control what goes into their mouths. Still others plant vegetables because they have happy memories of the gardens of their childhood. Many people think they save money by growing their own produce (and a small number actually do save, significantly in some cases).

ORIGINS Vegetables have been cultivated for many thousands of years. Fossil records indicate that the common bean was grown in Mexico 6,000 years ago; cucumbers were introduced in China over 2,000 years ago. Illustrations in Egyptian tombs dating to 3200-2700 B.C. show laborers eating onions, and the Egyptians are known to have cultivated cabbage between 2500 and 2000 B.C. Vegetables were equally important to the civilizations of ancient Greece and Rome; they are mentioned in the writings of many statesmen and poets, often accompanied by recipes.

When we choose vegetables for our gardens, we are choosing from the bounty of the world, past and present. Many of the vegetables that we commonly eat today—including asparagus, cabbage, beets, lettuce, onions, peas, and turnips—originated in the Mediterranean region. From southern Mexico and Central America came the bean, lima bean, pepper, and sweet potato. From South America we got the pumpkin and the tomato. Cucumber, lettuce, and eggplant came from India; China and Central Asia offered the carrot, onion, radish, and spinach.

DEFINITION In the most general terms, a vegetable is any kind of edible plant or plant product. A more commonly accepted definition is that a vegetable is the edible portion of an herbaceous plant that is eaten either raw or cooked. In popular usage, the difference between a fruit and vegetable is often hazy, but in everyday language a fruit is considered to be much sweeter.

Botanically, a fruit is the mature ovary of a flowering plant and often contains seeds. Thus, produce such as tomatoes and peppers that contain seeds are actually mature fruits.

Many different plant parts are eaten as vegetables. The most delicious part may be the root, as in beets or carrots, or the storage tuber, such as a potato. It could be the stem, as in asparagus, or the bulb like onion and garlic. The edible portion may be a petiole, or leaf stem, such as in celery or rhubarb. Brussels sprouts are actually buds of the flower, and broccoli and cauliflower are harvested as immature flowers. Sometimes we eat immature fruits such as eggplant or cucumber, or seeds such as sweet corn and shell beans.

VEGETABLE FAMILIES Most of the vegetables we eat fall into 8 major families. Although they seem very different, the vegetables in each of these families share botanical characteristics such as floral structure.

Chenopodiaceae, the goosefoot family, contains many herbs, shrubs, and vegetables such as beets, Swiss chard, and spinach.

Asteraceae (Compositae), the sunflower family, is comprised of about 950 genera, many of them ornamentals such as achillea, asters, and coneflowers; it also includes artichokes, lettuce, and sunflowers.

Brassicaceae (Crucifera), also known as the brassica or mustard family, is the source of many important vegetables–broccoli, cabbage, cauliflower, collards, kale, mustard greens, arugula, garden cress, horseradish, and radish. The popular flowers alyssum and candytuft are also members of this family.

Cucurbitaceae, the gourd family, includes many tendril-bearing vines. Cucumber, melons, pumpkins, and squash are contained in this group.

Poaceae (Gramineae), the grass family, includes many important economic crops: corn, sugar cane, grasses, wheat, and bamboos.

Fabaceae (Leguminosae), the pea family, is another important source of food such as beans, peanuts, and peas as well as timber, fiber, and ornamental plants.

Solanacea, the nightshade family, has many plants with medicinal or poisonous properties, some ornamentals, and such popular vegetables as eggplants, tomatoes, potatoes, and peppers.

Apiaceae (Umbelliferae), the parsley or carrot family, includes many plants with strong flavors or pungent odors. Carrots and celery are among the members of this family.

Vegetables like these come to our gardens and tables from all over the world–corn and tomatoes from South America, beans from tropical America, cabbages and turnips from Europe, radishes and spinach from Central Asia.

HISTORICAL NOTES

When and where people first learned to partake of nature's bounty we have no idea, but a combination of hunger and accident seems the likely precipitating event. Wild harvests persisted for some millennia, until someone thought to plant seeds deliberately. As in much of human history, the connection between idea and resulting effect often took time to establish itself. It was a long and chancy road from spontaneous gathering of crops of berries to purposely sowing wheat in the soil of Jericho and other sites in the Middle East.

The vegetables we eat today were greatly changed by human intervention, both in how and where they grow. Plants were originally transported by wind and ocean currents and by birds and animals. But as early societies flourished, they tended to expand and to become more mobile. Naturally, they sought to surround themselves with that which was familiar and to indulge in foodstuffs that they already knew. Humans introduced new crops by taking them from one site to another and sometimes sought them out in the wild for transplantation.

The discovery of the New World exposed a whole new world of vegetation as well. Early explorers in South America found elaborate gardens filled with maize, squash, beans, and other crops. Many of these vegetables were entirely new to the Europeans, and others were grown more expertly than they had ever seen; by all accounts, the gardens in the New World far surpassed those of Europe. Native Americans depended on vegetables for a large part of their diets. They had developed effective farming practices as well as folk methods; one remedy for preventing cutworms was to have a naked woman walk around the crops, inscribing a magic circle that no worm would dare cross.

It was immediately recognized that some of the new species could become important in Europe, and a brisk trade developed. At the same time, traders brought previously unknown foods *to* the Americas; apples and peaches were among the first crops to become naturalized here.

Early colonists were experienced gardeners who brought seeds and tools with them. Some of the earliest advertisements in Colonial publications were for seeds. George Washington and Thomas Jefferson both started legendary vegetable gardens (in Mount Vernon and Monticello) that are still maintained today; both actively engaged in investigating and experimenting with new plants and corresponded with other farmers in Europe and America. Horticulture in America was advanced by entrepreneurs

Seed catalogs have always reflected our interest in vegetable gardening. Many new printing techniques were first applied to these catalogs. *Below:* Chromolithographed cover of *Vick's Garden and Floral Guide,* 1909.

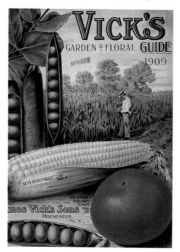

like John Bartram, a botanist and explorer who established the Bartram Botanic Garden in 1728 and sent many American specimens to Europe.

In addition to plant introductions, hybridization and improvements in agriculture have changed the vegetables that nature provided. For one thing, head cabbage was not developed until the Middle Ages; until that time, it remained loose, leafy, and bitter, not yet having been tamed by cultivation. Early flavors were generally stronger and harsher, rarely ever the smooth, pleasant products we know today.

And let us not forget some of our true wizards of the plant world. George Washington Carver, born into slavery, became one of the 19th century's most ingenious chemists, and extracted a myriad of different products–including paint, textiles, and peanut butter–from the humble peanut while working as director of agriculture of the Tuskegee Institute, and later as head of the Bureau for Plant Industries of the United States Department of Agriculture.

Another plant researcher, Luther Burbank, began as a market gardener and improved the potato crop with the development of the Burbank potato. Captivated by his plant experiments, he then moved from Massachusetts to the more congenial climate of Santa Rosa, California, where he quickly demonstrated the almost unbelievable versatility possible through plant breeding. Thanks to him, we gained new strains of plums, berries, roses, corn, squash, and tomatoes. Through the efforts of men like Burbank and Carver we have some idea of what can be done in the future.

FRANK J. ANDERSON

BASIC NEEDS We're used to seeing beautiful produce lined up in the supermarket all year long, and the availability of a dozen kinds of lettuce 12 months of the year may make us forget that it takes water, sunshine, a spot of ground, and 6-12 weeks for a head of lettuce to be ready for harvest.

Like most plants, vegetables require sunlight, water, and nutrients. Many flowering plants grown for aesthetic purposes are tolerant of a wide range of environmental conditions, including variations in temperatures, soil fertility, and light. Indeed, a flower can be found to fit almost any garden situation.

Vegetables are not so adaptable. Almost all vegetables need at least 6-8 hours of sunlight every day during the growing season. Exceptions to this are the fast-growing leafy vegetables such as spinach, lettuce, oriental greens (particularly Mizuna mustard greens, Chinese cabbages, and bok choys), or root crops such as carrots or potatoes, which will still produce well with slightly less sunlight—but even these need at least 5-6 hours each day. In very hot climates, like that of Phoenix, home of the the Desert Botanical Garden, most plants need to be shaded from the brutal sun at least part of the day. (See pages 210-211 for information on gardening in the desert.)

Some vegetables need a lot of room to grow. Squash, pumpkin, and melon vines sprawl and crawl for months before they are ready to harvest, so plenty of space should be provided for them. Other vegetables can be grown in tiny, postage-stamp-sized plots, or in containers; some varieties have been bred for this ability. (See pages 204-05 for more information on small plots.)

Since most vegetables are a least 70 percent water, constant moisture is a basic necessity in a vegetable garden. Some vegetables are so particular that they will never recover if their roots and stems are allowed to dry out.

Soil composition is also an important factor in the successful growing of vegetable crops. Different vegetables need different nutrients, making soil improvements desirable for the best home gardens. (See pages 172-77 for a full explanation of different types of soil and how to improve them.)

HOW HARD IS IT? As with most rewarding undertakings, gardening requires time and work. Although many people talk about shortcuts—and there are, indeed, many ways to minimize toil—you cannot realistically expect to reap without first sowing. Similarly, although many people possess the legendary "green thumb"—an innate knack for making things grow—there is no substitute for acquiring basic skills by reading, taking courses, visiting botanic gardens and nurseries, talking to other gardeners, and learning from your own mistakes and successes.

Unreasonable expectations are among the frequent causes for failure. Some gardeners assume that they can bring plants home from the nursery, stick them into the ground, and enjoy a full crop of vegetables without any further work. They are surprised and often discouraged by midsummer, when pests, diseases, and weeds that thrive in hot weather slow production and gardening turns into a real chore. More experienced gardeners prepare their plots and improve their soil *before* they plant; they take the time to maintain their gardens and enjoy both the work and its rewards.

SCIENTIFIC NOMENCLATURE
Botanists and horticulturists use a binomial, or two-name, system to label the over 250,000 species of living plants. Because the names are in Latin, this system crosses both time and language barriers and allows people all over the world to communicate about plants. Occasionally, a scientific name will be changed to reflect additions to our knowledge about plants. A scientific name consists of the genus (singular; genera is plural) and the species—as in *Phaseolus vulgaris* (snap beans). The genus name is always first and always capitalized; the species name follows and is generally not capitalized. A particular plant may have many common names—snap bean, green bean, string bean—but it has only one correct scientific name.

Above: Mr. and Mrs. Cason Callaway, founders of Callaway Gardens. *Above right:* A view of Mr. Cason's Vegetable Garden from the air.

The information in this volume comes from the gardeners at Mr. Cason's Vegetable Garden at Callaway Gardens in Pine Mountain, Georgia; gardeners in other regions added extensively to it. Mr. Cason's Vegetable Garden is a highly cultivated, labor-intensive, 3-season garden that emphasizes growing and displaying the best vegetables in the best ways and sharing gardening knowledge through guided walks, workshops, printed information, television, and interaction with visitors. The garden is the southern site for the popular PBS television program *The Victory Garden.* The garden is run by David Chambers, manager of Mr. Cason's Vegetable Garden, and Lucinda Mays, curator of Victory Garden South and host of the southern segments of *The Victory Garden.* David, who has been working in the vegetable garden for over 20 years, is responsible for the hundreds of varieties of vegetables; Lucinda looks after the smaller gardens dotted throughout the vegetable garden's 7½ acres.

Lucinda and David employ gardening practices that are both efficient and environmentally safe. They do not spray regularly because they believe that scheduled spraying is costly, time-consuming, and spreads more chemicals than are needed. Instead, they monitor crops carefully, use alternative pest-

DAVID CHAMBERS

David Chambers started gardening by "helping out" as a little boy spending summers at his grandparents' house. He learned how one gardens when winter meals depend on the gardens' crops. The experience stayed with him, and when he went to college he studied agribusiness.

Talking about his experience at Callaway Gardens, he says, "Because Mr. Cason's Vegetable Garden is mostly for display, I don't have to worry about making a profit the way a farmer does, so there's less pressure to produce marketable vegetables and more freedom to experiment with new crops and techniques." He gets calls and letters from all over the country. "I especially enjoy talking with visitors–they are sincere in looking for information and in sharing their own experiences. Everyone learns something in this exchange of information.

"And I like the tractor work; for me, it is like going fishing is for other people. When I'm tilling on the tractor, I know there will be no telephone calls, no interruptions.

"But my favorite time in the garden is in the spring, when you can see the young plants growing in their different shades of green."

control methods (see pages 196-98), and apply dusts or sprays only when necessary. They do mulch regularly because it allows them to reduce weeding and watering dramatically. They rotate crops to improve yield and quality of vegetables while reducing the need for chemical fertilizer. Succession planting of different varieties insures a constant stream of vegetables. Soil at Mr. Cason's garden is tended carefully; David and Lucinda use cover crops and compost to improve the soil. You will find information about these practices throughout this book.

   With their staff of gardeners and volunteers, Lucinda and David produce garden displays for hundreds of thousands of visitors as well as provide vegetables for Callaway Garden's many restaurants. In this book, they hope to share the information and experiences they have gathered with an even larger audience.

Above: The Sibley Horticultural Center at Callaway Gardens. *Left:* The vegetable garden in midsummer.

LUCINDA MAYS

When she was a child, Lucinda Mays' father allowed her to plant whatever was left over in the seed packs in her own little plot. "Whatever he did in the big garden, I did in my garden," she recalls. "It never occurred to me not to garden; I was surrounded by an extended family of gardeners, each with a specialty—my mother's cut flowers, my grandmother's white sweet corn, Uncle Bill's tomatoes, Aunt Rena's moss roses, Granny Griffin's irises. I have gardened every year of my life that I can recall."

   Today, Lucinda feels fortunate to make her living doing something she would do anyway. Engrossed in whatever task is at hand, she often loses track of time and derives a true sense of well-being when surrounded by singing birds and the subtle fragrances of fresh-tilled soil and individual plants—even the scents of the weeds please her. "I like to garden because it keeps me in the middle of a living, growing, dynamic sort of sculpture. I get to play at being an artist with the most forgiving of media—soil, plants, structures, and wild animals. And there's nothing more satisfying than bringing a bouquet of fresh homegrown flowers or a basket of new potatoes into the house."

PLANT SELECTOR 2

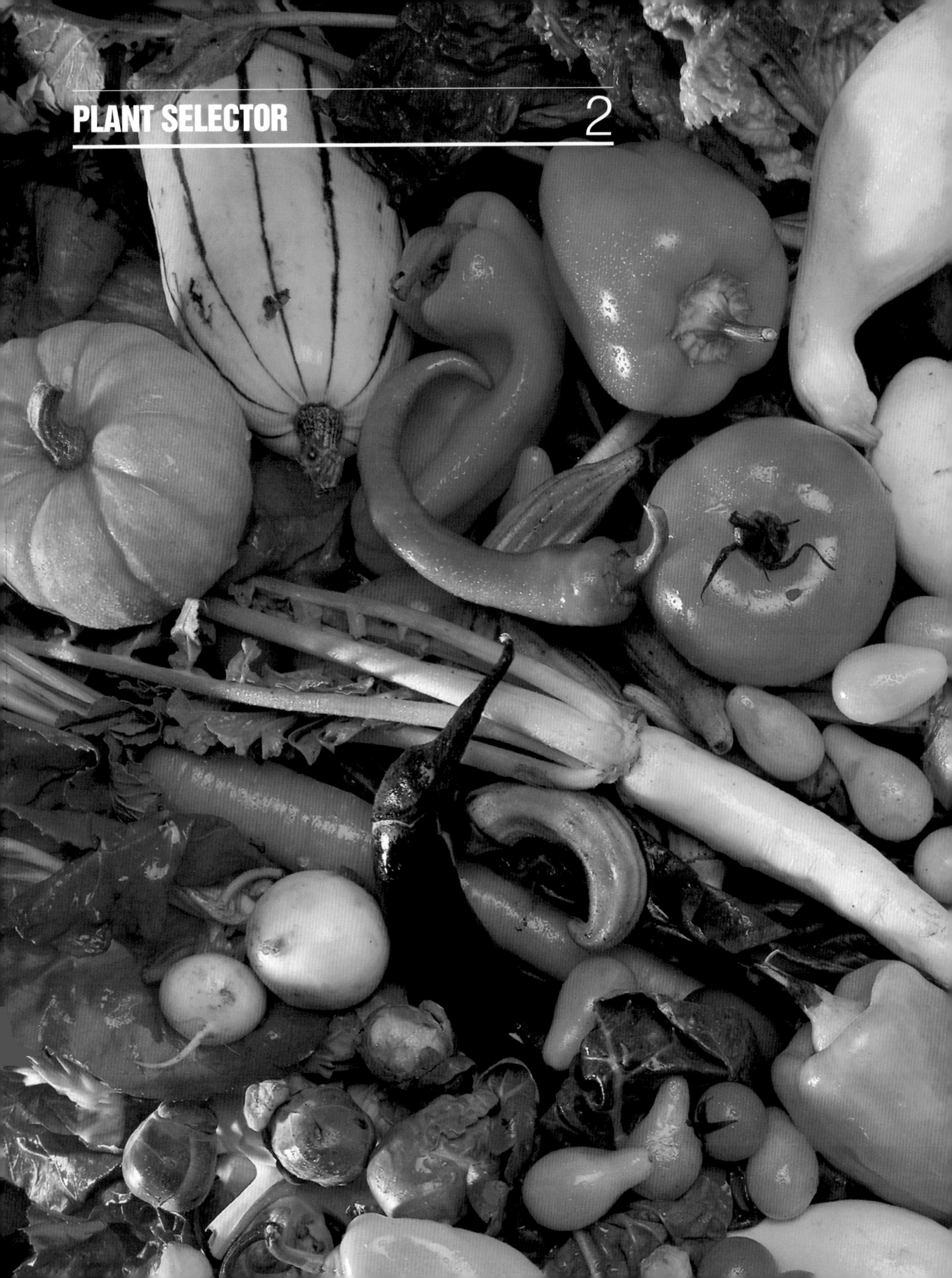

The vegetables in this book are arranged alphabetically by their common names. Certain vegetables are grouped:

Beans include snap beans, dry or shell beans, fava or broad beans, and lima beans.

Cover crops include winter wheat, Austrian peas, and crimson clover.

Greens include varieties that are generally cooked before they are eaten—collards, kale, mustard greens, spinach, New Zealand spinach, turnip greens, Swiss chard.

Lettuce includes other salad greens, such as arugula, endives, garden cress, chicory, corn salad.

Melons include canteloupe, watermelon, and honeydew.

Squash include pumpkins, summer squash (including zucchini), winter squash, and gourds.

Gardeners don't always enjoy every part of the gardening process—but finding a great new vegetable is pure pleasure for just about everyone. Since thousands of different varieties and cultivars are currently being sold, and nurseries, botanists, and private gardeners all over the world are busy finding and creating more (and rediscovering important heirloom varieties), there will never be a shortage of new plants to discover. The key is finding out which ones are right for you.

This plant selector chapter is designed to give you basic information about vegetables to grow in your own garden. For information on techniques on how to plant or how to start seeds indoors, see Chapter 3; for information on how to design a garden, see Chapter 4. In this chapter, you will find portraits of individual vegetables. Lucinda Mays and David Chambers of Callaway Gardens selected about 150 varieties that work well for them; they mixed some common, easy-to-find varieties with others that you might not know about, but should. Gardeners from other botanic gardens around the country added varieties that do well in their regions.

There are many ways to determine the kind of plants to put in your garden. Some of the questions you want to ask yourself are:

1. What do I like to eat? Don't plant what you don't like.

2. How much space will it take up?—if you have only a tiny frontyard space, melons are not a good choice.

3. For which crops do I have the right conditions? If you are blessed with good loamy or sandy soils, you can grow almost anything. If your soil is poor, you might consider improving it or using raised beds—or choosing vegetables that will do well in less-than-great soil, such as radishes, beets, and lettuce.

4. What is my climate zone? Do I live in the right geographical region for this crop? If you live in a temperate region, you may be able to grow artichokes, but not asparagus; northern gardeners may have to skip artichokes—but their asparagus will thrive. If you are not sure about your climate zone, talk to your county extension service, local nursery, or botanic garden. But don't forget that your site is unique; it has its own "microclimate," and conditions may be different from those 2 blocks away let alone at the nursery 10 miles down the road. Even within your own yard, the climate in a sheltered spot near the house might be different from the site on the other side of hill. (See page 152 for information on choosing a site, and Chapter 5 for information on growing vegetables in difficult climates.)

5. How much care will this plant take? And how much time do I wish to spend caring for it? Is it susceptible to a disease that is rampant in my area? Will it need staking? Pruning? Extra watering? Tomatoes can be a high-maintenance crop, zucchini is easier. How much care is it worth? You can grow almost anything if you are willing to take the time to pamper it.

6. Can I find the plants and seeds I want in regional catalogs and local nurseries? Regionally grown plants are already acclimated to your climate

and will be easier to care for.

Answer these questions honestly. It's easy to fudge–but the plant will know. Much heartache and wasted effort can be saved by putting the right plants in the right place right from the start.

CHOOSING PLANTS

When choosing plants, you will find dozens or even hundreds or thousands of varieties available for each vegetable. Every gardener has his or her personal favorites; one gardener's heaviest yielder is another's certain failure. We have listed varieties that have worked for our gardeners; the only way to find the ones that will work for you is to try them yourself.

Some of the vegetables that appear here are open-pollinated; that is, they were developed without the aid of human beings. Breeders choose the strongest plant to encourage the best possible strain of the variety, but do not otherwise alter the plant. Varieties reproduce through open pollination, that is, they are pollinated by the wind or by animals. They will usually not produce exact copies at each planting. *Cultivars* are cultivated varieties, named, man-made forms, bred for qualities such as resistance to disease, cold- or drought-hardiness, color, or size of fruit; they usually appear in print within single quotation marks, like 'Better Boy' tomatoes. Although there are obvious reasons to choose these cultivars, particularly if they are resistant to a disease or pest that is rampant in your area, there are also good reasons to keep the old varieties alive–see page 215 for more information on heirloom varieties.

Throughout this book, you will find references to AAS winners. These varieties, chosen by a committee of seed industry professionals, have been selected as superior "All-America Selections" and can be depended upon to produce healthy and tasty crops in most areas.

The U.S. Department of Agriculture has prepared this map, which separates the country into climate zones; many seed companies use these zone numbers to indicate where a particular variety will survive the winter. Find out what zone you're in and pay attention to the growers' recommendations–but remember that climate zone is only one part of the picture.

RANGE OF AVERAGE ANNUAL MINIMUM TEMPERATURES FOR EACH ZONE	
ZONE 1	BELOW –50°F
ZONE 2	–50° TO –40°
ZONE 3	–40° TO –30°
ZONE 4	–30° TO –20°
ZONE 5	–20° TO –10°
ZONE 6	–10° TO 0°
ZONE 7	0° TO 10°
ZONE 8	10° TO 20°
ZONE 9	20° TO 30°
ZONE 10	30° TO 40°
ZONE 11	ABOVE 40°

This chart is designed to provide an overview of the planting requirements and growing times of the major vegetable crops. It does not provide full information, which is contained in the rest of this chapter.

CROP	SEAON/TYPE	PLANTING	DAYS TO HARVEST	COMMENTS
Asparagus	Cool/ Perennial	Sow seeds after danger of frost has passed; or plant divisions in trenches	First harvest after 3 years	Prepare bed carefully
Beans	Warm/ Annual	Direct seed 2-3 weeks after frost, 1-1/2-2" deep, 2' apart, thin to 4-5"	50-65	Pole beans need support
Beets	Cool/ Biennial, grown as annual	Direct seed 2-3 weeks before last frost, again 2-3 weeks before first fall frost; 1/2" apart, 1/4-1/2" deep; thin to 4-6" apart	50-60	Needs light, rich, well-tilled soil
Broccoli	Cool/ Biennial, grown as annual	Start seeds indoors; sow 1/4-1/2" deep, 8-10 weeks before last frost; transplant seedlings to garden 4 weeks before last frost, 1-2' apart	55-58	Good fall crop; Needs even moisture
Brussels Sprouts	Cool/ Biennial, grown as annual	Same as for broccoli	90-97	Grows best in cool weather
Cabbage	Cool/ Annual	Start seeds indoors; sow 1/4-1/2" deep, 6-8 weeks before last frost; transplant seedlings to garden 2 weeks before last frost, 12-24' apart	60-90	Tolerates partial shade and frost
Carrots	Cool/ Biennial, grown as annual	Direct seed 2-3 weeks before last frost, again 6 weeks before first frost; scatter seed lightly in rows 2-3' apart; cover with 1/4" of soil	60-75	Needs well-tilled soil
Cauliflower	Cool/ Biennial, grown as annual	Start seeds indoors; sow 2-3 seeds 1/4-1/2" deep, 6-8 weeks before last frost; transplant 2 weeks before last frost, 2' apart	75	One-harvest vegetable; pull up after head is cut
Corn	Warm/ Annual	Start indoors, sow 2-4" deep; transplant when 2-4" tall; or direct seed 1" deep in furrow	70-100	Wind-pollinated; isolate different cultivars to avoid cross-pollination
Cucumber	Warm/ Annual	Start indoors and transplant 1-2 weeks after frost, or direct seed, 4-5 seeds per hill	60-80	Can be trellised
Eggplant	Warm/ Perennial, grown as annual	Start seeds indoors, transplant 8-10 weeks later, 2 weeks after frost, 3' apart	64-85	Requires long growing season
Greens	Cool/ Annual	Start seeds indoors; or direct seed 4 weeks after last spring frost and again in fall	40-70	Many greens taste better if grown in frost

CROP	SEASON/TYPE	PLANTING	DAYS TO HARVEST	COMMENTS
Lettuce and other salad greens	Cool/ Annual	Start seeds indoors; transplant after 3-4 weeks, 2 weeks before last frost; or direct seed 1/4-1/2" deep	50-80	Plant successively, 3 weeks apart; bolts in hot weather
Melons	Warm/ Annual	Start seeds indoors; transplant after 3-4 weeks, when first true leaves develop; or direct seed in hills	65-95	Allow lots of room; do not grow in waterlogged soils
Okra	Warm/ Annual	Start seeds indoors 2 weeks after last frost; transplant when soil reaches 65° F., in clumps 2-3' apart	55-60	Soak seeds overnight for improved germination
Onions	Full/ Annual	Start seeds indoors 12-14 weeks before last frost; transplant when soil is 45°F. or warmer; or direct seed, 1/4" deep 2 weeks before last frost	90-120	Can be planted from sets; germinates faster in warm soils
Peanuts	Warm/ Annual	Direct seed, 1-1/2-2" deep, 6" apart	120	Plants develop pegs beneath soil. Won't tolerate frost
Peas	Cool/ Annual	Direct seed 6 weeks before last spring frost, 6 weeks before first fall frost, 1/2-1" deep, 1" apart	55-90	Most need trellis or support
Southern Peas	Warm/ Annual	Direct seed 3 weeks after last frost, again every 2 weeks until 2 weeks before first frost 1" deep, 2" apart	55-65	Thrive in poor soil
Peppers	Warm/ Annual	Start seeds indoors, 1/2" deep, transplant after 6-8 weeks, 4 weeks after last frost, 1-2' apart. Or direct seed 4 weeks after last frost	63-75	Start indoors for best results
Potatoes	Warm/ Annual	Plant seed potatoes 8" deep in early spring, 12" apart	90-120	Till deeply; apply mulch; purchase disease-free seed potatoes
Radishes	Cool/Biennial grown as annual	Scatter seeds thinly, 1/2" deep, 3-4 weeks before last frost, 2-3 weeks before first fall frost	25-40	Need well-tilled, light soil. Germinate and grow quickly
Squash	Warm/ Annual	Start seeds indoors; transplant when true leaves appear. For later plantings, direct seed in hills 3' apart	48-120	Deep planting will produce stronger plants
Strawberries	Full/ Perennial	Plant virus-free rootstock, and plant in early spring or late fall, 12-18" apart		Different varieties suitable for different climate regions
Tomatoes	Warm/ Annual	Start seeds indoors 6-8 weeks before last frost; repot when set of true leaves appear.	61-90	Indeterminate (vining) varieties require support

ARTICHOKE CYNARA SCOLYMUS *Asteraceae*

COOL-SEASON PERENNIAL The delicious, edible artichoke, native to the Mediterranean region, is really the immature flower of a thistle plant. If left on the plant, the artichoke bud will open into a large, beautiful purple flower.

Homegrown artichokes are more tender than those found in the local market, which are usually bigger because they are not picked until past their prime. Artichokes require at least 2 years to harvest the first heads. After 3-4 years of cultivation and harvest, production decreases.

BEST CONDITIONS Artichokes need mild winters and a long, cool growing season; they do best in California and some parts of the South. In the North, they are usually grown as annuals. Rich, well-drained soil is a must; when the roots stay wet too long, they rot and the plants die. Amend soil with generous amounts of compost. In early spring, apply a balanced fertilizer, and water generously, especially in dry weather.

PLANTING Artichokes can be started from seeds or root divisions called offsets. Sow seeds outdoors just before the last frost is expected. Plant ¼ inch deep but do not expect germination for 12-15 days. Or start indoors in late winter in small peat pots. Plant offsets 2-3 weeks after the last spring frost.

PESTS AND DISEASES In warm climates: powdery mildew, crown and stem rot.

HARVEST In the second growing season, harvest when the immature head is the size of a golf ball but before it reaches fist-size.

VARIETY 'Green Globe' is an easy-to-find variety. In areas where summers are very hot it can be grown as an annual if watered heavily during dry spells.

At The New York Botanical Garden, cardoon (*Cynara cardunculus*) is grown instead of artichokes. The flowers are similar-looking, but the leaf stalk of cardoon is eaten.

ASPARAGUS ASPARAGUS OFFICINALIS *Liliacea*

COOL-SEASON PERENNIAL Garden asparagus, native to Europe, Asia, and Northern Africa, is the most long-lived of all garden vegetables. An established planting that is well-composted and mulched can produce large, tender spears daily over a 2-month season for 10, 15, or more years. Homegrown asparagus is more tender and less expensive than store-bought.

BEST CONDITIONS Asparagus must be grown in areas where winter temperatures are below freezing because it must go through a dormant period to keep producing. It is a favored crop at Fetzer and Chicago botanic gardens, where it needs little attention once established; it produces for a shorter period in Callaway's southern climate. The best soils are very rich in organic matter and drain well.

PLANTING Start from seeds or divisions of crowns. Roots will be marked either 1- or 2-year plants; both need to be in the ground at least 2 years before spears are harvested, though 2-year roots produce more in the first harvest.

Start seeds outdoors in spring after the danger of frost has passed. Germination is slow, taking 2-3 weeks. Thin seedlings to 3-5 inches apart. Soon after the last spring frost, plant transplants in 6-inch-deep trenches; fill in soil around spears as they grow until the trench is full. Water thoroughly.

Spare that spear! Don't harvest asparagus spears at this size; leave them to provide carbohydrates for subsequent root growth. Wait 3 or 4 years, until spears are at least finger-sized before you harvest; the plant needs that time to develop a strong mat of roots. You will be rewarded for your patience, as a healthy asparagus plant will produce for 10-20 years.

ARTICHOKE 'GREEN GLOBE' Open-pollinated. 2½-3 (sometimes 5) feet tall. Needs full sun, ample water, well-drained soil. Yields 3-4 heads per plant in second growing season. Harvest in spring (April). Zones 8-10. Days to harvest: 180.

ASPARAGUS 'JERSEY GIANT' All-male hybrid. Plant 3-4 feet tall produces stalks 8-10 inches tall, 1 inch thick. Needs full sun or partial shade, cool winters. 20 crowns yield 2-3 pounds every week for 1 month. Harvest in early spring.

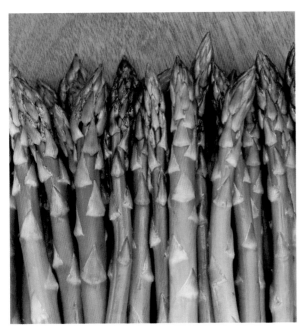

ASPARAGUS 'MARY WASHINGTON' Hybrid. Plant 3-4 feet tall at maturity produces 6- to 8-inch-long stalks, pencil-size or larger. Needs full sun, cool winters. 20 crowns yield 1-2 pounds every other week for 1 month. Resists rust.

BUSH SNAP BEAN 'BLUE LAKE 274' Hybrid. Compact bush, 2 feet tall, 18 inches wide, produces smooth pods 5-6 inches long with white seeds. Needs full sun. Peak yield: 1 quart per plant. Good for multiple plantings. Resists Southern mosaic. Days to harvest: 50-60.

Beans grow in the 2 habits shown below: short stocky bushes or long leafy vines. Bush beans are compact, a plus for small gardens, and are ready about 2 weeks before pole beans. They produce for only about 3 weeks, but can be replanted every 3 weeks for successive harvests. Pole beans require some support, but produce over a much longer period.

CARE Time spent preparing an asparagus bed is well invested. Make sure drainage is good, or improve it by raising the bed or adding sharp sand. Amend soil generously with compost or other organic material. Add phosphates if a soil test indicates they are necessary.

Cutting back brown stems in the fall helps prevent the spread of disease and makes spring harvesting easier. Be sure to wait until stems turn brown, or growth will continue through the year and stems will get long and spindly and will not produce well. Each fall after cutting back old stems, add 2 inches of well-rotted compost. A thicker compost layer may delay sprouting until warm weather. Mulch helps control weeds.

PESTS AND DISEASES Rust is often a problem in hot weather; control by cutting out affected plant parts. The same treatment should be used for bean mosaic, indicated by curled leaf tips. Black-and-orange asparagus beetles can be hand-picked; destroy any spears with whisker-shaped black eggs.

HARVEST A few spears can be harvested after 2 years, a few more after 3, but the optimum waiting period is 4 years. In early spring, begin cutting spears that are pencil-sized or larger. To harvest, either snap off the spears or cut them with a knife just under soil level. Early harvest will be heaviest.

VARIETIES 'Mary Washington' is easily obtained by the home gardener.

'Viking KB3', a female hybrid, is hardier in both hot and sub-zero climates and more tolerant of rust and fusarium than male cultivars.

'Jersey Knight', a male hybrid, is tolerant of rust, wilt, crown rot, and fusarium.

'UC157', another male hybrid, was developed for the southern and western parts of the country. Male hybrids are heavier producers than female.

BEANS

SNAP BEANS PHASEOLUS VULGARIS *Fabaceae*
BROAD BEANS VICIA FAVA *Fabaceae*
RUNNER BEANS PHASEOLUS COCCINEUS *Fabaceae*
DRY (SHELL) BEANS PHASEOLUS VULGARIS *Fabaceae*
LIMA BEANS PHASEOLUS LUNATUS *Fabaceae*
BUTTERBEANS PHASEOLUS LUNATUS *Fabaceae*

WARM-SEASON ANNUALS From the Boston baked bean to the lima bean, this diverse vegetable is grown, eaten, and loved throughout the world. Columbus discovered not only the New World, but a new bean, too, which he considered of "good and pleasant taste." The French were so enthralled with the beans from America that they renamed them the French bean. The broad, or fava, bean was so important during the Middle Ages that the penalty for robbing a beanfield was death. The origin of the word *bean* shows the high esteem this vegetable has always enjoyed. The name comes from a Greek word meaning "to eat."

Beans may be eaten in the immature stage, shell and all, as in the snap or pole bean; in the mature stage when only the bean itself is consumed, as with the lima; or left on the vine to dry and then cooked, as with the pinto bean.

BUSH SNAP BEAN 'DERBY' Hybrid. Bush 18 inches wide, 18 inches tall, produces 5- to 6-inch rounded pods with dark green beans. Needs full sun. Early and continuous harvest; beans and blooms appear simultaneously. Days to harvest: 50.

BUSH SNAP BEAN 'GOLDEN WAX' Produces heavy, flat pods, 5-6 inches long. Resists rust. Days to harvest: 50-60.

POLE SNAP BEAN 'BLUE LAKE FM1' Vine 6 feet tall, 18 inches wide, produces rounded, medium green pods, 6 inches long. Yields 2 quarts per plant. Days to harvest: 60-65.

POLE SNAP BEAN 'KENTUCKY BLUE' Hybrid. Vine 8 feet tall, 2 feet wide, produces round pods 8 inches long. Yields 2 quarts per plant. Vigorous grower. Very large leaves; requires support. Days to harvest: 58.

Beans come in a large range of shapes, sizes, and colors. *Right (left to right):* 'Royal Burgundy', 'Tenderette', and 'Golden Wax' bush beans; thin haricots verts; broad, flat 'Romano' pole beans; red-speckled French Horticultural pole beans; fava beans; and cranberry shell beans.

BUSH SNAP BEANS

Snap beans are eaten in the immature stage, so the pod and beans are both eaten. They are also called green beans, French beans, and string beans (though few modern varieties have the "string" along the seam that has to be removed before cooking). Bush snap beans are grown on stocky bushes that can reach a height of about 3 feet.

BEST CONDITIONS Fertile, well-drained soil is necessary because heavy, poorly drained, compacted soils promote root disease in beans. Plants will not produce pods without full sun.

PLANTING Seed directly into the garden site. Beans do not transplant well but are easy to grow from seeds. Germination should take 4-8 days depending on the soil temperature. Germination of early seeding is generally not as good as in later plantings because the soil is cooler. Plant 2 weeks after the last frost (or when soil temperatures reach 55° F.) 2 inches apart to a depth of 1½-2 inches in rows 3-4 feet apart; ¼-½ pound will seed a 100-foot row. Thin to 6 inches. For continuous harvest, plant several times during the summer, about 3 weeks apart. Beans can be planted in rows or hills. To plant in hills: remove a trowel-full of soil, plant 3-4 seeds, and cover with an inch or two of soil. Space hills 1 foot apart.

Gardeners at Fetzer Organic Gardens, located in nonhumid Northern California, find that planting in rows 10 inches apart is sufficient.

CARE Because snap beans have a relatively short garden life, mulching is not generally needed. For protection from a late frost or to keep the hot sun off new plants, use a floating row cover; other coverings might crush the plants.

Water heavily immediately after planting and as much as needed after germination; 1 inch per week is ideal. Spraying water on the plants when beans are in full bloom may knock blossoms or pollen from the plant, thus reducing pollination and production. Handling the plants when they are wet may promote disease. Weed to maintain vigorous plants.

Two to 3 days before planting, apply a balanced 8-8-8 or 10-10-10 fertilizer to the soil. Either till it in or side-dress the row where the beans will be planted. Once the beans have foliage (in 3-4 weeks), use a high-nitrogen mix, such as 20-10-10 and fertilize again.

PESTS AND DISEASES Early plantings have fewer insect problems because they mature before the insect populations are high. Mosaic is a common bean disease but resistant varieties are available. To help prevent bean diseases, do not plant beans in the same spot in the garden more than once every 4 years—plant beans 1 year, then plant something else in that spot for the next 3 years.

HARVEST Beans are ready when the pods are 4-6 inches long. They are most tender when the pod is ¼ inch wide. They can still be harvested when the seeds start to form in the pod, but the pods may be tough, the flavor stronger, and yields are often reduced. For best harvest results, don't pull off the entire cluster. Pick individual pods when ready; leave smaller pods to mature. To avoid spreading leaf disease, don't harvest when the plants are wet.

VARIETIES 'Blue Lake 274' is slower to mature in the pod, but gives a long harvest. Each plant yields 1 quart during peak season, but will continue to produce a limited amount if kept harvested. It is resistant to Southern mosaic disease.

'**Derby**' is an easy variety to harvest because the beans are presented above the foliage (unlike other bush beans) and will have a longer continuous harvest, producing both beans and blooms on the plant at the same time. It has a heavy first crop yield and forms a second harvest quickly.

'**Golden Wax**' bears heavy yields of pale yellow beans (sometimes called wax beans) on compact bushes.

'**Provider**', grown at the University of Nebraska, germinates well in cooler soils for earlier harvest. Plants have strong root systems and are disease-resistant.

'**Royal Burgundy**' bears unusual purple pods that turn green when cooked. This plant does well in cooler soils.

'**Tenderette**' yields tender pods with a strong bean flavor. The pods are dark green, 5½ inches long, and slender. Each plant should yield 2 quarts and should continue to produce at a reduced rate for about 1 month after peak.

POLE SNAP BEANS

Pole snap beans are grown for their young, edible pods (and sometimes for their mature seed). They are vining plants that need support in order to climb. Pole beans, once mature, will produce for 8-12 weeks, given sufficient water. Choosing varieties that produce in early, mid, and late season will provide an extended harvest. These take a little longer to mature than bush varieties—generally 60-65 days—but the pods are smoother, cleaner, and easier to harvest because they are high off the ground.

BEST CONDITIONS Pole beans need rich, well-drained soil of pH 6.0-7.0. Poor drainage promotes root disease in beans.

PLANTING Sow these large seeds directly into the garden where you want them to grow. They should germinate in 6-10 days depending on the temperature of the soil. Seedlings usually do not transplant well. They are easy to grow from seed, and fresh seed germinates well. Sow seeds 3 weeks after frost 1½-2 inches deep 6 inches apart in rows 4 feet apart; ¼-½ pound of seed will plant a 100-foot row. Be sure to leave enough room between rows to cultivate and harvest easily.

CARE After the plants have started to grow on the trellis or other support,

POLE SNAP BEAN 'MCCASLAN' Vine 5-7 feet long produces flat, dark green pods with white seeds, 7½ inches long. Stringless; good flavor, fresh or dry. Days to harvest: 61-66.

POLE SNAP BEAN 'YARD LONG' (also called 'Asparagus Bean') Vine 5- to 7-feet long produces very long slender pods with nutty flavor. Needs strong poles or trellis support. Days to harvest: 50.

RUNNER BEAN 'SCARLET RUNNER' Vine up to 12 feet long produces flat pods, 3-8 inches long, and showy red (sometimes white) flowers. Beans can be eaten fresh or dried. Days to harvest: 65-70.

BROAD (FAVA) BEAN 'IPRO' Open-pollinated. Bush 3-4 feet tall, 18-24 inches wide, produces 6- to 8-inch pods with about 5 beans per pod. Yields 1 pint of beans per plant. Days to harvest: 90-100.

mulch 2-3 inches deep with rotted composted leaves or dried grass clippings. The mulch will help retain moisture, help keep down the weeds, and creates a good walking surface to keep the soil from compacting during the extended harvest season. Immediately after planting, water heavily, and as needed after germination (1 inch per week of rain or water is ideal). Do not water heavily with overhead sprinklers when beans are in full bloom, because blossoms or pollen are knocked from the plant, reducing pollination and pod production.

Two to 3 days before planting, add a good balanced 8-8-8 or 10-10-10 fertilizer to the soil. Till it in or side-dress the rows where beans will be planted. Fertilize again every 4 weeks by side-dressing with a high-nitrogen mixture (such as 20-10-10) directly on top of the mulch throughout the growing season. Be careful not to hit the foliage with granular fertilizer.

PESTS AND DISEASES Early plantings have fewer insect problems. To avoid mosaic disease, select resistant varieties. Be sure to rotate bean crops–don't plant beans in the same spot until 3 or 4 years have passed.

Mildew is sometimes a problem on large-leaved varieties, indicating poor air circulation. Late in the season, rust is sometimes a problem. Select rust-resistant varieties or be prepared to pull and remove heavily affected plants. Mexican bean beetles are also often a problem. These pencil-eraser-sized copper-colored beetles appear midsummer. Early crops are rarely infested. Keeping the pods picked discourages pod worm infestation. Avoid getting water on leaves by watering the soil at the plant's base.

HARVEST When the pods are 6-8 inches long and ¼ inch wide for flat pods, or pencil sized for round pods, they are ready to pick. Harvest frequently (every 3 days) to ensure continued production. Pick individual pods, leaving smaller ones on the vine to mature. A 100-foot row will yield 30-40 pounds of beans.

VARIETIES 'Blue Lake FM1' The unusual round bean pods of this variety take longer than usual to mature. It requires continual picking over a 4-6 week production period to maintain continuous harvest. Because the plants produce for such a long time, mulching for water and weed control is recommended.

'French Horticultural' pole beans are most often planted for their attractive striped red pods. They should be harvested when 4-7 inches long. This variety is slightly shorter than other pole beans and has less foliage. Each plant should yield 2 quarts, taking 60-65 days to mature. It is resistant to mosaic disease

'Kentucky Blue' This variety is more resistant to mosaic because it is a vigorous grower, continuously putting on new growth. Bean beetles can become a pest because the upper leaves provide a good hiding place. The bottom leaves drop as the plants age. This hybrid was combined from 'Kentucky Wonder' and 'Blue Lake' and was a 1991 AAS winner.

'McCaslan' is a 1930s variety with white seeds; it can be used fresh or dry.

'Purple Pod' Lavender flowers and deep purple beans and pods make this 6-foot vine attractive as well as productive. (New York Botanical Garden)

'Yard Long' beans ('Asparagus Bean') produce very long pods on vigorously growing vines and need very hot summer weather. (Chicago Botanic Garden)

Pole beans require a trellis or other support structure. Poles, bamboo posts, branches, wooden stakes, twine, netting, or 4-inch wire fencing can all be used for support. Callaway gardeners use wires stretched at the top and bottom between 6-foot poles. They then weave twine over and under the wires, creating a zigzag trellis with twine contacting the support wires every 12 inches. There is no need to cut strings except at the end of the row. For long rows, this is an effective and inexpensive trellis.

Plant the beans so that they will grow within a few inches of the structure–the plant will twine onto strings, wires, or poles. You can give the plant some assistance by wrapping the vine onto your support, but most plants are able to accomplish this task quite well.

Many gardeners like to support their pole beans on bamboo "tepees" like the one above, which is supporting a vigorous 'Yard Long' bean at the Chicago Botanic Garden. Although more expensive than homemade supporting structures, many trellises are attractive, easy to assemble, and get the job done well.

RUNNER BEANS

The flowers of runner beans are so showy that the plants are more often grown as ornamentals than as vegetables. But the beans are delicious; the young tender pods are eaten, as well as the seeds, which can be used freshly shelled or dried. Runner beans are grown the same way as pole snap beans.

VARIETIES 'Painted Lady' is an heirloom variety with red and white flowers. It produces 9- to 12-inch pods in about 90 days.

'Red Knight', a modern cultivar, produces a 10- to 12-foot vine covered with red blossoms and a heavy crop of stringless beans throughout the summer.

'Scarlet Runner' is another heirloom cultivar, developed before 1750. It produces 20-40 red flowers and dark green, coarse-textured pods.

BROAD BEANS (Also called fava beans)

Cultivated by ancient Old World cultures, these beans are not always easy to find in local markets. Some people of non-Mediterranean descent have an allergy (called "favaism") to these beans. They can be planted early in the growing season. Although slow to start growing, once the plants are established, they seem to have a quick growth spurt. The beans are not ready to harvest until 100 days from planting, but they can be started outdoors as soon as soil can be worked, making harvest possible by midsummer. These beans need full sun, good soil and air circulation, and generous amounts of fertilizer high in nitrogen. They are subject to viral wilt in the heat of the summer.

VARIETY 'Ipro' is a heat-resistant cultivated variety.

DRY BEANS (Also called shell beans)

Dry beans are left on the vine until the pods dry. The beans are varied in color (white, black, yellow, pink, brown, or speckled) and offer many different flavors. They are often used as storage beans, harvested dry for later use. Many are compact plants that can be grown in small gardens.

BEST CONDITIONS Dry shell beans need full sun, fertile, well-drained soil, and at least 1 inch of water each week. Keep them free of weeds.

PLANTING Two weeks after the last frost, sow seeds directly into the garden 1-1½ inches deep in rows 3-4 feet apart. Successive plantings can be done every 3 weeks for varieties that produce quickly, but remember that beans will need time to dry before the end of the season. If the soil is heavy, plant only 1 inch deep. Seeds should germinate in 6-10 days. Thin seedlings to about 5-6 inches apart. Because the pods must dry out thoroughly at harvest time, it is best not to mulch because mulch tends to hold in moisture.

CARE Two to 3 days before planting, add a good balanced 8-8-8 or 10-10-10 fertilizer. Till it in or side-dress the row where the beans will be planted. When the plants have foliage (3-4 weeks) fertilize again using a high-nitrogen mix. Do not water with overhead sprinklers when the plants are in full bloom, and discontinue watering when the pods start to wrinkle, crack open, or turn

POLE DRY BEANS 'KENTUCKY WONDER' Vigorous vine produces smooth, flat 8- to 9-inch green pods, with large brown seeds. Stringless when young. Heavy yielder. Use fresh or dry. For best flavor, harvest promptly. Days to harvest: 65.

BUSH DRY BEAN 'VERMONT HORTICULTURAL' Heirloom variety. Compact bush produces 5- to 6-inch-long pods with 5- to 6½-inch-long oval brown beans with purple speckles. Does well in all climates. Days to harvest: 60-90.

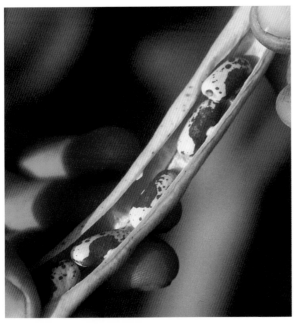

BUSH DRY BEAN 'JACOB'S CATTLE' Open-pollinated. Bush 2 feet tall, 18 inches wide, produces pods with large, red-speckled white beans. Needs good soil, ample water. Yields 1 cup shelled beans per plant. Days to harvest: 90-100.

BUSH DRY BEAN 'MIDNIGHT BLACK' (Turtle Soup) Open-pollinated. Bush 18 inches tall, 12 inches wide, produces dry pods, 4-6 inches long, with small black beans. Yields 1 cup shelled beans per plant. Days to harvest: 90-100

BUSH LIMA 'EASTLAND' Upright bush 18 inches tall, 18-24 inches wide, produces 3- to 4-inch flat green pods. Yields 1 quart of shelled beans per plant. Days to harvest: 68.

BUSH LIMA 'THOROGREEN' Bush 15-16 inches tall, 18-24 inches wide, with glossy green foliage, produces 3- to 4-inch pods with 2-4 pale green beans in each. Yields 1 quart shelled beans per plant. Tolerant of heat and drought. Days to harvest: 67.

POLE LIMA 'KING OF THE GARDEN' Twining vine with very large leaves, 6-8 feet tall, 2 feet wide, produces broad pods 6-9 inches long with 4-5 creamy white beans in each. Yield 2 quarts shelled beans per plant. Days to harvest: 84.

BUSH LIMA 'HENDERSON' Bush 2 feet tall, 2 feet wide, produces 3-inch pods with 3-4 creamy white beans per pod. Yields 1 quart shelled beans per plant. Days to harvest: 65.

yellow, which are signs of maturing seeds.

PESTS AND DISEASES To avoid disease, do not plant shell or pole beans in the same spot year after year. Rotate in other types of crops for 3 years before you plants beans there again. Floating row covers are an alternative to chemical dusts and sprays to keep insects from plants. Hand-pick Mexican bean beetles. Early generations of soft-bodied pests such as mites and aphids can be controlled by using a soap spray.

HARVEST Harvest when the pods start to wrinkle, crack open, or turn yellow. Usually all the pods are ready to harvest at the same time. Store the shelled beans in a cool, dry place. Gardeners at Fetzer Organic Gardens advise that beans should not be harvested until very dry, but before they shatter. They should then be shelled, cleaned, and frozen in sealed containers for a week to kill latent bean weevils that might otherwise hatch in storage. Warm to room temperature before using.

Harvested plants may be removed from the garden anytime, but the earlier the better. Older plants attract pests and insects to the garden. A 100-foot row should yield 10-15 pounds of shelled beans.

VARIETIES 'Dutch Brown' is an excellent producer of light brown beans with a nutty-beany-potato flavor. (Fetzer)

'Jacob's Cattle' Plant seeds for this large, handsome bean 2 weeks after the last frost. It matures slowly, so it is subject to greater damage from weevils that get into the mature beans as they dry, Mexican bean beetles that feed on the foliage, and mosaic.

'Kentucky Wonder' produces rounded light green pods and oblong light green beans; it is used as both a snap bean and a dry bean.

'Midnight Black' is faster growing than other dry shell beans, so it has fewer pest problems. This is a good variety for multiple plantings. It is a vigorous grower even in cool weather and has several beans per pod.

'Vermont Horticultural' won the taste test at Fetzer Organic Gardens in Hopland, California, 2 years running. Its speckled brown-red beans taste like raw peanuts and retain color after cooking. It is a vigorous grower, quick to mature and easy to harvest.

LIMA BEANS, BUTTERBEANS

In cultivation for over 6,000 years, lima beans grow on bushes or vines. Both large-seeded limas and small-seeded butterbeans are shelled before eating. The large beans are difficult to grow in northern areas because they need a long, hot growing season, but butterbeans do well at the Minnesota Landscape Arboretum if sown as soon as the soil is reliably warm. Lima beans have similar cultural requirements to bush and pole beans.

BEST CONDITIONS Full sun is required. Soil should be well-drained, rich in organic matter, with pH of 6.0-7.0.

PLANTING Plant seeds once the soil has warmed in the spring and after all danger of frost has passed. Seeds treated with a fungicide can be planted slightly

Trellising beans on arches is decorative as well as practical. Beans planted on either side of the arch will clamber up the support and meet on top.

Before yet any woodchuck or squirrel had run across the road, or the sun had got above the shrub oaks, while all the dew was on, though the farmers warned me against it—I would advise you to do all your work if possible while the dew is on—I began to level the heads of haughty weeds in my bean-field and throw dust upon their heads. Early in the morning I worked barefooted, dabbling like a plastic artist in the dewy and crumbling sand, but later in the day the sun blistered my feet. There the sun lighted me to hoe beans, pacing slowly backward and forward over that gravelly upland, between the long green rows, fifteen rods, the one end terminating in a shrub oak copse where I could rest in the shade, the other in a blackberry field where the green berries deepened their tints by the time I had made another bout. Removing the weeds, putting fresh soil about the bean stems, and encouraging this weed which I had sown, making the yellow soil express its summer thought in bean leaves and blossoms rather than in wormwood and piper and millet grass, making the earth say beans instead of grass—this was my daily work. . . . But labor of the hands, even when pursued to the verge of drudgery, is perhaps never the worst form of idleness. It has a constant and imperishable moral, and to the scholar it yields a classic result. From *Walden,* by Henry David Thoreau, 1854

Opposite: 'Sieva' butterbeans growing at Callaway Gardens.

earlier. Plant seeds 1½-2 inches deep; they should germinate in 7-10 days. Thin both bush and pole varieties to 9 inches apart in rows 3-4 feet apart. Successive plantings of bush varieties can be made every 3 weeks until 2 months before the first expected frost.

CARE Till in or side-dress the row 2-3 days before planting with 10-10-10 fertilizer. Treat again once a month during the growing season.

Add mulch to pole varieties to conserve water and keep weeds in check. Fertilize these plants on top of the mulch—it will filter through. Provide support for pole varieties.

PESTS AND DISEASES Lima beans are subject to the same pests as bush and pole beans (mosaic, rust, and Mexican bean beetle). In addition, red spider mites cause leaf curl and drying. Downy mildew may be a problem in wet conditions. Rust often occurs when a wet period is followed by hot weather.

HARVEST Keep beans picked to stimulate further yield. Lima bean pods should not be fed to livestock—pointed ends may damage mouths and stomachs.

VARIETIES BUSH LIMAS: 'Eastland' limas are easier to pick because the pods are high on the plant. The pods continue to bear for continual harvest throughout the summer. It does best if planted when warm weather has set in and growing conditions are not wet.

'Fordhook 242' produces large-seeded beans. Though the beans are slower to form than other cultivars, it has fewer problems with mosaics and rusts. It does well in hot, dry conditions. Harvest continues until frost, with fewer beans each time.

'Thorogreen' produces a green seed with a mild flavor and a texture that is not as mealy as other limas. It is more difficult to shell but slower to lose moisture and color after shelling; excellent for freezing and canning. Seeds can be planted 2-4 weeks after frost. More heat- and drought-tolerant than other bush limas.

POLE LIMAS: 'Hopi' White, gray, red, and yellow versions, distributed by Native Seeds/SEARCH, tolerate salt and alkaline soils. (Desert Botanic Garden)

'King of the Garden' must be supported by a trellis or wire. It produces large flat, creamy white seeds, 4-5 per pod, that can be used either green or dry.

'Willow Leaf', an heirloom variety, has long narrow foliage and a rich-flavored, large white bean seed. Harvest will continue until frost. Because of the narrow shape of the leaves, it can withstand drier conditions (loses less moisture through the leaves) and has fewer problems with whiteflies.

BUTTERBEANS: 'Henderson' plants are small and have less foliage than other lima bean cultivars and tend to put out side runners bearing beans—which can become a problem because beans rest on the soil and become moldy. The 3-inch pods open easily for shelling. This lima will set pods in dry conditions.

'Sieva' is a pole variety, producing a vine 5-6 feet long with small, dense leaves that need support to grow. It is a fast grower with heavy production. If seeds are planted too soon in cool, wet soil, they tend to rot. Seeds are found in 3- to 4-inch pods and can be harvested from midsummer until frost.

BEET 'CHIOGGA' Produces 3-inch orange-skinned beets with dark pink-and-white-striped interior. Green tops with shaded red stems. Good flavor. Days to harvest: 55.

BEET 'GOLDEN' Produces orange-yellow beet that does not bleed; exceptionally sweet flavor. Tops are used as greens. Slow to germinate; sow heavily. Days to harvest: 55.

BEET 'MOBILE' Hybrid. Red stem with green foliage, 18-20 inches tall. Each plant yields 1 smooth 2- to 3-inch round beet. Partial shade ok in hot climates. Days to harvest: 55.

BEET 'RED ACE' Hybrid. Red stem with green foliage, 12 inches tall. Each plant yields 1 smooth dark red, 2½-inch round beet. Partial shade ok in hot climates. Days to harvest: 54.

BEETS BETA VULGARIS *Chenopodiaceae*

COOL-SEASON BIENNIAL GROWN AS AN ANNUAL The popular expression "red as a beet" does not adequately describe this vegetable's range of colors. Beets can be the common red or purple, or a more unusual gold or white. In addition to the roots, the tops are also sometimes cooked and eaten.

Beets, native to Europe and parts of Asia, were originally used only for medicine, such as a salve for broken bones. Over the centuries, the Romans began to realize its culinary value and enjoyed it to the extent that even as late as the 16th century, it was known as the "Roman beet."

BEST CONDITIONS As with all root crops, a light, rich, well-drained soil is beneficial. The soil should be evenly moist, well tilled, and free of rocks, debris, and hard clumps of dirt. Although beets prefer full sun, they can be grown in partial afternoon shade in hot climates.

PLANTING Beets should be grown from seeds sown directly into the garden; the large roots may not form well if transplanted. Seeds can be planted 2-3 weeks before the last expected frost; repeat every 2 weeks until the onset of hot weather and resume for an autumn crop 6-8 weeks before the first fall frost. Seeds should germinate in 7-10 days. One ounce of seeds is sufficient for a 100-foot row. The rows should be 12-24 inches apart, the seeds sown ½ inch apart, ¼-½ inch deep. When the small seedlings are 1-2 inches tall, it is important to thin to 4-6 inches apart; otherwise roots won't form properly. The thinned seedlings are delicious eaten raw in salads or cooked in soups and stews.

CARE Keep soil evenly moist and weed frequently by hand-pulling between plants. Cultivate with a hoe between rows. Protect from light frosts with floating row covers or 2 inches of hay. Thinned plants are less likely to bolt.

A general 8-8-8 or 10-10-10 fertilizer should be worked into the soil 2 days before planting and again once the tops have begun to put on height. At Fetzer Organic Gardens, compost is applied instead of fertilizer.

PESTS AND DISEASES Beets are generally highly resistant but are sometimes affected by leaf miners and black spot. If this is a problem in your area, choose varieties that are resistant to these pests. Floating row covers provide insect protection. Close to harvest time, insect damage on foliage will not affect production of roots.

HARVEST Check the roots to see if they are full-sized by gently pulling the soil away from the root. Harvest at desired size. When harvesting, pull up the entire plant. When harvesting and cooking beets, leave at least 1 inch of leaf tops on them to help prevent loss of moisture and flavor.

VARIETIES Different varieties can be chosen that will display characteristics such as early maturation, greater resistance to disease, longer storage, better tolerance to heat and drought, or ability to be preserved well. Beets grown for greens do best in cool seasons. Faster-maturing beets have fewer problems with cracking and can be raised in heavier soils.

'Chiogga', with an orange-red exterior and a pink-and-white striped interior is

Because most beet seeds come in clusters, beet seedlings must be thinned. Some hybrids, like 'Red Ace' produce unclustered seeds that can be easily spaced at planting time.

not as productive as some other varieties, but is very sweet and unusual.
'Golden' has golden-yellow roots and unusual colored tops that are good for eating. It does best in light, rich soils and requires longer cultivation than other kinds. 'Golden' is a notoriously poor germinator; sow twice as many seeds as usual. It needs diligent thinning or the roots will become cylindrical rather than round. It is prone to cracking if not thinned. Excellent flavor.
'Little Bell' is good for canning and will grow in heavier soils. Because the root is smaller, it takes less space and can be grown in containers. The roots develop quickly.
'Lutz Green Leaf Beetroot' has a huge and somewhat asymmetrically shaped root—a single beet will suffice for a large family dinner. The roots can be left in the ground to harvest through the winter, although heavy mulching is needed in colder climates. Gardeners at Fetzer Organic Gardens find it to be the sweetest beet they've ever grown. It is not suitable for the South, where it often bolts in the heat.
'Mobile' requires less thinning because, as a hybrid, its seeds are sown individually rather than in clusters. The roots, which mature quickly, resist cracking.
'Red Ace' is resistant to bolting in hot weather and is tolerant to leaf spot caused by humidity or damp conditions.
'Ruby Queen' thrives in a wide variety of growing conditions. The seeds are easy to find and inexpensive.

BROCCOLI BRASSICA OLERACEA VAR. BOTRYTIS *Brassicaceae*

COOL-SEASON BIENNIAL GROWN AS AN ANNUAL Broccoli, one of America's favorite health foods, did not become popular in the United States until the 1930s. The word *broccoli* comes form the Latin *bracchium*, meaning "branch." Broccoli is thought to have been introduced to the .French court in the 1500s by Catherine de Medici. During the 19th century, gardeners grew brown, red, and purple as well as the familiar green.

Broccoli is grown for the upper stalks and the immature flower heads, or florets, that appear in terminal clusters on the plants.

Broccoli grown in the heat is tougher and has stronger flavor than plants grown under cooler temperatures. Hot spells in the spring cause heads to become loose and rapidly go to flower. Broccoli is an excellent fall crop and will not be injured by a light frost. It is one of the few vegetables grown in both spring and fall at the Chicago Botanic Garden.

"Sprouting" types of broccoli have smaller but more numerous flower buds; some are purple or white.

BEST CONDITIONS Broccoli needs loose, well-prepared soils—sand, clay, or loam. Ideal pH is of 6.0-6.8. Broccoli grows best in full sun. Ample moisture is also needed throughout the growing season.

PLANTING To start seeds indoors, place 2-3 seeds ¼-½ inch deep in a 2-inch fiber or plastic pot. Water thoroughly and supply enough light for the plants to produce strong, stocky stems. The young seedlings should be fed every 7-10 days with liquid 10-10-10 or 13-13-13 fertilizer. Seedlings will be ready to

Broccoli will form side shoots if it is harvested when baseball-sized. Side shoots will reach almost the same size, and extend the harvest for weeks. *Below:* 'Packman' side shoots.

BEET 'RUBY QUEEN' Open-pollinated. Red-stemmed foliage presented in an open bunch, 16-18 inches tall. Each plant yields 1 ringless 2-inch round beet with tapered end. Days to harvest: 52.

BROCCOLI 'GREEN COMET' Hybrid. Plant 2 feet tall, 18 inches wide, produces head 8 inches across. Yields 1-1½ pounds per plant. Needs good, rich soil and thrives with frequent cultivation. Days to harvest: 55 after transplanting.

BROCCOLI 'PACKMAN' Hybrid. Compact, uniform plant produces large, heavy, blue-green head with medium beading, 7-8 inches across. Adapts to most climates. Early to mid season. Days to harvest: 65.

BROCCOLI 'PREMIUM CROP' Hybrid. Plant 2-2½ feet tall, 18 inches wide, produces 1 large, 8-inch head and several small side shoots. 1-1½ pounds per plant. Days to harvest: 58.

BROCCOLI RAAB Traditional Italian broccoli with leaves and flowers clustered together. Extremely early. 6- to 12-inch-tall plants, medium green, with no central head. Strong, somewhat bitter flavor, similar to broccoli and mustard greens; must be cooked before eating. Days to harvest: 42.

ROMANESCO BROCCOLI 'MINARET' Hybrid. Also called sprouting broccoli. Leafy erect plants, 3 feet tall, with yellow-green pyramid-shaped heads, 3-5 inches in diameter. Days to harvest: 60-85.

BRUSSELS SPROUTS 'JADE CROSS HYBRID'. Stalk 26 inches high produces firm blue-green sprouts. Very cold-hardy. Days to harvest: 95.

BRUSSELS SPROUTS 'PRINCE MARVEL' Hybrid. Stalk 35 inches tall produces firm, well-spaced, dark green sprouts. Days to harvest: 90-97.

transplant in 4-6 weeks. Stressed transplants with woody-looking stems and yellow leaves will not produce a good crop and might bolt early. Harden off transplants before placing in the garden.

Transplants should be put in the garden in spring 4 weeks after the last frost and in fall 4 weeks before the first frost; fall transplants are difficult to establish in late summer heat. Space 2 feet apart in rows 3-4 feet apart. (At Fetzer Organic Gardens, broccoli plants are placed only 18 inches apart; commercial growers often leave only 12 inches of space.)

CARE Two days before placing the transplants in the garden, treat the soil with a fertilizer rich in nitrogen and repeat every 3-4 weeks thereafter. After fertilizing, the soil should be cultivated to incorporate fertilizer in the soil and to remove weeds. Maintaining adequate levels of nitrogen and soil moisture ensures the best crop.

PESTS AND DISEASES In some areas downy mildew is a problem. To combat, use mildew-resistant varieties. If cabbage loopers become a problem, dust the plants with Bt; check early for damaged leaves. Insect damage is often worse on the side shoots because they mature later in the season. Covering with straw also protects from frost damage; be sure to remove the straw as soon as the threat of frost is over. Floating row covers can also be used. To protect young transplants from cutworms, place a cardboard or plastic collar around the plant, pressing the collar at least 1 inch into the soil.

HARVEST Cut the center head and 4-6 inches of stalk, which is where the first larger leaves appear. This allows the side shoots to form smaller heads. Broccoli will yield 1-2 bushels per 100-foot row.

VARIETIES 'Emperor' is adapted to a wide variety of climates and does well planted in either spring or fall. Transplant no later that 4 weeks before the last expected frost, well before warm weather sets in.

'Green Comet', somewhat shorter than most, is a good variety for hot areas because the tight heads resist early flowering. Side shoots develop with small harvestable heads. Thrives with frequent cultivation of soil; place ring-paper or Styrofoam cup 1-inch down in soil.

'Packman' is an early-maturing variety; it is best in areas with long winters.

'Premium Crop' is particularly nice because the stem is thick and resists wilting after harvest. Several small side shoots are also generally produced.

Romanesco 'Minaret' broccoli is yellow-green and has an unusual spiraled head; it is somewhat difficult to grow in hot climates.

Broccoli Raab does not form a large central head the way regular broccoli does; instead, shoots of yellow flowers rise from the stem. The buds and leaves are both eaten; the taste is somewhat bitter. Harvest the shoots from the main stem when the flowers begin to open.

BRUSSELS SPROUTS BRASSICA OLERACEA VAR.
GEMMIFERA *Brassicaceae*

COOL-SEASON ANNUAL Brussels sprouts have been called the "thousand-headed cabbage," an appropriate name for these vegetables since they are tiny cab-

Brussels sprouts produce many small cabbagelike heads on a tall stalk. *Below:* 'Rubine Red' Brussels sprouts, growing with lemon verbena.

CABBAGE 'DARKRI' Hybrid. Plant 18-inch tall, 18-inch wide, produces very early, firm 8- to 10-inch heads. Few outer leaves, less insect damage. Very heat-tolerant Yields 1 2-lb head per plant. Days to harvest: 67 from seed, 42 from transplants.

CABBAGE 'HEADS UP' Hybrid. Plant 14 inches tall, 18 inches wide, produces compact, globe-shaped heads. Yields 1 3-pound head per plant. Tolerates light shade. Days to harvest: 60 from transplanting.

CABBAGE 'STONEHEAD' Hybrid. Plant 18 inches wide produces tight, small heads with small outer leaves. Yields 1 2- to 3-pound head per plant. Days to harvest: 60.

RED CABBAGE 'LASSO' Hybrid. Plant 18 inches wide produces compact, round head with few outer leaves. Yields 1 1½ - to 2-pound head per plant. Days to harvest: 70.

bages growing from a central stalk. Several small cabbage-shaped heads are grown along stalks 3-3½ feet tall and 2 feet wide.

BEST CONDITIONS Loose, well-prepared soils are necessary to grow this vegetable, but it will grow in sand, clay, or loam; pH should be 6.0-7.0. Brussels sprouts grow best in cool temperatures.

PLANTING Brussels sprouts perform best when started indoors and transplanted. Start seeds indoors 6-8 weeks before transplanting. Plant 2-3 seeds in a 2-inch fiber or plastic pot, ¼-½ inch deep, and water gently and thoroughly. Seeds should germinate in 6-8 days. Supply sufficient light for the plants to develop stocky stems. Fertilize seedlings every 7-10 days with a balanced liquid fertilizer (10-10-10) or add a balanced granular fertilizer at half the recommended rate to the potting mix before sowing seed.

The seedlings should be ready to transplant in 6-8 weeks and can be put into the garden 4 weeks before the last frost, or as soon as the soil can be worked; at the Minnesota Landscape Arboretum, Brussels sprouts are usually transplanted around June 1. Plant 2 feet apart in rows 3-4 feet apart.

CARE When the plants are 10-12 inches tall, add 2 inches of mulch around the root zone of the plant to keep the soil cool. Fertilize 2-3 days before planting time and once a month thereafter, using a high-nitrogen mix (such as 15-5-5). Cultivate after each application of fertilizer to keep areas free of weeds and to incorporate the fertilizer into the soil. Because Brussels sprouts have a long growing season, they will eventually need more fertilizer than other crops.

PESTS AND DISEASES Look for varieties that tolerate black rot. Downy mildew-resistant varieties do best in cool growing conditions. Dust with Bt as needed for cabbage loopers. Hand-pick bugs if there are only a few of them, and do not apply insecticide.

HARVEST Sprouts will be ready to harvest when the stems are firm, approximately 120 days from planting. Sprouts first appear at the base and then higher up the stem as the plant continues to produce. Pop individual heads from stem as they are ready. For the last harvest, pull the entire plant. As small heads (½- to 1-inch wide) are harvested, it's a good idea to cut off the leaves up to the point on the stalk where new heads are beginning to form. Continue to do this throughout the harvest period to let in sunlight, producing fuller sprouts.

VARIETIES 'Jade Cross Hybrid' produces medium-size sprouts quickly.

'Prince Marvel' is tolerant of black rot; produces smooth, well-spaced sprouts.

CABBAGE BRASSICA OLERACEA VAR. CAPITATA *Brassicaceae*

COOL-SEASON ANNUAL Cabbages have been in cultivation for thousands of years and were greatly prized by the Romans. According to Roman folklore, cabbages were formed from Jupiter's tears, which he shed when trying to understand two oracles who proclaimed opposite views. Today's cabbages are said to have been developed from a curly-leaved nonheading cabbage similar to collard greens. Both red and green cabbages were known to Roman soldiers and were carried with them when they invaded Britain.

Because cabbages have high nutrient requirements and are slow growers, staying in the garden a long time, they need to be cultivated. Leaving ample space between cabbage rows will make cultivation easier.

The word for cabbage in Chinese is *choi*. Chinese cabbages, which are a different species (*Brassica pekinensis*) than European ones, come in several forms. Bok choi (also known as pak choi; at right in the above picture) have a form somewhat like celery, with tall white ribs and droopy leaves that look and taste a little like kale. Napa forms, such as the one on the left, form tighter upright heads.

Cabbages grow 2- to 4-pound heads on plants that are 12-18 inches tall and 2 feet wide.

BEST CONDITIONS Although cabbage grows best in loose, well-prepared soils, it will adapt to sandy, clay, or loamy soils. For best results, the soil should be slightly acidic (pH of 6.0-6.8) and well-drained, as wet soils offer conditions for many soil-borne diseases. Cabbages need full sun and at least 1 inch of water per week. A cool-season crop, cabbages do best when grown in spring or fall; avoid midsummer heat, particularly for Savoys. They should be planted in early spring, and again for a fall crop in late June or early July. Once established, cabbages can withstand temperatures as low as 27° F. in the fall.

PLANTING Seeds should be started indoors 4-6 weeks before transplant time (2 weeks before the last expected frost). Plant 2-3 seeds in a 2-inch fiber or plastic pot, ¼-½ inch deep. Water thoroughly and keep moist. Seeds will germinate in 6-8 days. Either mix granular fertilizer at half the recommended rate into the potting mix before sowing seed or feed seedlings with a 10-10-10 liquid fertilizer every 7-10 days. Supply plenty of light, or spindly stems will be produced.

When transplanting seedlings into the garden, place plants 12-24 inches apart (space larger heads more widely), placing rows 3-4 feet apart. Select transplants with no yellow leaves, flexible stems, bright white fibrous root systems; pot-bound plants may not develop heads.

CARE Fertilize soil 2-3 days before planting and once a month thereafter with a high-nitrogen mix, such as 15-10-10. Be sure to apply nitrogen when heads first appear, as this is when the plant requires it most. Gardeners at Fetzer Organic Gardens find that applying fertilizer in the fall causes cabbages to rot in storage. Cultivate after each application of fertilizer; when cultivating, move soil up around base of stem to stabilize plant. Floating row covers offer frost protection as well as insect barriers.

PESTS AND DISEASES "Yellows" (yellow-spotted leaves on head and outer leaves eventually causing the plant to die) and black rot as well as insects such as aphids and cabbage loopers are sometimes a problem when growing cabbage. Choose varieties resistant to these pests and diseases. At the Chicago Botanic Garden and Callaway Gardens, Bt is used to control cabbage loopers.

HARVEST Cabbage is generally ready to harvest 60-80 days after transplanting; they are ready when the heads are firm. At harvest time, decrease water to prevent cracking of the heads. Usually, there is only 1 harvest, and each plant produces only 1 head. Cut the stalk at the base of the plant and then trim outer leaves. Harvested cabbages store well in cool, dark places.

At The New York Botanical Garden, gardeners have found that if they make a shallow crosscut in the stump after they harvest the early cabbage, a second crop of smaller cabbages may form by autumn.

VARIETIES GREEN CABBAGES: 'Bravo', a main-season blue-green cabbage, is very cold-tolerant and holds well without splitting. (University of Nebraska)
'Conquest' is an early-midseason medium-sized cabbage with a very mild, sweet flavor, excellent for cole slaw. Its tender leaves are susceptible to insect dam-

Few and singly blessed are those whom Jupiter has destined to be cabbage planters. For they've always one foot on the ground and the other not far from it.
RABELAIS, GARGANTUA AND PANTAGRUEL

Cabbages are among the most ornamental of vegetables both in form and color. This bed of blue cabbages planted with red and green lettuces rivals the beauty of most flower beds.

RED CABBAGE 'RED ROOKIE' Hybrid. Plant 18 inches wide produces 6-inch round head, deep red. Days to harvest: 70.

SAVOY CABBAGE 'ACE' Hybrid. Yields 1 head, weighing up to 5 pounds; allow 1 square foot per plant. Withstands summer heat. Days to harvest: 70-90.

SAVOY CABBAGE 'KING' Hybrid. Plant 2 feet tall, 18-20 inches wide, produces large, loose, leafy head, white inside. Yields 3-4 pounds per head. Best in spring but heat-resistant. Days to harvest: 65.

CHINESE CABBAGE 'MEI QUING CHOI' (BABY PAK CHOI) Hybrid. Produces attractive heads with green petioles. Vigorous and early, upright and compact, tolerant of heat and cold. Days to harvest: 45.

Savoy cabbages, such as the one on the right in this picture, have crinkled leaves. The cabbage on the left is a red variety. Savoy, red, and green cabbages have the same cultural requirements. Cabbages contain a chemical called anthocyanin, which turns the heads blue, green, or red depending on its concentration. All cabbages have outer leaves called wrappers. The wrapper leaves protect the cabbages from pests and diseases, retain water and nutrients, and aid the process of "heading." Most late-season cabbages form more efficient wrapper leaves than earlier ones.

age. 70-75 days to harvest. (University of Nebraska)

'Darkri' produces 8- to10-inch heads 42 days after transplanting.

'Early Jersey Wakefield' is ready for harvest 8-10 days sooner than other cabbage varieties. Because the head is loose, it is susceptible to damage from cabbage loopers. Size and flavor are best when fall-planted.

'Heads Up' matures early and is resistant to insect damage.

'Stonehead' is an older, dependable variety and heads well under many different growing conditions, resisting cracking even when rainy. Because the head forms quickly, insects cannot easily get down into it. It is also resistant to cabbage loopers. Plant 18 inches apart. This prize-winning selection should be fertilized 3 times during the growing season.

'Tropic Giant' is an easy-to-grow variety that produces 12-inch heads weighing up to 15 pounds. It can be grown in spring or fall, but needs extra growing time to reach its full size. (New York Botanical Garden)

RED CABBAGES: 'Lasso' can withstand colder temperatures and stay longer in the field without splitting. This variety does particularly well when planted in late summer and allowed to mature in fall. Having few outer leaves, it is resistant to insect damage.

'Red Rookie' is a cool-season hybrid that forms a 6-inch head approximately 70 days from transplanting. The outer leaves of this variety are tough, making it more resistant to damage from insects. This variety resists cracking and has a small core and a milder flavor than most other red cabbages.

SAVOY CABBAGE: 'Ace' is a crinkled-head Savoy, excellent for stir-fry and resistant to insect damage because of its well-filled head.

'King' has sweet, tender, flavorful leaves that mature approximately 65 days from transplanting. The crinkly leaves of this cabbage make a good hiding place for aphids and loopers, and insect damage is sometimes a problem. This variety should be spaced 24 inches apart and fertilized 3 times during the growing season; more heat resistant than other Savoys.

ORIENTAL CABBAGES: 'Blues' is a reliable and easy-to-grow Chinese cabbage that

Carrots are formed underground; only their lacy foliage shows above the soil. Like other root vegetables, they need loose well-tilled soil that is free of rocks; roots will be stunted or deformed if they encounter obstacles in the soil. If your soil is heavy, grow carrots in raised beds.

produces large heads and is slow to bolt, making it a good variety to grow in the spring. (New York Botanical Garden)

'Jade Pagoda' is best grown from transplants rather than seeds sown directly into the garden because it requires a long growing season. At the Minnesota Landscape Arboretum, it does best as a fall crop.

Mei Quing Choi is a hybrid green-stemmed baby pak choi with a compact, upright growth habit that makes it easy to harvest. It is easy to grow and very flavorful. Resists bolting.

CARROT DAUCUS CAROTA VAR. SATIVUS *Apiaceae*

COOL-SEASON BIENNIAL GROWN AS AN ANNUAL The original carrot was probably developed from the wild carrot, often called Queen Anne's lace, a pretty wildflower. The first cultivated carrots were branched and red, purple, white, or black and were grown by early Greeks and Romans. Substances within the carrot were thought to be useful as an aphrodisiac.

Carrots are very high in vitamin A (a single carrot supplies the adult daily requirement) and have a high sugar content. The sweetness of carrots makes them popular in cooking such dishes as cakes, puddings, and marmalade. This vegetable is so sweet that the Irish called it "underground honey."

Carrots produce a tapered underground root and lacy foliage that stands 1-2 feet tall and spreads 6-8 inches wide.

BEST CONDITIONS Carrots need very well-tilled, deep, sandy soils, at a pH of 6.0-6.8. A generous amount of compost added to the soil is beneficial. They grow best when there are no rocks and the soil is soft and easy to push through. For heavier, clay soils, try "ball" or mini types with short roots.

Carrots need full sun for good root formation and do best grown during cooler months. Though they can also be grown in warm weather, heat often results in bitter, woody carrots. At Callaway Gardens, carrots produce the sweetest flavor when grown as a spring and early summer crop; summers at Callaway are too hot for the tender carrot seedlings. Ideally, carrots should receive 1 inch of water per week.

PLANTING Carrot seeds should be planted directly into the ground. Indoor propagation is not recommended. Sow the seeds directly into the garden 2-3 weeks before the last frost and again as a fall crop 6 weeks before the first frost is expected. Seeds should be scattered lightly in rows 2-3 feet apart. Before planting, firm the soil so the seeds will not sink too far down in the freshly tilled soil. Cover with no more than ¼-inch soil and water gently but thoroughly. The seeds are difficult to space because they are so small, and seedlings should be thinned to 1-2 inches apart. Seeds should germinate in 6-8 days. One-quarter to one-half ounce of seeds will plant a 100-foot row.

CARE A floating row cover will protect young seedlings from a late frost. Once established, the plants can withstand temperatures down to 35° F.; at the Chicago Botanic Garden, carrots have survived frosts down to 25-32° F. in the fall.

For best root growth, a fertilizer high in potash (rather than high in nitro-

CARROT 'DANVERS HALF-LONG' Open-pollinated. Ferny foliage, 10-14 inches tall, 10 inches wide, produces 1 red-cored carrot, 6-7 inches long, 1 inch wide. Good for heavy soils. Days to harvest: 75.

CARROT 'SCARLET NANTES' Open-pollinated. Ferny foliage 10-14 inches tall, 8-10 inches wide, produces 1 short, coreless, bright orange carrot, 6-7 inches long, 1 inch wide, per plant. Days to harvest: 70.

CARROTS 'SUPREME CHANTENAY' Produces deep orange carrots 6 ½-7½ inches long, with broad shoulders and tapered roots; best for loose soils. Good for juicing. Days to harvest: 70.

CARROT 'THUMBELINA' Ferny foliage, 6-8 inches tall, 6-8 inches wide, produces 2-inch round bright-orange root. Very sweet. Good for heavy or rocky soils. Days to harvest: 60-70.

CAULIFLOWER 'SNOWBALL 123' Hybrid. Medium-sized heads, lightly packed, creamy white. Very crunchy when eaten raw. Plant is 2 feet tall, 18 inches wide. Tolerates heat. Days to harvest: 65.

CAULIFLOWER 'SNOW CROWN' Hybrid. Medium-sized, dome-shaped heads on upright plant, 2-2½ feet tall. Resistant to moderate fall frost. Days to harvest: 50.

CAULIFLOWER 'VIOLET QUEEN' Hybrid. Small 7- to 9-inch heads, with violet tops that turn green when cooked. Grows and tastes like broccoli. Easy to grow; reaches harvestable size quickly. Days to harvest: 54.

CELERY 'UTAH 52-7R' Tall, vigorous, broad-ribbed stalks, bred for resistance to disease. 24 inches tall, up to 12 inches to first joint. Days to harvest: 120-135.

gen) should be applied; 5-10-15 or 10-10-15 is ideal. Spread fertilizer or well-rotted manure over soil 2-3 days before sowing and rake into the top 1-2 inches. Fertilize again every 4 weeks until harvest.

Cultivate between the rows with a tiller or hoe. Between the plants, pull weeds by hand. Keep the soil cultivated and loose to promote even root development. Heavy or rocky soils cause the bottoms of the roots to split. When the carrots grow too quickly as a result of too much nitrogen, they tend to split from the crown all the way down.

PESTS AND DISEASES Mildew can develop if the seedlings are not thinned or if the foliage is too heavy from overfertilization or overwatering.

HARVEST Carrots are ready to harvest in 60-70 days. When the foliage begins to turn light green and the soil around the top of the root begins to crack, the carrots are probably ready to harvest. To remove carrots from the ground, loosen the soil around each plant with a fork and hand-pull each carrot. A 100-foot row should yield 1½ bushels.

VARIETIES 'A+' produces 9- to 10-inch carrots that have a very high vitamin A content. Recent crop failures have made the seed hard to find. (New York Botanical Garden)

'Danver's Half-Long' is good for heavier soils and for planting in hot areas, where it can be planted in spring and fall and develops quickly.

'Gold Pak' is good for juicing. This "coreless" carrot can remain in the soil without cracking.

'Lady Finger' is sweet and tender and often cooked whole. It is good for a variety of soils because it is fast-growing and small-rooted.

'Nantes Half-Long' has closely grained flesh.

'Scarlet Nantes' has a handsome "coreless" interior. It grows quickly in a variety of soils and is easy to harvest.

'Supreme Chantenay' is a large plump carrot with a very smooth skin. It can be used fresh and stores well.

'Thumbelina' is good for growing in heavy soils. This thin-skinned, ball-shaped carrot was a 1992 AAS winner.

Before harvesting carrots, check the circumference of the top with your finger. If the carrot is the right size (which this 'A+' carrot is not), loosen soil and pull carrot firmly from the soil.

CAULIFLOWER BRASSICA OLERACEA VAR. BOTRYTIS

Brassicaceae

COOL-SEASON BIENNIAL GROWN AS AN ANNUAL Mark Twain called the cauliflower "nothing but a cabbage with a college education." Unlike broccoli, which will eventually form tiny yellow flowers, the cauliflower head is incapable of opening and putting forth flowers. It has been cultivated since at least the 12th century. During the 1700s, both red and purple cauliflowers were grown.

Cauliflower is grown for the 7- to 8-inch white head (called a curd) produced in the center of a 2-foot-tall and 2-foot-wide plant. Cauliflower grow best in spring and fall.

BEST CONDITIONS Cauliflower needs loose, well-prepared, neutral-pH soils but can grow in sand, clay, or loam. Soils that are too acidic produce plants with

When cauliflower heads are the sizes of golf balls, pull the side leaves up over the head and bind with twine or a rubber band. This is called blanching and keeps the head white. Celery requires blanching as well. Some varieties of each are "self-blanching." Blanch celery by banking soil against the plant as it grows. Start banking soil when plants reach 12 inches tall or 7-10 days before harvest. Soil piled halfway up the stalk produces pale, tender stems.

yellow leaves and a brown or purplish cast to the heads. Before planting, take a soil sample of the garden plot, for this vegetable is particularly sensitive to the level of trace elements in the soil and will respond adversely to deficiencies. Amend as recommended by the soil test results. Full sun is necessary to produce cauliflower.

PLANTING Seeds can be started indoors 6-8 weeks before the last frost. Plant 2-3 seeds ¼-½ inch deep in a 2-inch fiber or plastic pot. Water thoroughly and supply with sufficient light to produce strong, stocky stems. Poor light or too much heat produces spindly plants. Seeds should germinate in 6-8 days. Indoors, fertilize every 7-10 days with a liquid fertilizer (10-10-10 or 13-13-13) or put a mixed balanced granular fertilizer at half the recommended rate into the potting mixture before the seeds are sown.

Seedlings or store-bought plants should be transplanted 2 weeks before the last frost, 2 feet apart in rows 3-4 feet apart. When choosing transplants from a garden center, avoid plants with yellow leaves, limp or woody stems.

CARE Use a high-nitrogen mix, such as 15-10-10, 2-3 days before planting time and once a month thereafter. Place straw around the plants, or use a floating row cover, to protect the plants from frost.

After each application of fertilizer, cultivate lightly around the plants and move soil 1-2 inches up the stem to help stabilize the plants.

PESTS AND DISEASES Because cauliflower takes so long to grow (75-100 days), it is often subject to pest and disease problems. Look for heat-tolerant varieties. Mildew is sometimes a problem, so select resistant varieties for cool growing conditions. For a serious infestation of cabbage loopers, dust with Bt as needed. Cutworms feed at soil level but can be deterred by placing a cardboard or plastic collar around the transplant; press the collar down 1 inch into soil.

HARVEST Heads are generally ready 75 days after transplanting. Blanch when the heads are about golf-ball size. Check the heads for maturity every 3-4 days. The heads should be harvested before they start to yellow.

To harvest, cut at the base of the stalk and trim the leaves and stem away from the head so as not to lose any of the head. A 100-foot row will yield 1-2 bushels. This is a one-harvest vegetable and should be pulled up after the head is cut.

VARIETIES 'Alert' is the earliest self-blanching variety with full, pure white heads.
'Snow Crown' is a reliably fast producer. It has an open, rather than compact, head and must be blanched for best results.
'Snowball 123' has heavy side leaves that are good for blanching.
'Violet Queen' produces dark purple heads. It does not need blanching.

CELERY
CELERY APIUM GRAVEOLENS VAR. DULCE *Apiaceae*
CUTTING CELERY APIUM GRAVEOLENS VAR SECALINUM A*piaceae*
CELERIAC APIUM GRAVEOLENS RAPACEUM *Apiaceae*
BIENNIAL GROWN AS AN ANNUAL In Greek and Roman times, celery was called ache; wreaths of it were rumored to cure hangovers. The Latin name *apium* comes from the word *bee*, for bees are attracted to its tiny white flowers.

Celery is a mounded leafy plant that grows to 30 inches tall, with light green or yellow 6- to 9-inch leaf stalks.

Celery is not an easy vegetable to grow and will not produce if its conditions are not met. It requires constant mulching, fertilization, watering, and a long, warm—but not hot—growing season. Cutting celery (also called leaf celery, seasoning celery, Chinese celery, or wild celery) is more adaptable; its leaves have the same taste as celery, but it does not produce the crisp stalks that celery is usually grown for. Celeriac, which is related to celery and has a similar taste, is grown for its bulbous root; it requires even more care than celery. Celeriac is often used in place of potatoes.

At Fetzer Gardens, celery thrives in raised beds, started indoors from seed.

BEST CONDITIONS Celery will grow only in moist, rich soil (pH 6.0-7.0). It needs a 4-month growing season. Celery is not suited to the warm, humid climates of the South.

PLANTING Plant celery from seeds started indoors 10-12 weeks before transplanting. Seeds take up to 25 days to germinate; soaking them overnight may speed germination. Be sure to buy fresh seeds, for celery seeds do not remain productive as long as most others. Transplants bought in nurseries can also be used, but are sometimes hard to find.

Transplant seedlings to the garden when the temperature exceeds 55° F. Space seedlings 8 inches apart, in rows at least 8 inches apart. Celery will bolt if subjected to fluctuations in temperature; protect with floating row covers if a change in weather is expected.

CARE Celery is a heavy feeder. Supply a 5-10-5 fertilizer before planting and at 6-week intervals during the season. Water frequently—celery needs moisture—but allow to drain. A constant drip irrigation system works well for celery and celeriac. Mulch to help keep the plants moist and cool. Although self-blanching varieties are available, most celery needs to be blanched to retain good color. Celeriac needs even more water than celery and has an even longer growing season—usually 5 months.

PESTS AND DISEASES Celery plants are subject to many pests, including mosaic, aphids, nematodes, and celery worms.

HARVEST Celery can be harvested by lifting the entire plant, or by cutting individual stalks. Celery left after maturity will become hollow. Seasoning celery can be cut as needed from the garden and will grow back.

VARIETIES CELERY: 'Golden Self-blanching', a readily available variety, is a compact plant with tender but solid stalks.

'Utah 52-7R' has thick dark green stalks and is resistant to mosaic.

CELERIAC: 'Alabaster' has large roots and does not discolor when cut.

CUTTING CELERY: 'Amsterdam' has a much smaller rib than most; it looks like a very large parsley plant. It has a strong celery flavor and is good for cooking.

'Par-Cel' produces abundant foliage with a strong celery taste. It can be grown in light shade.

BOLTING

When a plant bolts, it produces nonharvestable flower and seed stalks. Bolting is a natural process; it is the way plants produce seeds for another year. But early bolting is often a problem for vegetable gardeners.

Although many people note that bolting follows dryness and heat, it is actually caused by a plant being under stress for a number of reasons: temperature fluctuations, drought, hot days, and tardy harvesting.

To prevent early bolting, schedule your planting and harvesting times carefully. For example, cabbages should be planted early enough to harvest before the heat of summer; okra should be harvested every 2 days to maintain production of fruit.

CUTTING CELERY 'PAR-CEL' Leafy green plant, reaches 12-24 inches tall, similar in appearance and growth habit to parsley; foliage looks and tastes like celery. Space 10-12 inches apart. Tolerates light shade. Harvest at 9-12 inches.

CORN 'GOLDEN QUEEN' Hybrid. Stalks 7-8 feet tall, 2 feet wide, produce yellow-kerneled ears, 8 inches long, 3 inches wide. Yields 2 ears per stalk. Days to harvest: 88.

CORN 'HOW SWEET IT IS' Hybrid. Stalks 6 feet tall, 2 feet wide, produce white-kerneled supersweet ears, 8 inches long, 3 inches wide, 2 ears per plant. Retains sweet flavor after harvest. Days to harvest: 85.

CORN 'MERIT' Hybrid. Stalks 7-8 feet tall, 2 feet wide, produce yellow-kerneled ears, 8 inches long. Yields 2 ears per stalk. Best early variety; germinates in cool soils. Days to harvest: 75.

CORN ZEA MAYS VAR. RUGOSA *Gramineae*

WARM-SEASON ANNUAL The name *corn* is given to the leading cereal crop of any region. In England, corn means wheat; in Scotland and Ireland, oats. The grain called corn in America is Indian corn, or maize. A descendant of wild New World grasses, the plant was domesticated and cultivated in America long before Columbus reached these shores. Ears of corn have been a motif of American art since prehistory, and Native Americans were so sophisticated in the cultivation of corn that they grew many different kinds–pop, sweet, dent, and flint. Corn was equally important to the first European settlers in the Americas. Sweet corn is grown to be cooked at an immature stage; popcorn is grown to maturity and then dried and stored; flint and dent corn are grown to maturity, dried, and ground for cornmeal; dent corn has a large depression on the top of each large kernel. Corn, high in sugar, begins to lose its sweet flavor as soon as the ears are picked from the plant (this explains the old country saying that you can stroll to the corn patch but you had better run back).

When leaves begin to appear on corn plants, mound the soil around the base of the plant. This keeps moisture in and allows the roots to develop and provide support against wind.

Corn is a tall annual grasslike plant grown for the "ears," which develop kernels or seeds in rows on a cob. Because corn depletes soil nutrients, corn crops should be rotated annually; do not return to the original site for 3 years. Most corn is wind-pollinated; it is important to not impede pollination. Plant at least 3 rows side by side or in blocks. The pollen of supersweet or ornamental corns can easily mix with that of other varieties, causing them all to become starchy and tasteless. If you are planting several types of corn, isolate them in distance or in time of planting. Because corn depletes soil nutrients, it should be rotated annually; do not return to the original site for 3 years.

At the Desert Botanic Garden in Phoenix, corn is a cool-season crop; if it is not established before the summer, the intense heat destroys the pollen, and pollination does not occur.

BEST CONDITIONS Corn seeds should not be planted until the soil is at least 55-60° F.; 65° is ideal. It will grow in several soil types, even in poorly drained soils, but does best in sandy loam with a pH of 6.5-7.0. Corn needs full sun; even partial shade will cause poor ear development. It will not tolerate frost.

PLANTING Corn is best grown from seeds sown directly into the soil. If it is necessary to start seeds indoors, use containers at least 2-4 inches deep to accommodate the extensive root system. Sow the seeds 1 inch deep in potting soil and keep evenly moist under lights. Transplant as quickly as possible (at the latest by the time they are 2-4 inches tall) to keep from growing pot-bound, spindly plants.

At Fetzer Organic Gardens, presoaked seed is sown at the beginning of March (8 weeks before frost-free date) and planted from a cool greenhouse into row-covered beds around April 1; corn is ready for harvest by early May.

When sowing seeds directly into the garden, plant 2 weeks after the last frost. Sow seeds 1 inch deep in a 4-inch-deep furrow. Space seeds 3-4 inches apart in rows 3-4 feet apart. Thin to 8-10 inches between plants. As plants grow, cultivate the soil on either side of the furrows and turn the soil up

CORN 'SILVER QUEEN' Hybrid. Stalks 8 feet tall, 2 feet wide, with dark green tight husks and abundant large leaves produce slender-eared small, white-kerneled ears, 8 inches long, 1½-2 inches wide. Yields 2 ears per stalk. Days to harvest: 90.

POPCORN 'STRAWBERRY' Open-pollinated. Stalks 3-4 feet tall, 2 feet wide, produce small red-kerneled ears, 2-3 inches long, 1½ inches wide. Yields 2 ears per stalk. Days to harvest: 80.

ORNAMENTAL INDIAN CORN 'FIESTA' Hybrid. Sturdy stalks, 7 feet tall, 2 feet wide, produce large multicolored kernels, on ears 8 inches long, 3 inches wide. Yields 2 large ears per stalk. Days to harvest: 102.

BROOM CORN Annual agricultural grass, 7-10 feet tall, 18 inches wide, grown for its loose wiry seedheads, which can be used for brooms, craft projects, or birdseed. Can be harvested green and dried indoors. Days to harvest: 100-110.

against the base of the plants. Sow additional furrows 2 weeks later to stagger harvests. Seeds should germinate in 5-7 days, but germination will be slower in cool soils. One-quarter pound of seeds will sow a 100 foot row.

HARVEST To harvest, snap the ear sharply downward in the early morning when the stalks are crisp. Leave the stalk to produce a smaller second ear. A 100-foot row should yield 2-2½ bushels in the first harvest.

VARIETIES SWEET CORN: 'Early Extra Sweet' is a fast producer. Loose shucks make it easy to clean. It is important to isolate this variety from other corn varieties or it will cross-pollinate, producing starchy kernels. 70 days to harvest.

'Encinal Blue', is a heat-tolerant variety; distributed by Native Seeds/SEARCH, it can be used as a warm-season crop even in the desert southwest.

'Golden Queen' holds its flavor well after harvest. The tight shucks keep insects from traveling down the ear, making it good to grow late in the season, but also making it more difficult to shuck. The silks generally do not turn brown at maturity, so check for harvest readiness by feeling for full ears.

'Honey 'n' Pearl', a "supersweet" corn has both yellow and white kernels, combining the best qualities of both. It is not necessary to isolate this corn from others. Good for freezing and canning and especially good as creamed corn.

'How Sweet It Is' is one of the sweetest corns and is still tender even when harvested a bit past the peak time. AAS winner. The silks do not turn brown.

'Kiss 'n' Tell' is a very sweet bicolor hybrid corn. It does not need to be isolated and is easy to pick. (Chicago Botanic Garden)

'Merit' reliably produces 2 full ears per stalk. It is also one of the easiest to shuck and rarely has earworm problems because it is an early producer with good leaf coverage and tight shucks; earworms show up later in the season. It is not recommended for growing in late summer.

'Silver Queen' is one of the most popular sweet corns. It is sweet and flavorful with a high yield. It has more foliage than other sweet corns, requiring more water and fertilizer in order to get 2 good filled ears of corn.

'Sugar Buns' is a sweet, early hybrid with rows of very rich, creamy bright yellow kernels. It holds extremely well both in the field and after picking.

POPCORN 'Strawberry' is best grown where humidity is low because it dries slowly. Constant moisture slows the drying process, affecting the quality of seed for storage. It is possible to pick the ears when the kernels first begin to harden and finish drying them in a cool, dry, well-ventilated spot. Used more as an ornamental corn than for popping.

'Iopop 12' produces good-sized yellow kernels. It is a good producer and especially well-suited to Northern gardens. (Minnesota Landscape Arboretum)

'White Cloud' is one of the best varieties, with flavorful, pointed, thin-skinned, "hull-less" kernels. (Minnesota Landscape Arboretum)

ORNAMENTAL INDIAN CORN: 'Fiesta' considered a "flint" corn, is highly ornamental, with multicolored kernels, the largest of the Indian corns.

BROOM CORN, actually sorghum, not corn, is cultivated and grown the same way as sweet corn, except that it can be sown closer together. Transplants of broom corn do better than transplants of sweet corn.

He partakes in the spring of the corn, in the rising and budding and earing of the corn. And when he eats his bread, at last, he recovers all he once sent forthe, and partakes again of the energies he called to the corn from out of the wide universe.

D. H. LAWRENCE, FROM *DANCE OF THE SPROUTING CORN*.

COVER CROPS

COOL- OR WARM-SEASON ANNUALS AND PERENNIALS Cover crops are shallow-rooted plants (though some have deep roots) grown close together for the purpose of covering the soil during unused times in the garden. They protect the soil against erosion and are generally tilled into the garden to enrich the soil. In general, they are grown as annuals started from seed. Cover crops can be planted in cool or warm seasons, depending on how the space is needed.

Benefits of cover crops include looser soil with more organic content, possible higher soil fertility, depending on the crop used, and quick prevention of soil erosion.

BEST CONDITIONS Full sun is best to encourage quick growth and full coverage. The crops most often used will grow in just about any kind of soil with normal (6.0-7.0) pH. Watering is necessary only for germination of seeds, except in dry areas.

A common problem is planting cool-season cover crops too late. When using cover crops, resist the temptation to seed too heavily. It is better to apply the seed at or under the recommended rates on packages because too thick a cover makes the crop difficult to till in. In most cases, be sure to till in the crops while the plants are still small to make tilling and subsequent breakdown of vegetative material easier.

Different cover crops are chosen for different reasons. If a fast-growing crop is needed, use rye or buckwheat. If your goal is to put more nitrogen into the soil use crimson clover, Austrian winter pea, alfalfa, or other members of the legume (pea) family.

PLANTING Cool-season cover crops (winter rye, crimson clover, etc.) should be sown soon after the first frost to reduce competition from warm-season weeds. The amount of seed necessary varies. For 1 acre use 50-60 pounds wheat, 20 pounds crimson clover, 50-60 pounds winter peas. For best results, till the soil in fall to break up the hardpan that has developed throughout the summer. Till again just before planting. Broadcast seeds evenly over the plot and rake to a depth of ½ inch. Germination should take only 3-5 days. Water until plants are established.

CARE In a plot that has not been frequently cultivated or fertilized, apply an 8-8-8 or 10-10-10 fertilizer at planting time or broadcast the seed; rake in. Weeds are seldom a problem since cover crops grow quickly and tend to shade out other plants. Likewise, pests and disease are generally not problems.

Cover crops are sometimes used as a windbreak to protect young vegetable transplants or seedlings. Wheat or rye, planted in 6- to 8-foot-wide strips between vegetable plots and allowed to grow to a mature height will slow down damaging winds.

When cover crops are grown in the vegetable bed, it is important to till them under at the correct stage. Wheat and rye should be tilled in early spring when 16-24 inches tall and still green. Clover and peas should be tilled in during early to mid spring at 10-12 inches high just before blooms open.

COVER CROP BUCKWHEAT Upright, fast-growing plant, 2-3 feet tall, 12-18 inches across. White blossoms attract butterflies. Can be sown, grown, and tilled under in 1 month.

COVER CROP CRIMSON CLOVER Round, large-leaved annual clover with bright red flowers in spring. 12-24 inches tall at harvest. A good nitrogen-fixing cover crop.

COVER CROP WINTER RYE Very cold-hardy, vigorous plant with extensive root system that provides erosion control and deposits organic matter deep in the soil. 6-7 feet at harvest; turn under when 12-14 inches tall.

CUCUMBER 'BURPLESS' Hybrid. Produces 9- to 12-inch dark green curved cucumbers, 2 inches in diameter. Mild flavor, no bitterness, good for slicing. Days to harvest: 62.

Cover crops, such as crimson clover (above), are not harvested conventionally; instead, they are turned into the soil, where they decompose and add nutrients that will be used by the next crop to be planted there. Cover crops are usually tilled in before they flower. If they do flower, it is important to till them in before the flowers go to seed because tilling in the seed essentially reseeds the crop. It is a good idea to till in cover crops before they mature and become tough and hard to work.

Buckwheat should be tilled in during summer at 2 feet high just as flowering begins. To till in cover crops, the entire plant needs to be turned into the top 6-8 inches of soil. Turning cover crops under deeper than that does not speed up the decomposition process.

VARIETIES Buckwheat is a fast-growing summer cover crop that is easy to till into the soil. Within 4-6 weeks it can be sown, grown, and tilled in. To grow buckwheat, till the soil, rake seeds into the soil to a depth of ½ inch, and water until seedlings are established. As flowering begins, till the entire plant into the soil. If allowed to go to seed, buckwheat will self-sow. Its white flowers attract butterflies and beneficial insects. Seeds are readily available through mail-order catalogs. Buckwheat can be sown spring through midsummer.

Austrian Winter Pea resembles garden peas with small round leaves and curling tendrils. This weak-stemmed, 12-inch-tall plant often tumbles over. To plant, till the soil and then sow inoculated seeds ½-1 inch deep. Winter peas break down quickly when tilled into the soil and help to increase the amount of available nitrogen in the soil. Winter peas are planted in the fall. Frost date is not critical, but winter peas need several months to grow.

Crimson Clover has deep red strawberry-shaped flowers and round leaves larger than other clovers. At maturity, it is 12-24 inches tall and is a good nitrogen-fixing plant. It is not necessary to till the soil to cover the seeds, but germination will be best if seeds are lightly covered with soil. Crimson clover is a very attractive plant when in bloom, and many southern states use it along roadsides. It is not, however, cold-hardy in northern states. The stems and leaves are tender and easy to till in. It is best planted in early fall.

Winter Rye is a vigorous annual cereal grain. As a cover crop it is grown to only 2 feet tall and then tilled in. If it is not cut and tilled in at this height, it will present a huge problem for the gardener because the root system becomes tough and hard to get out, and the amount of organic matter is so great it will have to be cut like hay and carried away. Even in the immature stage, it takes rye longer to break down than other cover crops. It should be tilled under twice—once to chop up the plants and mix them with the soil and again 2 weeks later to encourage faster decay. Winter rye is planted in the fall.

CUCUMBER CUCUMIS SATIVUS *Cucurbitaceae*

WARM-SEASON ANNUAL Cucumbers were grown more than 3,000 years ago in India; carbon dating of seeds found in a cave near the Thailand-Burma border indicates that this vegetable may have been cultivated as early as 9750 B.C. Ancient Romans venerated the cucumber; Virgil wrote about cucumbers in his *Georgics*, and the gourmet Apicius included 3 recipes for them—1 using calf's brains—in his famous cookbook. Samuel Johnson had less use for them. "A cucumber," he wrote, "should be well-sliced, and dressed with pepper and vinegar, and then thrown out, as good for nothing." Columbus brought cucumber seeds with him to the New World and planted them in Haiti in 1494. Called "cowcumbers," they had a place in the gardens of early colonists.

CUCUMBER 'EDMONSON' 1913 heirloom variety. Produces 4-inch cucumbers. Resists disease, insects, and drought. Days to harvest: 70.

CUCUMBER 'LEMON' Heirloom variety with white flesh and yellow rind. Produces 3-inch round fruits. Days to harvest: 64

CUCUMBER 'SALAD BUSH' Hybrid. Dark green, smooth-skinned slicing cucumbers on bushy plant, 18 inches tall, 2-3 feet wide. Disease-resistant. Days to harvest: 57.

CUCUMBER 'SWEET SUCCESS' Hybrid. Vines 5-6 feet long, 2 feet wide, produce 8- to 14-inch-long fruits. Seedless unless pollinated. Heavy producer; disease-resistant. Days to harvest: 58.

BEST CONDITIONS Cucumbers need full sun; plants grown in shady areas produce few fruits. At least 6-8 hours of sun a day is ideal. Loose, loamy soils are best, and good drainage is important. If growing in heavy clay, add generous amounts of compost to soil. Cucumbers prefer a soil pH of 6.0-6.5. The soil temperature at planting time must be 65° F. or higher. Cucumbers need 1 inch of water per week for even production. Uneven watering or poor pollination causes misshapen fruits to develop. They will not grow well in low spots. In the Great Plains, poor pollination is often caused by high winds or the absence of bees.

PLANTING To start indoors, sow 2-3 seeds each in 2-inch pots and keep soil evenly moist, though not wet. Supply with good light and transplant as soon as they are ready, usually in 3-4 weeks. Because the garden soil has to be warm before these plants will thrive, do not plant until 1-2 weeks after the last frost.

Cucumbers take up a lot of room. Transplant 2-3 seedlings in small hills, leaving 3 feet between hills in rows 4 feet apart. Seeds can be sown directly in the garden, ½-1 inch deep. Plant 4-5 seeds per hill and thin to 2-3. Gardeners at Callaway Gardens pinch off the unwanted plants rather than pulling them up in order to avoid disturbing the root system of the remaining plants.

CARE Straw spread 2-3 inches deep around the hills gives the fruits a resting place so they are not in contact with the soil. Work a balanced (10-10-10) fertilizer into the soil 2-3 days prior to planting seeds or transplants. Side-dress with calcium nitrate or potassium nitrate to encourage good blossom and fruit production. Apply fertilizer when the vines begin to run.

The area around cucumber plants should be kept weeded until the plants start running. Weeding after this can damage the plants by crushing leaves or nicking stems, which affects the plants' production. Keep cucumber production high by pruning off all damaged or diseased leaves.

Cucumber vines can be trellised on fences or 5- to 6-foot trellises. Large-fruited cucumbers, such as slicers, sometimes need the support of a trellis or fence in order to produce well-shaped fruit.

PESTS AND DISEASES Beetles often damage young cucumber plants; control with a floating row cover or insecticides. Row covers should be removed once flowers appear so that pollination can occur. White flies generally appear late in the season. Hose flies off the leaves with water and prune the affected foliage.

Gardeners at Fezter find that straw mulches encourage slugs, and side-dressing after planting encourages mites; they avoid both practices.

HARVEST Cucumbers can be picked when the fruits reach the desired size. Pull carefully or cut stems when harvesting so the vines will not be damaged.

VARIETIES 'Armenian' is a light green cucumber that never gets bitter; a tasting favorite at Fetzer Gardens.

'Burpless' has a mild flavor and no bitterness. It has a small seed cavity and is good for slicing.

'Dasher' is a highly productive slicing cucumber with good dark green color and a minimum of yellow belly. (University of Nebraska)

'Edmonson', an heirloom variety from 1913, has an odd greenish white skin; it tolerates diseases, insects, and drought.

'Kyoto' Oriental cucumbers are much thinner, crisper, and longer–up to 18 inches–than most. The climbing vines need trellising and produce heavy yields of fancy fruit.

'Lemon' produces yellow fruit.

'Pot Luck' can be grown in small garden spaces or in containers.

'Salad Bush', a non-runner-forming, mild-flavored variety, needs to be picked promptly to keep production high.

'Sweet Success', an AAS winner, is "seedless" and extremely productive.

EGGPLANT SOLANUM MELONGENA VAR. ESCULENTUM

Solanaceae

WARM-SEASON PERENNIAL GROWN AS AN ANNUAL The first eggplant was probably developed from a bitter, spiny fruit found growing in central Asia. It was introduced to the kitchens of China in the 3rd century A.D. but was not considered good–or even safe–to eat until it reached the Middle East.

Eggplant produces fruit on a multibranched shrubby 2- to 4-foot-tall plant.

BEST CONDITIONS Eggplant will not produce fruit in cool temperatures and must be grown in full sun to be productive. Eggplant is tolerant of a wide range of soil types, but prefers a pH of 6.0-6.8.

PLANTING Eggplant requires a long growing season. It should be grown from transplants rather than seed sown directly in the garden. Seeds sown indoors take 6-8 weeks before they are ready to transplant. Seeds should be planted at a depth of ¼-½ inch and should germinate in 7-10 days. It is essential to supply sufficient light indoors because they are in the greenhouse longer than most crops. The young seedlings are prone to damping off, so be careful to use sterile potting soil and not crowd or overwater. Multiple seedlings should be thinned to 1 per 2-inch pot.

Transplants should not be planted in the garden until 2 weeks after the last

He had been eight years upon a project for extracting sunbeams from cucumbers, which were to be put into vials, hermetically sealed, and let out to warm the air in raw or inclement weather. FROM *GULLIVER'S TRAVELS,* BY JONATHAN SWIFT

Eggplants are available in a large range of sizes and colors from pure white to almost black. Long, thin eggplants are usually used in Oriental cooking; Italian dishes are usually made with medium-sized eggplants.

EGGPLANT 'BLACK BEAUTY' Open-pollinated. Plant 3 feet tall, 3 feet wide, produces dark glossy oval fruit, 10 inches long, 8 inches wide. Yields 8-10 pounds per plant. Days to harvest: 85.

EGGPLANT 'GHOSTBUSTER' Hybrid. Plant 2½ feet tall, 3 feet wide, produces oval white fruits, 6-7 inches long, 5-6 inches wide, weighing 1½ pounds each. Yields 5 bushels per 100-foot row. Days to harvest: 75.

EGGPLANT 'ICHIBAN' Hybrid. Plant 3 feet tall, 3 feet wide, produces long, slender purple-skinned fruits, 12 inches long, 2-3 inches wide, weighing ½ pound each. Yields 5-6 pounds per plant. Days to harvest: 64.

EGGPLANT 'VIOLETTA DI FIRENZE' Plant 3 feet tall produces large fruits, 9 inches in diameter. Beautifully shaped, lavender-colored, sometimes with wide white stripes. Good for slicing. Days to harvest: 60-80.

frost or when soil temperature is 65° F. or higher. A 100-foot row will take 35 plants, allowing 3 feet between plants and 3-4 feet between rows. (At Fetzer Organic Gardens, they are spaced 18-24 inches apart.)

In the South, a second crop of eggplant can be grown by taking early summer cuttings of the first crop and rooting them in sterile peat-lite mix or vermiculite before planting outdoors.

CARE Apply a 10-10-10 fertilizer to the soil 2-3 days before planting. At 4 weeks and 8 weeks, side-dress with 13-13-13 for continued production.

It is important to keep the plants free of weeds until they create a leaf canopy that shades out the weeds. Don't cultivate the soil around the plants once they begin to produce fruit. Mulch will help keep weeds down and retain moisture. These plants need at least ½ inch of water per week if mulched, 1 inch without mulch.

PESTS AND DISEASES Flea beetles are usually a problem with young eggplants. Young transplants can be protected with floating row covers until they are tall enough (about 1 foot) to withstand a minimal amount of damaged foliage. Even when infested with these small beetles, the mature plants will continue to produce fruit. White flies may be a problem later in the season; they can be sprayed off with water or an insecticidal soap spray.

HARVEST Begin to gather fruits when they have reached the expected size. Early harvest of the first fruit encourages production; unharvested plants shut down. Cut, rather than pull, the fruit to reduce damage to the main plant. A 100-foot row should yield 5 or more bushels of fruit.

VARIETIES 'Black Beauty' produces glossy, dark, oval fruit with yellow-green flesh. It produces heavy crops, which should be harvested promptly to extend the harvest (though this eggplant will continue to produce in any case). A second crop can be grown by taking cuttings of this early-producing eggplant. A good variety for slicing and frying.

'Easter Egg' is a small (16- to 20-inch) plant that produces 10-12 small white fruits that turn golden yellow when left on the vine too long; gardeners at The New York Botanical Garden like its egg-shaped fruits.

'Ghostbuster' has oval white fruits, produced quickly and abundantly throughout the growing season on spreading branches that hold the fruit well. Dense green foliage protects the creamy white color of the skin. The flesh is mild-flavored and tender. It is often grown by home gardeners because it is hard to find in stores.

'Ichiban' has a thin, tender dark purple, not black, skin. It is more tender than most eggplants and has fewer seeds. It is a quick producer and begins fruit production on very young plants. It should be harvested promptly and refrigerated right away because fruits wilt quickly. This variety seems to have less foliage damage from beetles than others.

'Violetta di Firenze' produces beautiful, globe-shaped, variegated purple, lavender, and cream-colored fruits. It is productive, disease-resistant in California, and very tasty.

'Listada di Gandia' is almost identical to 'Violetta di Firenze'. (Fetzer)

Eggplants look lovely in the garden, but they should be harvested promptly or the plant will stop producing. To avoid damaging vine, clip rather than twist off fruits.

FENNEL FOENICULUM VULGARE *Apiaceae*

Florence fennel or *finocchio* is a perennial grown as an annual for its enlarged leaf bases; it looks like swollen celery at the bottom and like dill on the top. It can be eaten raw or cooked and has a licorice flavor.

Fennel herb (*Foeniculum vulgare*) is a 5-foot perennial plant that looks like a huge dill; it does not form a bulb. It grows just about anywhere, is very attractive, and has the same licorice taste as Florence fennel.

BEST CONDITIONS Florence fennel grows best in light, fertile, well-drained soil.

PLANTING Fennel can be started from seeds or sowed directly into the garden. If sowing indoors, transplant when the seedlings have 2-3 true leaves.

CARE Fennel can be unpredictable; it often bolts without forming bulbs.

VARIETY 'Zefa Fino' is a slow-bolting variety, making the spring crop more successful than most. It forms large, tender bulbs.

GREENS

COLLARDS BRASSICA OLERACEAE VAR ACEPHALA *Brassicaceae*
KALE BRASSICA OLERACEAE VAR ACEPHALA *Brassicaceae*
MUSTARD GREENS BRASSICA OLERACEAE VAR ACEPHALA
Brassicaceae
NEW ZEALAND SPINACH TETRAGONIA TETRAGONIOIDES
Tetragoniaceae
SPINACH SPINACIA OLERACEAE *Chenopodiacea*
SWISS CHARD BETA VULGARIS *Chenopodiacea*
TURNIP GREENS BRASSICA RAPA *Brassicaceae* (See also: TURNIPS)

COOL-SEASON ANNUALS Greens are grown for their large leaves, which are usually eaten cooked. Most plants are 2-3 feet tall and 2-3 feet wide.

Collard greens are most often grown and eaten in the southern United States, but can be grown successfully in most areas. When cooking collard greens, it is necessary to reach a high cooking temperature quickly to help avoid a bitter taste. Kale was probably the first of all the brassicas to be cultivated. It is similar to collard greens and produces thick, crinkly leaves from a central stalk. Kale is eaten for its impressive nutritional value (high in calcium, and vitamins A and C) and is also used extensively as fodder for livestock. It is very cold-tolerant and can be harvested after leaves have been exposed to freezing temperatures and early snow.

Spinach originated in southwest Asia and has been grown in North America since the early 17th century. Originally, spinach produced seeds covered with tiny hairs or prickles, but during the 16th century a plant was discovered that produced seeds without these prickles, leading to the introduction of smooth-seeded cultivars such as 'Bloomsdale'.

New Zealand spinach is a low-branching plant that produces brittle, fuzzy, triangular leaves. It is not a true spinach, but serves as a substitute for spinach in hot weather.

BEST CONDITIONS Greens produce in a wide variety of soils, but ideal pH is 6.0-

Many greens are cold-hardy; some, like kale and collards, actually taste better if they survive frost. *Below:* 'Vates' kale, dusted with frost.

FENNEL 'ZEFA FINO' Plant 1-2½ feet tall with fine, needlelike foliage (resembling dill) forms robust, tender bulbs composed of overlapping leaf stalks. Slow bolting. Days to harvest: 85-100.

COLLARD GREENS 'GEORGIA' Open-pollinated. Plant 2-3 feet tall, 2 feet wide, produces round, blue-green leaves. Yields 10 bushels per 100-foot row in one-time harvest. Days to harvest: 70-80.

COLLARD GREENS 'VATES' Open-pollinated. Plant 3-4 feet tall, 2 feet wide, produces medium-green, curly leaves. Yields 10 bushels per 100-foot row in multiple harvests. Days to harvest: 55-80.

KALE 'DWARF BLUE CURLED VATES' Open-pollinated. Plant 12-18 inches tall, 24 inches wide, produces very ruffled blue leaves. Yields 10 bushels per 100-foot row in one-time harvest. Days to harvest: 55.

KALE 'RED RUSSIAN' Open-pollinated. Plant 2 feet tall, 2 feet wide, produces beautiful blue-green leaves that turn to purple in cold weather. Heat- and cold-tolerant. Yields 10 bushels per 100-foot row in one-time harvest. Days to harvest: 50.

MUSTARD GREENS 'RED GIANT' Open-pollinated. Plant 18-24 inches tall, 12-18 inches wide, produces purple smooth-edged crinkled leaves. Yields 4 bushels per 100-foot row in multiple harvests. Days to harvest: 35.

MUSTARD GREENS 'SAVANNAH' Hybrid. Plant 2 feet tall, 18 inches wide, produces broad, thick-leaved greens. Yields 5 bushels per 100-foot row in multiple harvests. Days to harvest: 30.

SWISS CHARD 'LUCULLUS' Open-pollinated. Plant 18 inches tall, 18 inches wide, produces white-stemmed and -veined smooth leaves. Yields 4 bushels per 100-foot row. Days to harvest: 60.

6.8. They need at least 6-8 hours of full sun each day. Collards, kale, and mustard greens can withstand cooler temperatures than other greens. Spinach can withstand light frost, but the foliage begins to "burn" at temperatures below 32° F. Spinach is most tender when grown in early spring or late fall, in cool weather.

Unlike most salad greens, New Zealand spinach tolerates extreme hot weather. It grows best planted thickly in soils that have not been fertilized.

Greens need more water when they are mature plants than in the transplant stage.

PLANTING The first crops of collards and kale should be planted early in the season (3-4 weeks before the expected last frost); seeds will germinate when garden soil temperatures are in the 40s. Or grow transplants indoors when the soil is still too cool for good seed germination. Place 2-3 seeds ¼-½ inch deep in a 2-inch plastic or fiber pot; water thoroughly and supply plenty of light. It takes 4-6 weeks to grow seedlings to transplant size. Set into the garden 12 inches apart in rows 3 feet apart. Later plantings of collards, kale, mustard, turnips, spinach, and Swiss chard can come from seeds sown directly into the garden. A fall crop can be planted in late summer when evenings begin to cool. Planted too soon, a fall crop will flower too quickly, and growth will be stunted. One-quarter ounce of seeds will direct sow a 100-foot row; spinach seeds are larger, and ½ ounce of seed is needed for a 100-foot row. The small seeds should be sown on a firm bed ¼-½ inch deep; they will germinate in 4-7 days. Seeds for New Zealand spinach should be soaked overnight before planting to speed germination.

Thin kale, collards, and Swiss chard seedlings to 12 inches apart (thinned

Ornamental kale has been bred for show; although it is edible, it is not at all tasty or tender. But it does make a striking addition to vegetable or flower beds, and usually lasts well into autumn.

Greens are nutritious, easy to grow, cold-hardy, and, as an added bonus, remarkably beautiful. *Above:* Swiss chard growing in the perennial border at New York's Central Park Conservatory Garden. *Opposite:* 'Rhubarb' chard's brilliant red midrib is a show-stopper in any garden.

seedlings can be eaten as first harvest). Thin spinach to 6 inches apart. There is no need to thin turnips or mustard greens (unless you want to use the turnip roots–see page 147).

Spinach seeds should be sown directly into the soil as transplants often have weak root systems and tend not to develop quickly. In beds, spinach can be sown thickly and will still produce well. Sow seeds 4 weeks before the last spring frost and again 4 weeks before the first fall frost. Seedlings should be thinned to 2-3 inches apart. Grow in double rows 6-8 inches apart. Plant seeds ¼ inch deep–if planted too deeply, seed germination rate will be reduced. Because the seeds are small, use a seeder for more even distribution. If seeding by hand, till the soil well, rake to create a smooth seed bed, and then drop the seeds and lightly rake them in. Seed beds should be kept evenly moist until germination takes place (5-7 days), and established plants should be watered at a rate of ½ inch per week.

CARE Fertilize garden soil with 10-10-10 fertilizer 2-3 days before planting seeds or transplants. Side-dress with 13-13-13 1 month after planting. For spinach, the second application can be either balanced (8-8-8) or a fertilizer high in nitrogen (15-10-10). Plants need at least 1 inch of water weekly throughout the growing season.

It is important to cultivate to remove weeds while greens are still young to reduce competition.

A floating row cover or a light covering of mulch such as straw will protect young plants to temperatures down to 25° F. Floating row covers also serve to protect tender plants from heat, and the cooler temperatures under the covers prevent them from early bolting in hot weather.

PESTS AND DISEASES Flea beetles, aphids, and cabbage loopers are often a problem on young plants. Early harvest keeps the rows open and reduces infestation. Early spring crops have fewer insect problems than late-summer crops.

HARVEST When harvest begins, cut down on watering so that soil does not become compacted. (At Fetzer, watering is increased at this point.)

Spinach plants are ready to harvest after 40 days, by which time they are 4-6 inches across and are at their most tender stage. You can harvest the entire plant by cutting just below soil level or you can harvest the outer leaves, and return again for a second harvest. Harvest promptly to avoid bolting in hot weather; bolting is rarely a problem with fall crops.

For other greens, cut greens with a knife when they reach the expected size. Refrigerate immediately to reduce wilting.

Greens yield 2-4 bushels per 100-foot row.

VARIETIES COLLARDS: 'Blue Max' is a high-yield variety with outstanding blue-green color on slightly crinkled, very erect leaves. 75 days to harvest.

'Champion' is compact, fast-growing, and less susceptible to insect damage and bolting. It should be grown from seeds sown directly into the garden. 70 days to harvest.

'Georgia' is a nonheading collard. The leaf starts close to the ground, resulting

SWISS CHARD 'RHUBARB' Plant 2 feet tall, 18 inches wide, produces red-stemmed, glossy crinkled leaves. Days to harvest: 60.

SPINACH 'BLOOMSDALE LONGSTANDING' Open-pollinated. Broad, dark-green leaves, 8-10 inches tall and wide. More cold-tolerant than most hybrids. Days to harvest: 50.

NEW ZEALAND SPINACH More heat-tolerant than regular spinach; thrives in heat and drought conditions. Fleshy, crisp green leaves. Days to harvest: 70.

MALABAR SPINACH Thick, dark green leaves produced throughout the summer. Heat-tolerant; needs warmth. Plant is 20-30 inches tall, can grow to 6 feet if trellised. Days to harvest: 35

in less stalk. Spring planting should be from transplants; direct-seed in fall. More heat-tolerant than others. Harvest leaf-by-leaf.

'Vates', an inexpensive, easy-to-find variety, has a sweet flavor and tender leaves. Its taste is stronger and its leaves tougher if grown into the summer. Its upright habit allows close spacing.

KALE: 'Dwarf Blue Curled Vates' is grown commercially for its leaf, which is used as a garnish. Not as tender as other kales, but it is easy to grow and produces an attractive dark blue-green leaf. More cold-hardy than most.

'Red Russian' has an upright growth habit and tender leaves that tend to wilt quickly after harvest. It is used in salads and stir-fry and is a very ornamental cut-leaf plant.

'Winterbor' has an extra-mild flavor and very frilly deep blue-green foliage. (Chicago Botanic Garden)

MUSTARD GREENS: 'Red Giant' has purple leaves that turn green when cooked. The purple color develops as the leaves mature. It is a pretty plant that grows quickly and can be harvested before insects become a problem. It can be harvested leaf by leaf, but will not be strong after the first harvest. Nice, sharp mustard flavor.

'Savannah' is an upright form and one of the few hybrid mustards developed to resist heat stress, resulting in large, flavorful leaves 4 weeks after other mustards are done. The wide, flat stem should be removed before cooking.

'Southern Giant Curled' takes longer to mature than other mustards. It is grown for its distinctive mustard "bite," a result of its long growing season. Because this takes so long to mature, there is usually only a single harvest.

'Tendergreens' is the variety name given by southern gardeners to any mild-flavored mustard. This grows best as a spring (rather than a fall) crop and has a very tender leaf and fast growth rate.

SWISS CHARD: 'Lucullus' can be substituted for spinach in cooking. Its leaves are smoother than other chards, making it easier to clean. It wilts quickly after picking, so harvest early in the morning.

'Rhubarb' has a tender leaf used like spinach. The midrib of the stem is generally removed before cooking, or cooked separately. This should be seeded 2 weeks before the last frost. If it has been hit by frost 2 or 3 times in spring, it will bolt quickly once warm weather arrives. Use quickly after harvest. Its bright-red stems add color to the garden. (This 'Rhubarb' is a variety of Swiss chard; do not confuse with real rhubarb–see page 121–which has poisonous leaves and is grown for its stalks.)

SPINACH: 'Melody' does not tolerate a wide range of temperatures (it bolts in warm weather, freezes in cold) but is particularly tasty and was developed for use in the home garden. It is best to harvest the entire plant at once by cutting the stem just below soil level.

'Bloomsdale Longstanding' is an old, easy-to-find standby, more cold-tolerant than other hybrids. If outer leaves are cut when they're harvestable size, it will pro-

Harvest cooking greens (and salad greens) early in the day or in the evening; they wilt quickly if harvested under hot sun.

duce multiple harvests. Its upright growth habit keeps leaves a bit cleaner.

SPINACH SUBSTITUTES: New Zealand Spinach thrives in heat and drought and supposedly has the same flavor as spinach, though many people don't like it.

Malabar Spinach is another spinach substitute that tolerates heat.

Dandelion Greens are long, green leaves, with a slightly bitter taste.

Orach, also called mountain spinach, is a hot-weather substitute for spinach. It tolerates heat, cold, drought, and most kinds of soil. Plant in narrow rows as soon as the soil is warm enough to work; does best in spring and fall.

TURNIP GREENS: 'Just Right' produces lots of leaves and white roots. If the leaves are left unharvested, larger roots will form. This is a hybrid, and seeds are expensive, but it produces 4 harvests of leaves, while other turnip greens produce only 2.

'Shogoin' produces only a small root, even when the leaves are not harvested. The smooth green leaves have a mild flavor. Insects tend to feed on the foliage. It bolts quickly. Best as a spring crop. Harvest at 30 days, and again 10-14 days later.

'White Lady' is a good dependable crop for both spring and fall and is a good variety to grow in both the North and South. It is grown mainly for its root, but the greens are good too.

ORIENTAL GREENS: 'Mizuna' (Kyona), a "cut-and-come-again" Japanese green,

Many vegetables that originated in Asia—such as cucumbers and eggplants—have been popular in the West for so long that they long ago lost their exotic touch. Over the past decade, many new Oriental vegetables have been introduced to North America and grown in our gardens. Staples in the Orient, they are moving steadily into wider use, particularly since most are easy to grow. The list of Oriental vegetables that have become popular in America includes beans (such as azuki and soybeans), bitter melons, radishes like the Daikon, and many cabbages and greens.

DANDELION GREENS Perennial plant (grown as an annual) produces clumps up to 8 inches wide of slender, pointed leaves, up to 12 inches long. Somewhat bitter; cold weather sweetens it. Plant can be invasive; do not let it flower; remove roots in midwinter. Days to harvest: 95.

ORACH Erect annual plant, growing up to 6 feet tall; very ornamental. Tender leaves are used as spinach substitute. Can be harvested throughout a long season. Sow every 2 weeks through spring and summer; cut leaves as they appear.

TURNIP GREENS 'JUST RIGHT' Hybrid. Plant 10-12 inches tall, 6-8 inches wide, produces leafy greens with small, white globe turnip roots. Average yield: 4 bushels per 100-foot row. Days to harvest: 40-45 for roots and greens.

TURNIP GREENS 'SHOGOIN' Plant 10-12 inches tall, 6-8 inches wide, produces only a small root, grown for its smooth-leaved, mild-flavored greens. Fastest turnip to produce harvestable greens. Days to first harvest: 30 for greens only.

ORIENTAL GREENS 'MIZUNA MUSTARD GREENS' Deeply cut, frilly greens, with narrow white stalks, 8- to 10-inch leaves. Ornamental and edible. Will regrow for extended harvest if cut. Days to harvest: 40.

ORIENTAL GREENS 'TATSOI' Low-growing flat, rosette-shaped cabbage, 12-18 inches across, with deep green, spoon-shaped, mild-flavored leaves. Can be planted early; cold-tolerant. Days to harvest: 40-50.

HORSERADISH 2- to 2½-foot plant with coarse leaves forms gnarled root up to 18 inches long. Strong-flavored root can be grated and used as flavoring. Somewhat invasive; harvest annually in spring and fall. Days to harvest: 120-150.

JERUSALEM ARTICHOKE Open-pollinated. Single-stalked plant, 6-8 feet tall, produces 3- to 4-inch round, knobby below-ground tubers. Yields 3-4 tubers per plant. Days to harvest: 150

forms upright rosettes of many serrated, deeply cut leaves on a white stalk. Excellent for winter greenhouses, it grows well under cool conditions and is disease-resistant. Tasty and crunchy, it is often added to salads. (Fetzer) **'Tatsoi'** (Tah Tsai) is used in both salads and stir-frys. It is a fast grower, excellent in fall gardens and cool climates, and can be harvested in one cut or as leaves picked over a long period. In the South, 'Tatsoi' is best grown in the spring. (Fetzer Organic Gardens)

HORSERADISH ARMORACIA RUSTICANA *Cruciferae*
COOL-SEASON PERENNIAL Horseradish adds zip to many dishes. It is easily grown and once planted should provide enough roots for you and your neighborhood. Cultivated horseradish is native to Europe but has also naturalized in waste places throughout North America.
BEST CONDITIONS Horseradish is most successfully grown separately from other vegetables as it is a bed-forming perennial. It needs rich, loamy soil and full sun. Heavy soils produce stunted roots. Expect the foliage to look tattered by summer's end.
PLANTING Horseradish is readily propagated by root cuttings that can be purchased through nurseries or from any small part of the the root remaining in the soil.
CARE Top dress with a 2-inch layer of compost or manure after harvest for best crops.
HARVEST Harvest in spring and fall. Roots are usually grated after they are cleaned and peeled. Grating usually produces tears; these can be avoided by using a food processor. A few drops of vinegar can be mixed to achieve desired consistency and preserve strength. Horseradish should be refrigerated.

JERUSALEM ARTICHOKE HELIANTHUS TUBEROSUS
Compositae
WARM-SEASON PERENNIAL, SOMETIMES GROWN AS AN ANNUAL Often grown for its lovely flowers rather than its edible root, this vegetable is neither an artichoke nor from Jerusalem. "Jerusalem" is actually a corruption of the Italian name for this plant, *girasole,* meaning "turning toward the sun," for many members of this genus keep their face toward the sun throughout the day. It is native to North America and was used by many Native American tribes. Early settlers called them "sunchokes" and cultivated them as early as 1605.

Jerusalem artichokes can be substituted for water chestnuts in almost any recipe and have the advantage of being low in calories and an excellent source of potassium and thiamine. They are most frequently eaten raw in salads. If cooked in an aluminum pot, they may turn black.

This plant grows to 6-8 feet tall and 3 feet wide. It is rather leggy with bright yellow sunflower blossoms that produce below-ground tubers. If the plants are grown in good soil and not harvested, they often become an invasive weed. There are no known named varieties.
BEST CONDITIONS For best results and easiest harvest, this plant should be grown

KOHLRABI 'GRAND DUKE' Hybrid. Upright green plant, 14 inches tall, 10 inches wide, with globe-shaped swollen stem with a white center. Sweet, turniplike flavor. Days to harvest: 45 from transplanting.

KOHLRABI 'RAPID' Hybrid. Red or purple upright plant, 16-18 inches tall, 8-10 inches wide, with globe-shaped swollen stem and leaves radiating from it. Globe has red skin, white center. Days to harvest: 55.

LEAF LETTUCE 'BLACK SEEDED SIMPSON' Open-pollinated. Plant 6-8 inches tall, 6-8 inches wide, produces pale green loose-leaved heads. Yields 2-3 bushels per 100-foot double row. Days to harvest: 45.

LEAF LETTUCE 'RED SAILS' Open-pollinated. Plant 8-10 inches tall, 8-10 inches wide, produces heads with loose, red-tinged ruffled leaves. Yields 2-3 bushels per 100-foot double row. Days to harvest: 45.

in rich, loamy soil. Plant in full sun.

PLANTING Like potatoes, Jerusalem artichokes grow from small "eyes" found on tubers. Small tubers can be planted, larger ones should be cut into pieces, each containing at least 1 "eye." Tubers should be planted 2 weeks before last frost, 12 inches apart in rows 3 feet apart.

This plant does not need a great deal of moisture, though watering is recommended when the ground dries out.

PESTS AND DISEASES Generally free of pests, Jerusalem artichoke is susceptible to root rot in wet soils. The leaves of affected plants blacken and drop.

HARVEST When the leaves begin to yellow and fall in late summer (July and August), harvest can begin. To harvest, dig all the way around each plant, then gently pull the entire root system from the soil.

Floating row covers protect young seedlings from frost and sun and maturing plants from insects and birds. They are available in many sizes, are relatively inexpensive, and can be easily folded and stored. They can be difficult to place and anchor properly and can cause breakage of tall crops. They sometimes promote mildew by retaining moisture and increasing humidity under the covers.

KOHLRABI BRASSICA OLERACEA GONGYLODES *Cruciferae*

COOL-SEASON BIENNIAL GROWN AS AN ANNUAL Used as a vegetable at least since Roman times, kohlrabi has recently enjoyed a surge in popularity. Sometimes called the turnip-rooted cabbage because of its unusual growth form, kohlrabi produces a swelling in the stem just above ground level. Because it looks so unusual when growing, nongardeners mistake the red varieties for beets, the green ones for turnips. Kohlrabi is an upright plant with a swollen tuberous stem.

BEST CONDITIONS Grow in full sun. Kohlrabi will tolerate some summer heat, though production will be slowed considerably; cool spring or fall weather produces the sweetest, most tender kohlrabi. Supply with ½ inch water per week. Rich, well-tilled garden soil, pH 6.0-6.5 (similar to that best for growing root crops) will give the best results.

PLANTING Transplanting saves time, but seeds can be sown directly into the garden soil. Always be sure to use fresh seed. If starting from seed indoors, sow 4 weeks before setting out. Transplants held in pots longer than 6 weeks have stunted growth and woody stems. Set out transplants 2 weeks before the last frost and again 4 weeks before the first frost of autumn. These can be planted 6 inches apart in rows 2-3 feet apart, or in double rows 6-8 inches apart. When setting out transplants, put the rootball deep into the soil, leaving the bottom set of leaves above ground. Seeds should be planted ¼-½ inch deep, depending on their size. They will germinate in 5-6 days in spring, 4-5 days in fall, and seedlings should be thinned to 6 inches apart.

CARE Fertilize with a balanced fertilizer, such as 10-10-10, 2-3 days before seeding or setting out transplants. DO NOT fertilize again as this may cause the stem to crack. Water thoroughly when setting out transplants or seeds, and supply at least ½ inch per week throughout the cool growing season.

Kohlrabi will withstand light frosts, but temperatures below 25° F. may damage the globe. Red varieties are more cold-tolerant than green.

PESTS AND DISEASES Because this is a quick-growing crop, it does not have the same problems with pests and diseases as other members of the cabbage fami-

BUTTERHEAD LETTUCE 'BUTTERCRUNCH' Hybrid. Plant 6-8 inches tall, 6 inches wide, produces dark green leaves with pale green heart. Slow to bolt. Days to harvest: 55-75.

BUTTERHEAD LETTUCE 'PIRAT' Hybrid. Loose, medium green heads, 8-10 inches across, edged with red. Buttery taste. Resists bolting; adapts to growing throughout the season. European variety. Days to harvest: 55.

BUTTERHEAD LETTUCE 'SUMMER BIBB' Open-pollinated. Plant 4 inches tall, 8-10 inches wide, produces loose-leaved butterhead with dark green leaves. Yields 2-3 bushels per 100-foot double row. Days to harvest: 60-70.

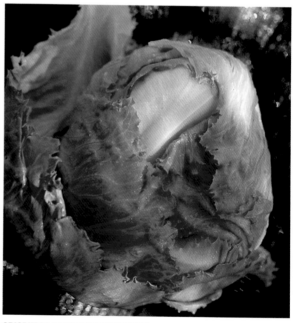

CRISPHEAD LETTUCE 'GREAT LAKES' Tight, bright green heads, 12-15 inches in diameter, large, erect outer leaves. Resistant to sunburn. Adapted to many climates. Days to harvest: 90-100.

ly. Also, cool-season weeds are not as prolific as summer weeds, making cultivating kohlrabi easier.

HARVEST Harvest 40-45 days after transplanting when the rounded stem is no
more than 3-4 inches in diameter. When not harvested promptly, the stem
becomes woody, and the globe cracks and loses its flavor. Use a sharp knife
and cut off the stem at soil level. Leaves kept on the plant will help extend its
shelf life. The tops can also be used as cooked greens.

VARIETIES 'Grand Duke' has a globe with a white center and a sweet turniplike flavor. It is used raw or cooked. Though the skins of the earliest harvest are
sweet and tender, fruit from subsequent harvests is tougher and will have to
be peeled. AAS winner.

'Rapid', a red variety, can handle more cold than green varieties, though the
globes tend to be smaller. The leaves are an attractive blue-green with distinct
red veins.

LETTUCE AND OTHER SALAD GREENS

LETTUCE LACTUCA SATIVA *Compositae*
ARUGULA ERUCA VESICARIA SUBSP. SATIVA *Cruciferae*
CHICORY, RADICCHIO CICHORIUM INTYBUS *Compositate*
CORN SALAD (MACHÉ) VALERIANELLA LOCUSTAE *Valerianacea*
ENDIVES CICHORIUM ENDIVA *Compositate*
ESCAROLE CHICORIUM ENDIVIA *Compositate*
GARDEN CRESS, UPLAND CRESS LEPIDIUM SATIVUM *Cruciferae*
WATERCRESS TROPAEOLEUM OFFICINALE *Nasturtium*

COOL-SEASON ANNUALS Generally cool-season crops, lettuce and other salad
greens can be grown in spring and fall; a few varieties can be grown during
the summer months. At The New York Botanical Garden, gardeners enjoy
lettuce all through the summer by using some nonbolting varieties, keeping
some plants in the shade, and sowing a succession of different varieties.

BEST CONDITIONS The best flavor is obtained when salad greens are grown at 60-
65° F.; they need at least 4-6 hours of sun daily. Salad greens are tolerant of
most soils but prefer a pH of 6.5-6.8; poor soils sometimes cause bitterness.
Soils that drain too quickly do not retain enough water for these plants, and
heavy, poorly drained soils may result in rotting of the roots. Callaway gardeners recommend placing beds in areas that haven't been recently planted
with other crops to avoid frequently-tilled, loose soils that splash or blow into
the leaves and make gritty salads. Salad greens thrive in raised beds where
soils drain well and the plants are not sitting in low spots.

PLANTING Salad greens can be grown successfully from either seeds or transplants. Seeds should be sown to a depth of ¼-½ inch into well-prepared soils.
Germination takes 4-6 days. If starting indoors, thin seedlings to 3 per pot. It
takes 3-4 weeks from seed to transplant size. Transplants can be put into the
garden 2 weeks before the last expected frost, but be prepared to cover them
with sheets or floating row covers; they will not tolerate even light frost. Plant
in double rows 12-18 inches apart, 3 feet between the double rows. Successive

Hundreds of varieties of lettuce are available to gardeners. They fall into 4 groups
(from top): crisphead, butterhead,
romaine, and looseleaf.

ROMAINE LETTUCE 'VALMAINE' Open-pollinated. Plant 8-10 inches tall, 8 inches wide, produces upright plants with dark flat leaves. Yields 2-3 bushels per 100-foot double row. Days to harvest: 75.

ARUGULA Open-pollinated. Also called roquette, rocket salad. Mounding leafy plant, 18 inches tall, 2 feet wide at harvest; harvest before fully mature. Leaves peppery when young, strong when mature. Days to harvest: 40.

CHICORY 'EARLY TREVISO' Forms a loose 8-inch head, similar to romaine, with a somewhat bitter taste. If let overwinter, will produce loose flowers on tall stems. Days to harvest: 85.

CHICORY 'GIULIO RADICCHIO' Compact plant produces 4- to 6-inch garnet-red heads, with white ribs. Resists bolting. Days to harvest: 60-80.

plantings can be done 3 weeks apart until the weather turns warm.

CARE Apply a balanced fertilizer such as 10-10-10 to the garden site 2-3 days before planting. Side-dress with the same fertilizer 4 weeks after planting. If heavy spring rains result in yellow leaves, fertilize again with high-nitrogen mix such as 15-10-10.

Cultivate to keep down weeds when plants are small. As the plants attain harvest size, hand-pull any weeds to prevent dirt from falling on the leaves. Callaway gardeners have found scuffle hoes are good to cultivate between rows of salad greens because they cut weeds off at soil level without kicking up the soil.

PESTS AND DISEASES Young tender lettuce are often the first green leaves to appear in the garden in spring and invariably attract rabbits and chipmunks. Chicken-wire barriers help protect the leaves from small animals. Rotating the site where you plant lettuce prevents disease.

HARVEST The first harvest will be thinnings. Later, hand-pick leaves from leaf lettuce as needed, beginning with the larger outer leaves. For the final harvest, cut just below ground level to get the entire bunch, and trim off unwanted leaves. Harvest early in the day to keep leaves from wilting. Lettuce is about 95 percent water, giving it its crisp texture, but also making it susceptible to quick wilting.

A 100-foot double row provides 2-3 bushels of lettuce or other salad greens.

VARIETIES LEAF LETTUCE: 'Black Seeded Simpson' is commonly grown in home and commercial gardens. Thinning this variety is not as important as for other lettuces, as the leaves are produced in an upright, open manner. Heat-tolerant.

'Lingue de Canarino' is a bright yellow-green looseleaf lettuce from Italy that is very slow to bolt. The name means "canary tongue." (New York Botanical Garden)

The pot sprouted all right, and right on schedule too, and I was thrilled—until it became plain even to my inexperienced eyes that the little green shoots weren't lettuce but weeds in embryo, and the lettuces when they did appear soon toppled and died. The miracle would have been if they hadn't because I had done everything wrong. The pot was much too large and deep and you don't plant a seed in unsterilized garden soil without inviting damping-off, a fungus disease that destroys young seedlings. You don't learn how to sow seed by studying ancient religious practices. You buy a book and read the directions.
FROM *GREEN THOUGHTS*.
BY ELEANOR PERENYI

Because they grow quickly and take up very little room, leaf lettuces are often interplanted between other vegetables, such as beets, as shown here.

'Lolla Rosa', another Italian favorite, is a very compact plant. It is slow to bolt and has ruffled red-tinged leaves. (New York Botanical Garden)

'Red Sails' is widely available and easy to grow. Keep outer leaves trimmed for maximum production. AAS winner.

BUTTERHEAD: 'Buttercrunch' has thick outer leaves with plenty of body for use in salads. It is good for successive crops in spring and fall, and seeds germinate well in garden soil in either season. It needs plenty of room to grow, so plants must be thinned or spaced correctly.

'Nancy' is a classic green butterhead with dull green leaves that grows very large in rich soil. It is a Fetzer Gardens tasting favorite, with semisweet flavor and a pleasing almost crunchy texture; very buttery.

'Pirat' yields a large head with bronze-brown leaf margins and rich lime-green interior. In addition to an excellent appearance, it is alive with flavors—nutty, sweet, semi-buttery—and has a soft interior texture. It was a favorite in taste tests at Fetzer Gardens. It is resistant to brown-rib or tip burn.

'Summer Bibb' has leaves tightly clustered in the center, effectively keeping soil and grit away from the harvestable part of the plant. It has a stronger flavor than most of the other butterhead lettuces.

Flowers grown in the garden add color, and some of them, such as nasturtiums, are edible as well. A word of caution: some flowers are highly poisonous; do not use any of them until checking against an approved list of safe flowers. Nigella—the blue flower in this picture on the right—was considered edible, but is now questionable. Although it is difficult to find definitive answers on the subject, it is always better not to take chances.

CORN SALAD (MACHÉ, LAMB'S LETTUCE) Shiny, spoon-shaped leaves 2-3 inches long. Delicate taste, rich in vitamins and minerals. Harvest leaves as needed. Days to harvest: 40-60.

ENDIVE 'GREEN CURLED' Open-pollinated. Fringed, wide-leaved, mounding plant 6-8 inches tall, 6-8 inches wide. Days to harvest: 90.

ENDIVE 'SALAD KING' Open-pollinated. Flat, spreading plant 6-8 inches tall, 6-8 inches wide, produces dark green curly leaves. Yields 2-3 bushels per 100-foot double row. Days to harvest: 52.

ESCAROLE 'NUVOL' Broad, wavy, dark green leaves with creamy yellow hearts. Large heads, 12-15 inches across. Resists bolting. Days to harvest: 50.

The term *mesclun* does not refer to any single type of lettuce. Mesclun is a combination of many greens, chosen for their taste, color, aroma, and texture. Mesclun often includes herbs such as basil, perilla, and oregano, edible flowers, squash blossoms, corn salad, and red and green leaf lettuces. In France, where mesclun originated, several towns have their own unique recipe for mesclun.

Opposite: One of the easiest ways to make your vegetable beds attractive as well as productive is to plant borders of bright red and green lettuce.

'Tom Thumb' produces small heads, each one making a serving. It produces more quickly than other head-type lettuces and should be sown in early spring or fall.

CRISPHEAD: 'Grand Rapids', a longtime favorite in northern gardens, has frilled medium green leaves with a sweet flavor that form loose heads. It is slower to bolt than other crisphead varieties.

'Great Lakes' is especially well-suited for fall crops in the North. Heads are tight and bright green.

ROMAINE: 'Valmaine' produces tall dark green heads and is mildew-tolerant. It is dependable and fast-growing, but needs proper spacing to produce well. Does best if transplanted in spring. It holds well in garden at harvestable size.

ARUGULA is a mounding, leafy plant with a peppery-nutty flavor that adds an interesting taste to salads. Old leaves are bitter, so harvest frequently to encourage growth of new leaves. At Callaway Gardens, arugula is planted in spring, as fall plantings tend to bolt in autumn heat. At Chicago Botanic Gardens, where autumns are not as hot, fall plantings do well; at Fetzer Organic Gardens, fall plantings are superior to spring plantings. It is a fast-growing crop, easily grown from seed with no noticeable insect damage.

CORN SALAD (Maché) is an open-mounded salad plant that produces a rosette of tender, hairy leaves and is often mixed with other salad greens for diversity. It is more cold-tolerant than lettuce and can be planted earlier. The seeds are slow to germinate, taking 10-14 days. It is best to sow seeds indoors in early spring and then transplant the small seedlings to the garden 2 weeks after the last frost. The plant grows quickly and has few problems with insects and diseases. (At Fetzer, it grows slowly and is hard to clean.) Harvest early when the leaves are still young and tender.

CHICORY is grown for its hard, carrotlike root (which can be ground for a coffee substitute) and for its foliage (used as a salad green). Roots are harvestable in late fall; leaf crop is harvested in spring from direct seed or from foliage cut from stored roots. To produce pale, tender, blanched leaves, bank soil halfway up the plants 7-10 days before harvesting from the garden.

RADICCHIO, also called red or leaf chicory, does better in the South than white varieties and adds bright color and spicy flavor to salads. Either homegrown or nursery transplants should be set out in early spring or fall. Radicchio often bolts in warm weather; if left to grow, it produces pretty blue flowers.

'Giulio' produces small, tight, garnet-red heads with white ribs and resists bolting. Its color and taste make it popular.

GARDEN CRESS has dark green leaves with a tangy, peppery flavor. Sow seeds inside and set out transplants early in spring. It is best grown during wet spring months, for it prefers cool, moist weather. The flavor tends to change at maturity. A fast grower, garden cress can be direct-seeded 2 weeks after last expected frost and 4 weeks before first expected frost. Gardeners at Fetzer Organic Gardens direct-seed because they find that garden cress bolts when transplanted.

WATERCRESS thrives as an aquatic plant, but will also do well in the ground as

long as soil is kept very moist and lightly shaded. It also does well as a container plant. Seeds or cuttings germinate quickly; thin to 10 inches apart.

ENDIVE, a long-growing, narrow-leaved plant, and **ESCAROLE,** which is taller and has broader leaves, are similar in many ways; both are varieties of *Cichorium endivia* (Belgian endive, also called witloof chicory, is *Cichorium intybus*). They are grown the same way as lettuce, though both are better at withstanding heat. Gardeners at The New York Botanical Garden find that plants grow faster if started indoors and then transplanted into the garden. To effect blanching, they place a round piece of cardboard or a small plastic container over the center of the plant; this reduces bitterness. The center of the plant must be kept dry because it rots easily.

'Green Curled' endive grows like dandelions but is slow to produce flowers. The entire plant should be harvested.

'Salad King' endive has white-ribbed stems and will produce even when planted thickly.

ESCAROLE: 'Catalogna', popular in Italy, has elongated leaves that resemble dandelions.

'Nuvol' escarole produces a large head with broad, wavy dark green leaves and a creamy yellow heart. It is slow to bolt, self-blanching, and sweeter than other varieties. (The New York Botanical Garden)

MELONS

CANTALOUPE CUCUMIS MELO VAR. CANTALUPENSIS *Cucurbitaceae*
HONEYDEW CUCUMIS MELO VAR. INODORUS *Cucurbitaceae*
WATERMELON CITRULLUS VULGARIS *Cucurbitaceae*

WARM-SEASON ANNUALS Melons are one of the most delicious crops grown in the vegetable garden. This has been known since the 16th century, when melons were cultivated extensively in Europe. In 1583 a scholarly work was printed listing 50 different methods of preparing melons.

Most of the melons grown in this country fall into the muskmelon group (which include cantaloupes and Persian melons and have a hard, strongly netted rind and orange or musky flesh) and the inodorus group (including casaba, crenshaw, and honeydew melons, which have smooth or wrinkled rinds and crisp white or green flesh). The word *cantaloupe* comes from the Italian word *cantalupo*, meaning "wolf howl"; it was named for Cantalupo, a papal villa outside Rome where they were grown. The honeydew was named *inodorus* due to its lack of scent compared to muskmelons or cantaloupes.

Watermelons have always enjoyed tremendous popularity. Mark Twain wrote of the watermelon, "When one has tasted it, he knows what angels eat." A tremendous number of watermelon varieties are available to us today, including seedless varieties, yellow-fleshed melons, and sizes varying from a few pounds to a hundred.

BEST CONDITIONS Melons need full sun—at least 6-8 hours a day; plants grown in shady areas produce few fruits and are less sweet. Loose, loamy soils are best, and good drainage is important. If growing in heavy clay soils, add generous

Melons need a lot of room to grow; each plant produces running vines with several melons. At Callaway, a 4 x 4 foot space is allowed for each melon; at Fetzer, they are spaced 1½-2 feet apart in rows that are 5 feet from center to center.

WATERCRESS Small leaves on tender stems, deep green. Grows vigorously in running water; can also be grown in moist soil. Tolerates light shade. Perennial; usually winter-hardy in water. Days to harvest: 60.

CANTALOUPE 'AMBROSIA' Hybrid. Long vines produce 6 ½ x 6-inch 5-pound melons, with very sweet deep orange flesh and small seed cavities. Heavily netted. Mildew-resistant. Days to harvest: 86.

CANTALOUPE 'SATICOY' Hybrid. 6½ x 5½-inch, 3- to 5-pound melons with hard rind, medium netting, and deep-orange flesh. Tolerates fusarium wilt and powdery mildew. Days to harvest: 90.

MELON CASABA Hybrid. 6- x 8-inch, 4- to 8-pound melons with ribbed, wrinkled golden rind. Very sweet. Can be harvested over a long period. Days to harvest: 110.

MELON CRENSHAW Hybrid. 6 x 8-inch, 5-pound melons with dark green rind that turns yellow when ripe. Green flesh (some varieties have pink flesh). Days to harvest: 90-110.

HONEYDEW 'HONEYBREW' Hybrid. Strong, vigorous vines produce 6 x 6-inch melons, 3-5 pounds each, with smooth ivory rind and pale green flesh. High yielder, even under cool conditions. Days to harvest: 110-112.

MELON SANTA CLAUS Hybrid. Long, vigorous vines produce 12 x 6-inch melons, 8-9 pounds each, with very sweet pale green flesh. Wrinkled gold and dark green rind. Days to harvest: 108.

WATERMELON 'CRIMSON SWEET' Hybrid. Long, vigorous vines produce large, almost round 20- to 25-pound melons, with bright red, very sweet flesh, medium green striped rind. Very few seeds. Resists fusarium and anthracnose. Days to harvest: 95.

amounts of compost at planting time. Melons prefer a pH of 6.0-6.5. The soil temperature at planting time must be 70° F. or higher. Melons do not grow well in low spots or waterlogged soils. Hot, sunny weather during the fruit's ripening time will result in sweet, flavorful melons.

PLANTING To start indoors, sow 2-3 seeds each in 2½-inch pots and keep evenly moist, though not wet; thin to 1 plant per pot. Supply with good light and transplant as soon as they are ready, usually in 3-4 weeks. Transplants are ready when 1 or more true leaves have developed; do not allow them to get too large, because plants will not develop properly if root growth is restricted. Because the soil has to be warmed before these plants will thrive, wait until 1-2 weeks after last frost before planting in the garden. Or sow seeds directly into the garden, ½-1 inch deep. Plant 4-5 seeds per hill and thin to 2-3.

Melons take a lot of room. A 4-foot-by-4-foot space is necessary for each plant; watermelons need a minimum of 32 square feet. Plant 2-3 cantaloupe or honeydew seedlings in small hills leaving 3 feet between hills in rows 4 feet apart; watermelon hills should be 3 feet apart, rows should be 5-6 feet apart. At Callaway Gardens they have found it best to pinch off the unwanted plants rather than pull them up so as not to disturb the root system of the remaining plants.

CARE A 2- to 3-inch-deep layer of straw spread around the hills gives the fruits a resting place so they are not in contact with the soil.

Work a balanced (10-10-10) fertilizer into the soil 2-3 days before planting. When the first blossoms appear, side-dress with calcium nitrate, potassium nitrate, or a 5-10-15 mix to encourage blossom and fruit production.

Melons need 1 inch of water per week for even production.

The areas around the melon plants should be kept weeded until the plants start running. Weeding after this can damage the stems. Care should be taken to prevent crushed leaves or nicked stems that may reduce production.

Cantaloupes and honeydews can be trellised on fences or 5- to 6-foot trellises. Large fruits require additional support, such as bags made of netting attached to the trellis. The bags hold the fruit and prevent tearing the stem.

PESTS AND DISEASES Cucumber beetles often damage melon plants and transmit diseases. They can be controlled with a floating row cover or insecticides. White flies generally appear on foliage late in the season. Spray off with water and prune off the affected foliage. Gardeners at Fetzer Organic Gardens find that mulching with straw attracts slugs and sowbugs.

HARVEST Melons can be picked when the fruits achieve their ripe color: green melons become a lighter shade of green; tan melons become darker. Cantaloupes are ripe when the fruit slips easily from the stem and fruit are yellow or tan in color. Melons that don't release easily on their own should be picked when blossom end is slightly soft under thumb pressure. Watermelons are ripe when the green rind becomes slightly dull and when the melon easily separates from the stem when gentle pressure is applied to the melon where it joins the stem. Pull carefully when harvesting so the vines will not be damaged. Unlike other melons, watermelon will not ripen if harvested a few days

Because they are so heavy, melons require special care at harvest. Place large melons on boards, and turn them occasionally to keep them from getting soft on the bottom. Secure hanging melons with cloth slings so their weight does not cause them to fall prematurely.

WATERMELON 'SUGAR BABY' Hybrid. 3- to 4-foot vines produce 8- x 10-inch melons, 8-12 pounds each, with very sweet, bright scarlet flesh, thin but tough dark green rind, and small seeds. Easy to grow. Days to harvest: 68-80.

WATERMELON 'YELLOW DOLL' Hybrid. 5- to 8-pound melons, with striped green rinds and crisp yellow flesh. Semi-compact vines can be trellised. Often first to produce. Days to harvest: 65-95.

OKRA 'BURGUNDY' Hybrid. Plant 3-4 feet high in South, 2-3 feet high in North, produces creamy white flowers and very ornamental, edible red pods, 6-8 inches long. Produces even in cool weather. Days to harvest: 50.

OKRA 'CLEMSON SPINELESS' Open-pollinated. Plant 4-5 feet tall produces rich green, slightly grooved pods 6-9 inches long. Very heavy yielder. Days to harvest: 55-60.

before it is field ripened. Watermelons do not increase in sweetness after harvesting.

VARIETIES CANTALOUPE: 'Ambrosia' has a very sweet flesh and heavy production. It is sweeter than most cantaloupes, but is susceptible to foliar diseases.

'Saticoy' is good for mid to late harvest; popular throughout the country.

'Sweet 'n' Early', ripens after only 75 days and has firm, bright peach-colored fruit that is sweet and juicy. It yields 6-8 4½- to 5-inch melons per plant and resists powdery mildew. (Chicago Botanic Garden)

'Jenny Lind' is a turban-shaped heirloom variety grown at The New York Botanical Garden. It was named for the famous singer because it was said to be as sweet as her voice.

CASABA melons have ribbed, wrinkled gold rinds and are exceptionally sweet.

CRENSHAW is usually grown in home gardens because its skin is too thin for shipping.

HONEYDEW: 'Honeybrew' is a medium-sized, oval-round melon with a smooth light green exterior and attractive lime-green flesh. It slips from the vine when ripe with medium to firm pressure on the stem. It has a rich abundance of fig, melon, lemon, "tropical" flavors and a semicrisp texture. A Fetzer tasting favorite.

'Snow Charm' has a complex flavor and a refreshing crisp texture. Wait for softness under thumb pressure at blossom end before harvesting. It is an "overwhelming favorite" in all taste trials at Fetzer Gardens.

SANTA CLAUS melons are particularly sweet and keep for months.

WATERMELON: 'Blue Ribbon Klondyke' is an old, open-pollinated strain of classic red watermelon; it is the usual large, oval watermelon size; top quality for the North California region of Fetzer Gardens.

'Crimson Sweet' produces good-sized fruit for market. Not much is wasted when these melons are cut.

'Sugar Baby' melons can sit directly on the ground if the soil drains well. Seeds are inexpensive and easy to find. Fruit are small and round.

'Yellow Doll' is a medium to small icebox type, with bright lemon-yellow flesh, small black seeds, a wonderfully refreshing, lemon sherbet flavor, and juicy sweetness. Very productive.

'Chinese Preserving Melon' (*Beninsocas hispida*), also called bitter melon, is used in making sweet preserves, or, if picked small, cooked like a squash.

'O'odham Ke:li Ba:so', a casaba-type with light green flesh, does well in desert areas. Distributed by Native Seeds/SEARCH. (Desert Botanical Garden)

OKRA ABELMOSCHUS ESCULENTUS *Malvaceae*

WARM-SEASON ANNUAL This tall, leafy plant produces hibiscuslike flowers; its pods are sometimes dried and used in flower arrangements.

BEST CONDITIONS Okra must be grown in hot weather—it needs warms days and nights and full sun; soil should be above 65° F. It grows well in most soil types and needs a pH of 6.0-6.8. Okra is a heavy feeder and needs fertile soil or

Okra, beautiful of flower, delightful to the taste, is from the tropics of the eastern hemisphere. It is eaten in stews and gumbos, particularly in the southeastern United States. Because of the great amount of mucilage it contains, it is sometimes used to thicken soups and broths.

additional fertilizers. Crowding or cool weather slows production.

PLANTING Plant from seeds or transplants. For areas with short growing seasons, start seeds indoors about 2 weeks after last frost. Sow 2-3 seeds ½ inch deep in 2½-inch pots in lightweight sterile potting soil. Seeds will germinate in 3-7 days inside. Keep evenly moist and supply plenty of light to keep seedlings from getting leggy. They will reach transplantable size in 3-4 weeks. Seeds can also be sown outdoors, where they will germinate in 7-10 days. Okra seeds are very hard and often shatter; germination is variable. Soak seeds overnight for improved germination.

Place transplants in the garden 1 month after last frost, but not until soil temperature reaches 65° F. Plant hills of 2-3 plants each 3 feet apart with 4 feet or more between rows. Leave plenty of space between rows for easy harvest and cultivation and to provide good air circulation, which will discourage insect infestation and diseases. Transplant carefully, because okra stems are hollow and easily damaged. Mulch to retard the soil compaction that could result from frequent harvesting.

CARE Apply a balanced (10-10-10) fertilizer 2-3 days before planting seeds or plants. Apply 15-10-10 fertilizer to this heavy feeder every 4 weeks. Okra needs 1 inch of water weekly until flower, pod, and leaf production slows. Okra grows slowly for the first few weeks. Be sure to keep surrounding soil well cultivated to encourage rapid growth and to prevent weed competition. Tall stalks may require staking; place 1 stake for each plant.

PESTS AND DISEASES Damping off sometimes occurs on tender stems, but can be avoided by not overwatering plants. If powdery mildew occurs, remove affected leaves. Use soap sprays to eliminate aphids. Diseases and insect problems usually do not affect production of okra.

HARVEST When plants are about 2 feet high and put on first pods, begin harvest. As plants mature, test for tenderness by pressing pods with thumbnail; if nail won't pierce, the okra is overripe. When pods reach 3 inches, harvest every other day. Cut stems, leaving half the stem on pod. Harvest early in the morning to reduce wilting.

VARIETIES 'Burgundy' has red leaves and pods. Dark red varieties of okra are sometimes grown for their ornamental qualities, and unpicked pods cause the plant to become top heavy. Keep pods picked to keep production high.
'Clemson Spineless' is easy to find, and its "spineless" quality makes it easier to harvest. It is sometimes used as an ornamental plant.

ONIONS, GARLIC, LEEKS, SCALLIONS, SHALLOTS
ONIONS ALLIUM CEPA *Amaryllidaceae*
GARLIC ALLIUM SATIVUM *Amaryllidacea*
LEEKS ALLIUM AMPELOPRASUM *Amaryllidacea*
SCALLIONS ALLIUM CEPA *Amaryllidacea*
SHALLOTS ALLIUM CEPA *Amaryllidacea*
FULL-SEASON PERENNIALS OR BIENNIALS The tangy members of the onion family are closely related to such beautiful (but poisonous) flowers as the amaryllis

Above ground, garlic plants produce edible, round white tops. Below the ground, they produce the clusters of cloves that are used in many cuisines.

ONION 'GRANEX 33' (VIDALIA) Hybrid. Plant with foliage 12 inches tall produces yellow bulbs 3-4 inches wide. Short-day onion, excellent flavor, adapted to hot, humid climates. Days to harvest: 110.

ONION 'WHITE SWEET SANDWICH' Hybrid. Long-day onion, adapted to northern areas. 4-5 inches across, light yellow with white skin, mild-flavored. Good storage onion. Days to harvest: 110.

ONION 'RED TORPEDO' Long, cylindrical onions, weighing up to 1 pound each, good for slicing, with purple skin and sweet white flesh. Day neutral. Stores well. Days to harvest: 75-110.

SHALLOTS Open-pollinated. Foliage 6-8 inches tall, in clumps 3 inches across, produces clusters of small 1- to 2-inch bulbs; often used as green onion. Tolerates partial shade. Days to harvest: 90-120.

To encourage good root development on onions and leeks, cut out the flowering stalk.

and narcissus. The word *onion* is from the Latin word *unio*, meaning "united," and refers to the growth habit of some members, such as shallots, which form clusters of small bulbs. Others, such as storage onions, grow as single bulbs.

Members of the allium family are cultivated for their edible bulbs and, in some varieties, their edible leaves and flowers. Onions respond to day length and temperature. Different cultivars respond to day length in different ways, making it necessary to choose cultivars suitable for the sunlight hours in your own area. (Summer days are longer in northern climates so short-day cultivars for southern climates form small bulbs when grown in the North.) One solution to this is to buy onion sets and seeds locally. If buying from a catalog, remember that northern gardens need "long-day" and southern gardens need "short-day" onions. Be sure to read the catalog descriptions.

BEST CONDITIONS Onions are generally best grown in full sun in spring or fall. Frost tolerance differs for various cultivars. They like loose, well-drained sandy loam of pH 6.0-6.8.

PLANTING When growing onion transplants from seed, sow thinly in potting soil and cover with ¼ inch of soil. Start seeds indoors 8 weeks before setting out. Onion seeds usually take 1-2 weeks to germinate. Thin to 1 inch apart in pots. If sowing directly into the garden, sow seeds ¼ inch deep into loose soil 2 weeks before the last frost or 4 weeks before the first frost.

Sets and seedlings should be planted outside 4-6 weeks before the last frost. Onion seed can be sown in soil that is 45° F. or warmer, and can be planted at the same time as cabbages. It will germinate faster in warmer soil, but a longer growing period is desired for large bulbs. (Onion plants can be purchased in bundles of 25-50 showing bare roots. Plant quickly after purchase.)

Space spring onion sets and other onion plants 2-3 inches apart, large-bulb types should go 6-8 inches apart in rows 1-2 feet apart. When putting in the plants, cover the white part of the plant completely with soil. When planting sets, push the bulb just under the soil level, allowing only the bulb's top point to show. Two pounds of sets, 400 transplants, or 400 bare-root plants should plant a double 100-foot row.

CARE Expect very slow growth during the first 30 days in the garden and do not "push" with fertilizer to get better results. After the first month growth should be rapid. Onions are fairly heavy feeders that need fertile soil to maintain active growth. Apply a balanced fertilizer, such as 10-10-10, 2-3 days before planting, then after about 4-6 weeks cultivate in a high-nitrogen fertilizer (15-10-10). In poor soils, frequent light applications of nitrogen will promote leaf development and larger bulbs.

Onions are very shallow-rooted, with most roots in the top 8-10 inches of soil. This top soil zone should be kept evenly moist for maximum bulb size; dryness will result in smaller bulbs.

Weed carefully around the roots to avoid harming the shallow root system. Soil that has been worked and is loose results in bigger onion bulbs. If the soil forms a crust, the bulbs will be smaller and more difficult to harvest. As you cultivate, pull soil away from the bulb rather than piling it around the onion.

GARLIC, ROCAMBOLE Plants 3-5 feet tall yield 4- to 6-inch bulbs with small, pungent cloves. Days to harvest: 90.

SCALLIONS 'EVERGREEN WHITE' Open-pollinated. Plant 10-12 inches long yields tender, white-stemmed spring onions, with ½-inch bulbs. Multiple clusters of leaves yield many scallions. Use fresh. Days to harvest: 120.

LEEK 'ELECTRA' Hybrid. Upright, dark blue-green leaves, 18 inches tall, 6-8 inches wide, with long white stem and 3- to 4-inch bulb. Very few side shoots. Tolerates partial shade. Days to harvest: 140 from seed.

PARSNIP 'HARRIS MODEL' Bushy plant 2-3 feet tall produces 10 x 3-inch smooth white root with superior flavor. Tolerates partial shade. Days to harvest: 100.

THE ONION IN WINTER
Gardeners at the Desert
Botanical Garden and Fetzer
Organic Gardens report that
onions grow best as a winter
crop for them. At Fetzer, which
is in northern California, they
are sown in August and over-
wintered; they are not bothered
by pests or diseases, unless they
are planted in soil that previously grew peas. At the Desert
Botanic Garden, which is in
Phoenix, successive plantings of
green onions are very productive and easy to grow. At the
Chicago Botanic Garden,
onions are planted in February
for late spring or summer harvest.

PESTS AND DISEASES To protect against disease, plant members of the onion family in a different location every year. Do not plant onions in the same location again for at least 2 years. Plant some from seeds and some from sets to stagger the harvest. Space the seed-grown onions, which have a long growing season, far from one another to help prevent the spread of disease.

HARVEST Harvesting methods differ according to variety. In general, the plants are ready to harvest when foliage begins to yellow or topple over. Loosen the soil around the plant with a spading fork and lift bulbs. Brush away the loose soil but leave tops on onions for a week to keep the drying process slow and even. Spread onions out to dry in an area with good air circulation. Onions should dry in 3-4 days. Store in open bags. Most rot problems occur during storage. In nonhumid climates, harvest garlic promptly or it will dry out and storage life will be greatly reduced.

Harvest bunching onions while the foliage is still green and tender.

VARIETIES ONIONS: 'Ebenezer' can be pulled for early "green" onions within a few weeks of planting. It has a strong onion flavor when eaten green. In the South this is usually used as a green onion rather than a storage onion. Sets are easily found in stores and through mail-order catalogs.

'Granex 33' is a yellow-bulb storage type used for cooking. It is a short-day onion with excellent flavor right from the garden and is also one of the best storage onions that can be grown in hot, humid conditions. It is easy to grow from seeds; this is the variety grown in Vidalia, Georgia.

'White Sweet Sandwich' is a mild onion that stores well and sweetens as it ages. It is commonly grown in northern gardens. (Minnesota Landscape Arboretum)

SHALLOTS produce multiple small bulbs which can be dried and stored or used fresh as green onions, tops and all. Grow as any green onion, from seed or sets.

ELEPHANT GARLIC produces large, mild-flavored cloves of garlic. It is best planted 12 inches apart in late summer or fall. New cloves should be planted each year to have strong, vigorous plants each spring. For convenience, garlic should be planted in beds rather than rows because the crop needs to stay in the ground several months for a summer or fall harvest. Harvest when foliage begins to yellow and droop.

Plant garlic in late summer or early fall so just a few leaves are formed before the ground freezes. If grown too large by late fall, it will winter kill or bolt in the spring.

CALIFORNIA LATE WHITE GARLIC is the most common culinary garlic. It has a sweet, pungent flavor, good disease resistance, and stores well. (Fetzer)

LEEKS: 'Carina' produces very large leeks; overwinter this variety to get beautiful round flower heads in the spring. It does well if grown indoors and trans-planted to the garden in shallow trenches. (New York Botanical Garden)

'Electra' The white stem of this is shorter than other leeks, so digging a plant-ing trench is not necessary. The bulbs grow deeply; harvest carefully.

'Varna' leeks are slender and very long, maturing in 50 days. They can be direct-seeded like bunching onions from early spring through fall.

SCALLIONS: 'Evergreen White' is a white-stemmed, "bulbless" spring onion that produces multiple clusters of very tender leaves, resulting in lots of scallions from 1 plant. The seed germinates easily, and is inexpensive and can be harvested year round in southern climates.

PARSNIPS PASTINACA SATIVA *Umbellifera*

COOL-SEASON BIENNIAL (GROWN AS AN ANNUAL) Native to the Old World, parsnips have been cultivated since Roman times for their long, fleshy root. Parsnips store well and were popular in this country when people had root cellars; today they are often overlooked. Unlike most vegetables, parsnips benefit from exposure to low temperatures, making them ideal for cooler areas. They don't develop a sweet taste in the warm climate of Fetzer Gardens.

BEST CONDITIONS: Like carrots, parsnips need deep, loose soil to develop slender roots; till the soil to a depth of 18 inches as parsnips grow as long as 15 inches. A pH level of 6.0-6.8 is best.

PLANTING Parsnips are usually planted in early spring and harvested in the fall and winter. Sow seeds as soon as soil temperature reaches 50° F. Sow seeds ½ inch deep, 1 inch apart, in rows 18-36 inches apart. Seeds may require 3-4 weeks to sprout; cover them with leaf mold, compost, or a mixture of sand and soil. Thin seedlings to 2-4 inches apart.

CARE Apply a balanced fertilizer 4-6 weeks after sowing seeds. Keep the soil moist; roots may split from rapid water intake following a heavy rain. Weed regularly.

PESTS AND DISEASES Parsnips are susceptible to army worms, cabbage root maggot, flea beetles, leaf hoppers, and nematodes. These can be avoided by not planting parsnips near carrots, celery, or caraway, since the pests and diseases that trouble those plants also affect parsnips. Companion plantings seem to help prevent trouble; use bush beans, peppers, potatoes, peas, radishes, onions, or garlic.

HARVEST When the tops of the roots have reached a diameter of 2-3 inches, the crop is ready. Since cold increases the sugar in mature parsnips, leave them in the ground until the first frost. Or you can leave them in the ground through winter, digging them up as needed; in that case, mound soil over the crowns in autumn. They yield about 100 pounds per 100-foot row.

VARIETIES 'All American' is tapered and shorter and broader at the shoulder than most varieties.

'Harris Model' has a 10- to 12-inch root with fine texture and flavor. This is the smoothest and whitest variety that is readily available.

PEANUT ARACHIS HYPOGEA *Labaceae*

WARM-SEASON ANNUAL Peanuts are not actually nuts at all. They are members of the pea, or legume, family and ripen underground. Peanuts have more protein than beef liver, more fat than heavy cream, more calories than sugar.

Peanuts have a unique way of developing, forming pegs that enter the soil in a rootlike fashion.

ROOT VEGETABLES
Root vegetables—including beets, carrots, parsnips, salsify, and rutabaga—will thrive where other crops fail. They do not need as much sun as summer vegetables like tomatoes and pepper—4 hours per day is enough—and so can make the more shaded areas of the garden productive. Because they grow under the cover of the earth, they are not affected by early frost; in many cases, they can be left in the ground well into winter and pulled as needed. Root vegetables can be planted in beds, making them perfect for small gardens.

It is, however, important to prepare soil carefully for root vegetables. Make sure that the soil is loose and free of stones or debris; obstructions in the soil will cause stunting and deformities. If your soil is heavy or clayey, mix a lighter planting medium—such as vermiculite or sand—into it before planting; add compost generously. Do not space more closely than recommended; although root vegetables do not need much space, overcrowding will affect production. Water thoroughly, so that the ground is moist to the bottom of the roots. Mulch to prevent soil compaction.

Most root vegetables store well. Indoor root cellars are a good place to store these useful and nutritious vegetables.

Young peanut plants need a lot of fertilizer; fertilize before planting and twice again before flowering. Once flowers appear, it is not necessary to fertilize further. While the flower blooms, a white peg, which is actually a fertilized ovary, develops. If this peg is close enough to the ground, the peg enters the soil and below-ground peanut development occurs. It will take at least 100 days before this plant produces harvestable goobers.

BEST CONDITIONS Peanuts need a long, warm season and should be planted in full sun; they will not produce in shade. Loose, sandy soil is ideal, and good drainage is important; soil pH should be 6.0-6.8.

PLANTING Buy seed inoculated with a fungicide to reduce rotting. Sow seed directly into the garden 1½-2 inches deep, and 6 inches apart in rows 3-4 feet apart. When the soil is warm (65-70° F.) it takes only 5-6 days for germination. 1¼ pounds shelled raw peanuts will plant a 100-foot row.

CARE Peanuts are heavy feeders. Prepare the soil by applying a balanced fertilizer (10-10-10) 2-3 days before planting. Apply again in 4 weeks. Four weeks after that apply a fertilizer lower in nitrogen such as 5-10-10. There is no need to fertilize after flowering. The plants are very tender and susceptible to frost damage. Constant weeding and cultivation is necessary to keep the soil loose so the pegs can easily penetrate the soil surface to form the underground peanut. Stop cultivation when flowering begins. Do not mulch.

Until the pegs are well-rooted, supply with 1 inch of water per week. After that, ½ inch is best so that the peanuts will not rot.

PESTS AND DISEASES Be sure to rotate peanuts from one site to another from one year to the next. Do not plant in an area where prior crops had problems with insects or disease.

HARVEST Four to 5 months after planting, when the plants begin to shed leaves and the stems start to dry out, it is time to harvest. Using a spading fork, loosen the soil, and then lift the entire root system of the plant along with the peanuts. Turn the plant upside down on top of the soil, exposing the peanut pods to the sun and dry air. After 2-3 days of field drying, pick the pods off and spread them out in a sunny, well-ventilated area to dry for 2 more weeks. They can then be stored for several months in a cool, dry place, or boiled or roasted for eating.

VARIETIES 'Valencia' has a brown hulls and red husks and a sweeter flavor than other peanuts. It dependably produces uniform, full pods.

PEAS PISUM SATIVUM *Fabaceae*

COOL-SEASON ANNUAL Peas have come a long way since their humble beginnings nearly 3,000 years ago. They are thought to have originally been grown in an area extending from the Mediterranean through the Near East to central Asia. These earliest peas were probably so hard that primitive cultures had to roast them to make them edible.

Garden peas were eaten by the Greeks and Romans and were later planted by Columbus in 1493 on Isabella Island. Peas soon became an important crop in the New World and were much loved by outstanding horticulturists such as Thomas Jefferson and George Washington

This cool-season annual is a tendril-climbing plant that produces green seeds and sometimes edible green pods.

BEST CONDITIONS Peas need to be grown during a cool season, either spring or fall, in full sun. They do best in rich, deeply worked, well-drained soils at a

PEANUT 'VALENCIA' Open-pollinated. Plant 2-2½ feet high, 2-2½ feet wide, produces peanuts with brown hulls and red husks. Yields 3-5 peanuts per pod. Days to harvest: 120, frost free.

PEA 'GREEN ARROW' Hybrid. Vines 24-28 inches long produce 4-inch-long pods with 9-12 very sweet bright green peas. High yields. Resists downy mildew and fusarium wilt. Mid to late season. Days to harvest: 62-70.

PEA 'TALL TELEPHONE' Heirloom variety. 5- to 10-foot vines produce very heavy yield of 5-inch pods, 8-9 peas per pod. Vines require support. Days to harvest: 70.

PEA 'WANDO' 2½-foot vines produce 5-inch pods with 7-8 peas per pod. Very productive; adapted to warm, dry, and cold climates. Days to harvest: 68.

We had not peas nor strawberries here till the 8th day of this month. On the same day I heard the first whip-poor-will whistle. Swallows and martins appeared here on the 21st day of April. When did they appear with you? And when had you peas, strawberries, and whip-poor-wills? Take notice hereafter whether the whip-poor-wills always come with the strawberries and peas.

LETTER FROM THOMAS JEFFERSON TO HIS DAUGHTER MARIA, JUNE 13, 1790

pH of 6.0-6.8. A lower pH causes yellowing and decreased pod production. Heavy, wet soil results in the rotting of the starchy seed peas. Too much nitrogen in the soil causes blossoms to drop early without setting pods.

PLANTING Two to 3 days before planting, apply 8-8-8 fertilizer to the bed. Plant newly purchased seeds that have been treated with a fungicide to keep them from rotting in damp, cool soil. Plant 6 weeks before the last frost of spring or 6 weeks before the first frost of fall. Plant seeds at a depth of ½-1 inch and thin to 1 inch apart in rows 3 feet apart. If it does not rain, gently water in the seeds. Seeds should germinate in 8-10 days in spring, 5-6 days in fall. Young plants will tolerate temperatures down to about 25° F. A floating row cover will give protection to 20° F. Even unprotected plants will come back after being hit by frost.

CARE Peas need approximately 1 inch of water per week; 3-4 weeks after germination, treat the plants to another application of 8-8-8 fertilizer. All pea varieties will produce better when trellised, even those advertised as needing no support. When the vines lie on the ground, flowers and pods drop off quickly. Peas have usually finished production and can be tilled directly into the soil in time to plant hot-weather vines, such as cucumbers, which benefit from the nitrogen set by the peas.

When weeding, do not cultivate too close to the plants once they begin to bloom. If the roots are disturbed, leaves and pods will drop quickly.

PESTS AND DISEASES Choose fast-growing varieties to avoid mildews and leaf wilts.

HARVEST Use both hands to carefully pull pods from the vines without jerking. Most varieties will yield 25-30 pounds shelled peas per 100-foot row.

VARIETIES SHELL PEAS: 'Green Arrow' is a bush variety that yields abundantly.

'Improved Laxton's Progress' grows on a dwarf vine; it does well without trellising at Chicago Botanic Garden. An early maturer, it bears pods that contain 7-9 good-quality peas.

'Knight', an early variety, has large pods and resists powdery mildew. (University of Nebraska)

'Little Marvel' is an older variety that is still popular because of its dependability. Its blunt-edged pods are of average size.

'Tall Telephone', an heirloom variety, is a 5- to 10-foot vine that produces into warm weather; it is used at the The New York Botanical Garden to extend the season.

'Wando' produces small pods, but is a heavy bearer. In northern gardens it is often used as a variety for late-season crops.

EDIBLE PODS: 'Sugar Ann', a low-growing variety, matures early and has thick, meaty pods. AAS winner.

'Sugar Snap' has sweet edible pods and grows on 6-foot vines; it was one of the first edible-pods peas available.

'Sugar Daddy' was the first stringless snap pea. It grows on compact plants.

Plant peas near a support and they will grab onto it. See page 33 for information on staking beans, which is similar.

Southern peas can be harvested green or allowed to dry on the vine. They are grown for the peas crowded inside. *Above:* 'California Black-eye' peas and 'Pink-Eye Purple Hull' peas.

SOUTHERN PEAS VIGNA UNGUICULATA *Fabaceae*

WARM-SEASON ANNUALS Hot-weather shelled beans, including black-eyed peas, cream peas, cowpeas, and crowders, are commonly called Southern peas.

BEST CONDITIONS Southern peas do well in almost any soil, including clay, rocky, or sandy soils; a pH level of 6.0-6.8 is best. Experienced gardeners plant their Southern peas in soils too poor to produce other crops. The peas' roots help improve the soil. Rich, fertile spots are actually disadvantageous—the plant will produce too much foliage. Southern peas need full sun, hot weather, and 1 inch of water per week until the pods are filled.

PLANTING Direct-seed into garden 3 weeks after last frost and again every 2 weeks until 6 weeks before the first frost. Plant seeds 1 inch deep, 2 inches apart, with 3-4 feet between rows. Do not thin; when closely planted, these peas support one another and tend to produce less foliage and bloom more heavily. The seeds will germinate in 3-4 days in warm soils.

CARE Two to 3 days before sowing, apply a balanced 10-10-10 fertilizer as a starter. After that, no fertilizer is needed.

Hand-weed when plants are young; stop weeding when vines begin to run.

PESTS AND DISEASES Southern peas are susceptible to Mexican bean beetles, which can be hand-picked, and mosaic in cool weather, which can be avoided by planting during hot periods.

HARVEST Peas will be ready for harvest about 65 days after planting if soil is warm. Hand-pick mature pods individually, leaving immature pods to develop. Harvest period lasts 2-4 weeks. For dry Southern peas, leave the last planting of peas in the garden; wait until the pods begin to rattle before you pick them.

VARIETIES 'California Black-eye' pea produces a bush-type vine with long, green pods filled with true "black-eyed" white seeds that are larger than most Southern peas. These peas, commonly found in markets, taste good shelled, green or dried.

'Corrientes' is one of several varieties of black-eyed peas distributed by Native Seeds/SEARCH. Black-eyed peas are a good crop for desert climates because they tolerate high heat and drought. (Desert Botanical Garden)

'Mississippi Silver' crowder is a short, upright vine producing several long pods held above the plant and filled with "square" beans. Crowder peas are "crowded" in the pod, producing the square shape. To tell when peas are ready, roll the pod in your fingers; harvest when the pod feels like it's letting go of the peas. It is highly productive, easy to harvest, and has excellent flavor.

'Pink-Eye Purple Hull' produces a bush-type vine with dark green leaves and pods that turn purple when ready to harvest; peas are creamy white with "pink eyes." This variety is best used fresh instead of dried. It matures early and has excellent disease resistance.

PEPPER CAPSICUM ANNUUM *Solanaceae*

WARM-SEASON PERENNIAL GROWN AS AN ANNUAL Hot peppers found growing in South America were received with instant popularity when brought back

PEA 'SUGAR DADDY' Short, compact climbing vine, 2-2½ feet tall, 2 feet wide, produces "stringless" edible-podded peas. Does not require much trellising. Not heat-tolerant; will produce 2 full harvests. Days to harvest: 72.

PEA 'SUGAR SNAP' Tendril-climbing annual vine, 4-6 feet long, 2 feet wide, produces sweet-flavored edible-podded peas. Very productive, continues to produce even in hot weather. Requires trellising. Days to harvest: 70.

PEA 'PINK-EYE PURPLE HULL' Open-pollinated. Bush-type vine with dark green leaves, 2½ feet tall, 2 feet wide, produces long purple pods. Days to harvest: 60.

PEA 'MISSISSIPPI SILVER' Open-pollinated. Short, vine-producing plant, 3-4 feet tall, 2-3 feet wide, produces pods 8-9 inches long with "square" beans. Days to harvest: 64-70.

SWEET PEPPER 'BELL BOY' Hybrid. 24-inch plant produces 4-lobed, thick-walled peppers, 3¼ inches x 3½ inches, glossy green turning to red. Resists tobacco mosaic. Yields 6-8 peppers per plant. Days to harvest: 63-70.

SWEET PEPPER 'CALIFORNIA WONDER' Hybrid. Produces big, blocky, thick-walled stuffing peppers, 4½ inches x 4 inches. Resists tobacco mosaic. Yields 8-10 peppers per plant. Days to harvest: 70.

SWEET PEPPER 'GYPSY' Hybrid. Plant 2 feet tall produces wedge-shaped, 3½-inch light green fruits that ripen to yellow; medium-thick walls. Adapts to cool climates. Yield 12-14 peppers per plant. Resists tobacco mosaic. Days to harvest: 62.

SWEET PEPPER 'LIPSTICK' 5-inch peppers with tapered points; superior sweet taste and thick flesh. Dark glossy green, ripening to red. Dependable heavy yields, even in cool summers. Good for roasting. Days to harvest: 60-75.

by New World explorers. They were soon in the gardens of Spanish monks and by the 16th century were also grown in Italy, France, and Germany.

Hot or pungent, peppers have unique flavors, and their hotness ranges from mild to truly unbearable. Peppers that lack pungency are called sweet or bell peppers. In addition to their pungent flavor, peppers are also high in vitamins C, A, E, B_1, B_2, and B_3.

Peppers grow on many-branched bushy plants that range in height from 8-10 inches to 4 feet.

BEST CONDITIONS Most peppers need warm nights, soil at least 65° F., and full sun, but some hot varieties will produce in light shade. Transplants grow well in most soils, but seeds have trouble germinating in heavy soil. The best soil pH is 6.0-6.8. Peppers need ½ inch of water per week, but there is no need to water when fruits are ripening. Peppers do poorly in cool, wet weather. In the extreme climate of the Desert Botanical Garden in Phoenix, they do best when grown in shade with cool roots; they are planted in pots that are moved to the coolest spot in the yard throughout the summer.

PLANTING For best results, start seeds indoors. Sow 2-3 seeds ½ inch deep in a 2½-inch pot in light sterile soil. Peppers take a long time to develop their strong root systems; plants will not grow to transplantable size for 6-8 weeks. Seeds will germinate in 6-8 days indoors, 8-14 days outdoors. Place transplants or seeds in garden 4 weeks after last frost. Space 1-2 feet apart in rows 3-4 feet apart. If sown directly in garden, sow ½ inch deep; thin to 2 feet apart. Mulch to keep weeds down and moisture level even.

Take extra care with pepper transplants. Their roots are slow to develop, and their tender top growth needs shading. Water carefully around the plant; hitting the leaves with water will cause them to tear or stick to the soil.

CARE Two to 3 days before planting or sowing, till in a balanced (10-10-10) fertilizer. Apply again every 4 weeks. Too much nitrogen will promote leaf growth at the expense of fruit production. Peppers should receive ample nitrogen early in the season, prior to flower development. A light side-dressing should be made after the first fruit is removed; stop fertilizing when fruits begin to change color. Don't use overhead water when plants are in bloom—it tends to wash away pollen, so flowers remain unfertilized and fruit does not appear.

Cultivate frequently, especially when plants are young. Caging for support is recommended for plants in rich soils, especially for tall varieties.

PESTS AND DISEASES Nematodes in the soil can destroy pepper crops; hybrid varieties are much less susceptible to diseases. Mosaic leaf curl often affects immature plants in cool, wet weather, but the plants usually grow out of this problem when the weather warms.

HARVEST Every variety has a best point of harvest. Pull individual peppers when they are the proper color and size. Large peppers yield 2-3 bushels per 100-foot row, small peppers yield 1½ bushels per 100-foot row. Peppers have a long, continuous harvest season; however, if fruits are not harvested regularly, fruit production will stop. Remaining peppers will turn red, yel-

Young pepper plants are fragile and need extra care if their roots are to develop properly. Shade them from strong sun and water carefully for their first 10-12 days in the garden.

Most green peppers turn red if left on the vine. For more unusual colors, like purple, yellow, orange, and white, specialty varieties must be planted. Many of these varieties are bred for their color and are not necessarily more tasty than plain green.

low, or orange depending on the variety. Days to harvest are counted from when transplants are set out.

VARIETIES BELL PEPPERS: 'Bell Boy' Fruit progresses from green to rust to red. Takes longer to get mature red fruits than other bell peppers. AAS winner.

'Bell Captain' is an easily available hybrid variety that produces well over a long season. Fruits turn from green to red and weigh as much as ½ pound each.

'California Wonder', which does particularly well in the West, consistently produces a true lobe-shaped fruit. The compact plant declines after first 2 or 3 pickings

'Golden Summer' has excellent sweet bell flavor. Fruit matures from pale green to golden yellow and looks beautiful in salads.

'Gypsy' can be harvested yellow, orange, or red. It resists tobacco mosaic and is very productive. AAS winner.

'Keystone Resistant Giant' is a green pepper that turns red when fully mature and resists tobacco mosaic virus.

'Lipstick', a recent introduction, is one of the sweetest peppers available and produces heavily even in cool summers.

'Sweet Banana' can be planted early, but plant and fruit may be smaller if grown in cool weather. Produces light green fruits that turn light yellow, orange, and red. Outer skin is thick and waxy, protecting fruit from insect

SWEET PEPPER 'SWEET BANANA' 18- to 22-inch plant produces tapered, 6-inch peppers with medium-thick walls and light, spicy taste; light green, ripening to yellow and red. Yields 20-25 peppers per plant. Days to harvest: 65.

HOT PEPPER 'HUNGARIAN YELLOW WAX' Open-pollinated. 14- to 22-inch bushy plant yields waxy canary yellow peppers ripening to red; 8 x 2 inches. Medium hot. Good pickled. Days to harvest: 75.

HOT PEPPER 'JALAPENO M' Open-pollinated. Produces dark green to red thick-walled peppers, 2 x ¾ inches. Best pepper for pickling; hottest when red. Yield 20-30 peppers per plant. Days to harvest: 75.

HOT PEPPER 'LONG RED CAYENNE' Open-pollinated. Spreading plant produces twisted, pointed dark green and bright red peppers 5 x ½ inches. Very hot. Yields 70 or more peppers per plant. Days to harvest: 70-75.

HOT PEPPER 'SCOTCH BONNET' Considered the very hottest pepper; also called 'Habanero'. Lantern-shaped 1½ inch long, 1 inch wide, light green pepper with wrinkled skin; turns bright orange when fully mature. Days to harvest: 95.

HOT PEPPER 'SUPER CHILE' Hybrid. Upright, ornamental, 12- to 24-inch plant produces 2½-inch green and red cone-shaped peppers. Hot. Good for containers. Yields 50-75 peppers per plant. AAS winner. Days to harvest: 75.

POTATO 'CHERRIES JUBILEE' Open-pollinated. Swedish heirloom variety. Plant with compact foliage 18 inches tall, 12 inches wide, produces small red-skinned potatoes with pink flesh. Excellent flavor, particularly as new potato cooked in skins. Days to harvest: 110

POTATO 'KENNEBEC WHITE' Open-pollinated. Medium-size plant produces large potatoes with excellent flavor, light tan skin, shallow eyes, white flesh. Good keeper. Yields 8-10 potatoes per plant, mid-season. Resists blight and mosaic. Days to harvest: 120.

damage. Transplants are generally easy to find in garden centers.

HOT PEPPERS: **'Hungarian Yellow Wax'** can withstand cool, wet weather better than most peppers. Fruit changes color from yellow to orange to red and gets progressively hotter. (Minneapolis)

'Jalapeno M' should not be overwatered or overfertilized. Takes a long time to turn red.

'Long Red Cayenne' does best in hot, dry areas and will produce for a long time. Turns from green to red quickly. One of the best hot peppers to dry for storage.

'Scotch Bonnet' peppers, which are very similar to 'Habanero', are about the hottest peppers available. They change from green to bright orange when fully mature.

'Super Chile', a 1988 AAS winner, must be grown in hot weather; will eventually turn red. It is both extremely prolific and very ornamental.

Chiltepines are wild relatives of cultivated peppers, native to North America. Their pea-sized fruits are very hot. They do well in sandy soil and need warmth; available through Native Seeds/SEARCH. (Desert Botanical Garden)

POTATO SOLANUM TUBEROSUM *Solanaceae*

WARM-SEASON PERENNIAL GROWN AS AN ANNUAL Potatoes were first grown in Peru over 6,000 years ago and were sometimes only the size of a chestnut. This vegetable, now considered the most popular in this country, was not always so loved. The English mistakenly ate the leaves and stems, which contain toxins and made them quite ill, and Scottish ministers forbade its consumption on the grounds that potatoes are not mentioned in the Bible. Luckily today the potato is not only accepted, but is enthusiastically appreciated by gardeners. Over 5,000 varieties of the common white potato have been developed.

Potatoes benefit from a mulch of straw, as shown below, or compost. This covering keeps the soil at the even temperature needed for formation of tubers.

Potatoes are edible underground tubers produced on green weak-stemmed plants. The tubers vary in size from 1 to 10 inches in length.

BEST CONDITIONS Potatoes do best in rich, very loose soils with a soil pH of 6.0-7.0 (worked to a depth of at least 8 inches). Production is best in sandy soils. If planted in heavy soils, "hill" soil around the plant as it grows so tubers develop in a well-drained mound.

PLANTING This vegetable is best started with "seed potatoes" or "spud buds" purchased at a garden center. These are disease-free and are not subject to potato scab, a common problem in cool, damp soils especially if kitchen potatoes are used to propagate new plants.

Potatoes perform best if planted in spring while it is still cool, though they mature satisfactorily during the warmer months. In early spring 4-6 weeks before the last frost prepare the bed by tilling deeply and applying 5-10-15 fertilizer 2-3 days before planting. Plant seed potatoes 8 inches deep, approximately 12 inches apart, in rows 3-4 feet apart. No thinning is required. As the plants grow, pile loose soil around them to keep tubers from being exposed to the sun.

For small gardens, a good way to hill (or hold soil around potato plants) is to set bottomless baskets over plants, adding compost and sand as plants grow. At harvest time, remove baskets and potatoes are easy to dig.

Compost makes a good mulch as it keeps the soil cool or warm as needed. Tubers formed in compost are easy to dig. Some gardeners plant the tubers directly into compost held in various containers such as plastic garbage bags or stacked tires.

CARE Depending on the weather, plants will sprout in 2-3 weeks. When they reach a height of 8-10 inches, till in a sidedressing of potassium nitrate or another low-nitrogen fertilizer such as 5-10-10; be careful to avoid cutting the potato roots. Till periodically to keep soil loose. Watering is not critical. Young plants will withstand light frost; tops may die back but the tubers will generally put forth new growth.

PESTS AND DISEASES Potatoes are in the same family as tomatoes and are subject to some of the same diseases such as wilts, blights, and mosaics. The best prevention is to plant certified disease-free seed potatoes or those bred to resist blight, wilts, and potato scab.

HARVEST Potatoes are usually ready to harvest in 90-120 days when the leaves and stems start to yellow and wilt. To harvest, loosen the soil around the base of the plant—12 inches from the stem—with a spading fork. Handle red-skinned potatoes carefully; their thin skins tear easily. Depending on the variety, yield may vary from 90-100 pounds per 100-foot row.

Potatoes grown in the deep South are not good "keepers" because of the heat and humidity. To prepare for storage, brush soil (do not wash) from the potatoes and store in a well-ventilated, cool, dry place. Potatoes harvested and then exposed to sunlight become "sunburned." The skins become green, bitter, and inedible.

VARIETIES 'Cherries Jubilee', an heirloom variety produces small, pink-skinned potatoes with excellent taste, particularly as new potatoes.

'Kennebec White' is a good "dry" potato for baking or frying and stores well. Relatively inexpensive and bred to resist blight.

'Norland' Early producer of small potatoes with red skin and white flesh.

'Red Pontiac' has an excellent "new potato" flavor and can be cooked in its

POTATO 'NORLAND' Medium-large tubers with very smooth red skin, white flesh. Does well under harsh conditions. Good yields. Days to harvest: 80-100.

POTATO 'RED PONTIAC' Open-pollinated Large plant with heavy foliage produces several medium-sized thin-skinned potatoes with excellent new potato flavor. Not good keepers; best cooked fresh. Good choice for heavy soils. Yields 8-10 potatoes per plant. Days to harvest: 70-80.

POTATO 'YUKON GOLD' Small, attractive, oval, smooth yellow-skinned and -fleshed potatoes, with waxy, buttery flavor, shallow eyes. Excellent keeper. Days to harvest: 60-80.

SWEET POTATO 'PORTO RICO' Space-saver bushes produce copper-colored sweet potatoes with deep orange flesh and high sugar content. Days to harvest: 100.

SWEET POTATO 'RED JEWEL' Bright copper skin and deep orange flesh. Highest yielding sweet potato. Days to harvest: 100.

RADISH 'APRIL CROSS' DAIKON Hybrid. 4-foot-wide plant produces enormous (18- to 20-inch), long-rooted radish. Very mild, thin-skinned, good cooked or raw. Extended growing season. Days to harvest: 60.

RADISH 'EARLY SCARLET GLOBE' Heavy 4- to 6-inch tall foliage produces small round solid red-skinned roots, 1½ inches across. Tender skin, white flesh. Easy to harvest. Days to harvest: 21.

RHUBARB 'VICTORIA' Bushy plant with 1½- to 2½-foot-long stalks and 1- to 2½-foot-wide red leaves. Leaves are poisonous. Tolerates light shade. Space 3 feet apart. Mulch in winter. Perennial; 2 years to first harvest.

tender thin skins when newly harvested. It has relatively few disease problems because the tubers mature so quickly.

'Yellow Finn' have yellow flesh and are good for boiling or baking.

'Yukon Gold' produces yellow-fleshed potatoes, early to mid season.

SWEET POTATO IPOMOEA BATATAS *Convolvulaceae*

WARM-SEASON TENDER PERENNIALS A relative of the morning glory, the sweet potato is originally from tropical America but is now grown in warm climates throughout the world. The genus name *Ipomoea* is from two Greek words meaning "worm" and "like" because the swollen stems of the mature vines resemble worms. Sweet potatoes have white or orange edible tuberous roots; they are generally the swollen roots of trailing vines, though bush or short vine types are also available.

BEST CONDITIONS Most varieties of sweet potatoes need at least 3 months of frost-free weather to produce a good crop. Row covers are recommended even in relatively warm climates. They need full sun and should have at least ½ inch water per week. Loose, sandy soil is ideal at a pH of 6.0-7.0. Overly rich soil produces abundant foliage but small, stringy potatoes. Insufficient sunlight also produces stringy fruit.

PLANTING Purchase certified disease-free "slips" with lots of small roots. Gardeners can start their own slips, but purchased disease-free slips give best results. The shoots are broken off the potato and placed in potting soil until they develop several small roots.

Two to 3 days before planting, till in balanced (8-8-8 or 10-10-10) fertilizer. Set out slips anytime from 2 weeks after the last frost through early summer, spacing 1 foot apart in rows 3-4 feet apart. Slips should be planted deep enough to cover all roots. Young plants are extremely sensitive to the cold and will not survive frost. Keep soil slightly moist for 1-2 weeks after the slips are planted.

CARE These vines are generally exuberant, and the excessive foliage tends to take over garden space. However, don't prune vines until just before harvest, as this slows or stops potato production.

PESTS AND DISEASES Plant sweet potatoes in a different location every year to guard against hematox infestation.

HARVEST To harvest, dig carefully with a spading fork after cutting the vines off and getting them out of the way. Sweet potatoes grown in clay soil must be harvested carefully or potatoes will break or bruise, causing spoilage. After harvest, brush soil (don't wash) from skins. Cure potatoes by storing in a cool dry place. After two weeks, store by spreading out in a cool, dry place. Sweet potato flavor is markedly improved by curing and storage.

In warm climates, old-fashioned gardeners sometimes stack cured potatoes out of doors between layers of straw and protected from the weather by corn shucks. A 100-foot row yields 90-100 pounds of potatoes.

VARIETIES 'Centennial' has a relatively short growing season, a real advantage since this cuts down on the possibility for pest infestation and diseases. Its

Radishes range in size from 1-inch balls to long, thin spears up to 1½ feet long. Japanese Daikon radishes are usually the largest. *Above, from top to bottom:* 'White Icicle', a mild-flavored radish; 'French Breakfast', which is shaded from red to white; Daikon 'Summer Cross'; small, perfectly round 'Cherry Bomb'; and 'Easter Egg', which will also bear pink, red, and purple radishes.

orange flesh is excellent for baking and has a tender, moist flavor.

'Porto Rico' is a bush type that produces fruit close to the center of the plant, all in one spot, making it easy to harvest. This variety is tolerant of a wide range of growing conditions.

'Red Jewel' prepares easily for cooking and has an excellent flavor.

RADISH RAPHANUS SATIVUS *Brassicaceae*

FULL-SEASON (SPRING AND FALL) BIENNIAL, GROWN AS AN ANNUAL The radish, a member of the mustard family, probably originated in western Asia. Early cultivated radishes were grown for a variety of reasons, including the seed pod, edible leaves, and oil-bearing seeds. The oil derived from the seeds was considered valuable in Roman times. The name *radish* is from the Latin for "root."

Radishes are a root crop generally served raw. Radishes mature quickly and can be planted at 2-week intervals during cool weather, providing a steady supply of mild, nonwoody radishes. Radishes grown in hot weather are hotter than those grown in cooler conditions.

BEST CONDITIONS Full sun is best, but most varieties will tolerate and produce in light shade. The best soils are loose, loamy, or sandy. Soil should be well cultivated and have a pH of 6.0-6.8. Heavy, clay soils cause radish deformities.

PLANTING Sow seeds directly into the garden in spring or fall, or during summer if the climate is mild. In spring plant 3-4 weeks before last spring frost; in fall, 2-3 weeks before the first frost is expected. Scatter seeds thinly ½ inch deep in rows 1 foot apart. Mulch, compost, and row covering are not needed.

Germination occurs after only 3-5 days. For the first planting, apply a balanced (10-10-10) fertilizer 2-3 days before sowing the seeds. Keep evenly moist until germination occurs.

CARE Keep weeds in check with hand cultivation.

PESTS AND DISEASES If any plants show signs of disease or pests, remove the affected plants immediately. Flea beetles attack radish foliage, but this does not seem to alter the productivity of the plant in the home garden.

HARVEST Harvest when radish root tops begin to show above the soil and root skin color is distinct. Radishes left past prime harvest time will quickly bolt and flavor becomes stronger.

VARIETIES, DAIKON: 'April Cross' is an enormous hybrid, white cooking radish that has a good flavor raw or cooked.

'Champion,' a red-skinned variety, does not become woody if allowed to grow larger than most others. Many gardeners sow this variety repeatedly for long-season enjoyment. (University of Minnesota)

'Early Scarlet Globe' takes only 21 days from seed to harvest. (Most globe types are early to harvest.) It has a pretty shape, tender red skin, and white flesh.

'Easter Egg' matures over a long period and stays mild even when large.

RHUBARB RHEUM RHABARBARUM *Polygonaceae*

COOL-SEASON PERENNIAL Rhubarb is a clumping plant whose juicy stalks are cooked and eaten as a fruit, often mixed with other fruits. Rhubarb will decline in any climate where the average summer temperature is over 75° F. and average winter temperature is over 40° F. Therefore, in the deep South it is best grown as an annual with spring and fall harvests.

BEST CONDITIONS Rhubarb is one of the few crops that does well in shade; it can easily be grown in spots near buildings and fences that are not usable for other vegetables. Rhubarb needs loose, well-drained soil and will not perform well in heavy soil that does not have good drainage. pH is not critical. First-year plants need 1 inch of water per week. Rhubarb is dormant in winter; in areas where there are warm winters and hot summers it is difficult to grow as a perennial.

PLANTING For southern gardens, where rhubarb is grown as an annual, it is best started from seed. In cooler areas, seeds, plants, or dormant roots can be used. To start seed indoors, sow 2-3 seeds per 2½-inch pot in sterile potting mix; start seeds 8 weeks before last frost. Outside, sow seeds 2 weeks after last frost; plant ½ inch deep, 6 inches apart, with 3-4 feet between rows. Seeds will germinate indoors in 5-6 days, outdoors 7-14 days. When plants are 4-6 inches tall, before the soil is very warm, spread 2 inches of mulch. When plants are 2 feet tall, thin to 1 feet apart and transplant the thinnings.

CARE Rhubarb does better without fertilizer. Hand-weed when plants are small. No staking is necessary.

PESTS AND DISEASES Avoid root and crown rot by planting in well-drained soils. Foliage damage by beetles doesn't affect productivity.

HARVEST For southern gardens, there will be 2 harvests. For first (spring) harvest, cut stalks on outer edge of clump. Leave short (2- to 3-feet tall) center stalks to grow for fall harvest. In early fall, harvest all stems of any size. To harvest, cut stem close to plant with a sharp knife. CUT OFF LEAVES BEFORE EATING; THEY ARE HIGHLY TOXIC.

VARIETY 'Victoria' produces tender juicy green and red stems. From seed, expect to harvest 6-8 stalks per plant.

RUTABAGA BRASSICA NAPUS *Brassicaceae*

COOL-SEASON BIENNIAL The rutabaga is grown extensively in Europe, where it is believed to have originated during the Middle Ages as a cross between the white turnip and the cabbage. The rutabaga is also known as the yellow turnip, Swedish turnip, or just the swede. Like parsnips, rutabagas are easy to grow and store well through winter. Also like parsnips, the taste of rutabagas improves with a light frost, and they are at their best in late fall or winter. The young leaves are eaten cooked or in salads.

BEST CONDITIONS Rutabagas need loose, well-drained soil (pH 6.0-6.9) that will not impede their growth or affect their root shape. They need plenty of space to allow their roots to reach their full weight of 3-5 pounds each.

Rhubarb grows in this place [Siam] and it is found thus: Twenty or twenty-five men gather together and they go into the forest, and when night falls, they climb into the trees, as much to catch the scent of the rhubarb as for fear of the lions, elephants, and other wild animals. And the wind carries the odor of the rhubarb to them from where it is growing, then when day comes, they go in that direction, and search until they find it.
ANTONIO PIGAFETTA, CHRONICLER OF THE MAGELLAN EXPEDITION, QUOTED IN *FOOD,* BY WAVERLY ROOT

Trellised loofah gourds produce straighter fruit than vines run on the ground. These huge fruits are too large for eating, but will soon be ready to be harvested and made into loofah sponges.

PLANTING Sow seeds in early to midsummer for an autumn harvest. Sow seeds about ½ inch deep, 1 inch apart, in rows spaced 18-36 inches apart; thin seedlings to 5-8 inches apart. If growing for greens, do not thin.

CARE The plants need about 1 inch of water per week; unwatered rutabagas are bitter tasting. Weed regularly.

PESTS AND DISEASES Rutabagas are susceptible to army worms, flea beetles, and leafhoppers.

HARVEST The plants are ready to harvest 90-120 days after sowing, when the roots are about 3 inches wide. After roots reach full size, they can stay in the ground, protected by a 6-inch mulch, and dug as needed.

VARIETIES 'Purple Top' ('America') has pale yellow flesh with purple shoulders; sweet and fine-grained, it stores well and is readily available.

'Laurentian' is one of the most popular varieties in North America; it stores well and has uniform roots.

'Canadian Gem' is extremely hardy, a good choice for northern gardens.

SALSIFY TRAGOPOGON PORRIFOLIUS *Compositae*

LONG-SEASON ANNUAL Salsify is grown for its long, fleshy roots, which have an oysterlike flavor. Indeed, salsify is also known as vegetable oyster and oyster plant. The genus name *Tragopogon* comes from two Greek words meaning "goatsbeard," a reference to the long, feathery hairs on the seeds, and salsify is also known as purple goatsbeard. The related meadow salsify, or yellow goatsbeard, is sometimes called John-go-to-bed-at-noon because the flower heads of salsifies close at noon. Salsify is an old-fashioned but satisfying vegetable.

BEST CONDITIONS Salsify prefers a deep, rich soil, deeply dug in the spring.

PLANTING Sow seeds in spring when soil has warmed. Sow ¼-inch deep in rows 24-30 inches apart. When the seedlings are small, thin to 4-5 inches apart.

HARVEST Salsify can be harvested whenever the roots reach a reasonable size. For storage in the fall, roots should be dug late in the fall; cut top to 1-2 inches from roots (like beets) and store in root-cellar conditions in slightly moist sand. In mild climates, salsify can be left in the ground over winter, covered with straw or hay, and harvested as needed.

VARIETIES 'Victoria' does well as an annual. It tolerates heat and humidity and produces very tender young stalks. Inexpensive seed is readily available.

SQUASH

PUMPKIN CUCURBITA PEPO *Cucurbitaceae*
SUMMER SQUASH CUCURBITA PEPO *Cucurbitaceae*
WINTER SQUASH CUCURBITA MAXIMA, C. MOSCHATA, C. PEPO
GOURDS CUCURBITA SPECIES, LAGENARIA SPECIES

Archaeologists have found squash seeds in Mexico that date back over 1,000 years, indicating that this is a very ancient crop. Native Americans baked squashes whole and then split them open, seasoning them with animal fat and maple syrup.

RUTABAGA 'PURPLE TOP' ('AMERICA') Large roots, up to 2 pounds each, with yellow flesh and purple shoulders. Sweet taste, fine texture, rich in vitamin A. Prefers cool weather, keeps well. Days to harvest: 90.

SALSIFY 'MAMMOTH SANDWICH ISLAND' Produces long, thick, dull-white roots, 6-8 inches long. Roots can be stored in moist sand. Days to harvest: 120-140.

PUMPKIN 'CONNECTICUT FIELD' Hybrid. Produces large, slightly ribbed pumpkins 10 x 14 inches, 25 pounds. Bright orange rind, orange-yellow flesh. Good for carving, flattened at ends. Days to harvest: 110-120.

PUMPKIN 'GHOSTRIDER' Medium to medium-large pumpkins, 10-20 pounds each, 16 inches across, deep orange rind and yellow-orange flesh. Good for baking or carvings. Days to harvest: 110.

PUMPKIN 'JACK BE LITTLE' produces 10-12 tiny 2-3 ounce pumpkins, 3 inches in diameter, flattened on both ends. Edible flesh, good for decorations. Days to harvest: 95

PUMPKIN 'PRIZE WINNER' Hybrid. 12- to 18-foot vines bear very large pumpkins, 30-36 inches across, weighing up to 100 pounds. Used for carving and competitions. Not easy to grow. Days to harvest: 120.

SUMMER SQUASH 'BUTTERBAR' Hybrid. 3-inch straightneck squash on compact, bush-type vines with space-saving but open habit. Solid flesh. Days to harvest: 50.

SUMMER SQUASH 'EARLY GOLDEN SUMMER' Short vines, 2½-3 feet tall, 3 feet wide, produce small crookneck squash with bumpy yellow skin, 4-5 inches across. Solid meaty fruit. Continues production if kept harvested. Later than most squash. Days to harvest: 48-53.

Squashes are divided into groups based on when they ripen. Summer squashes–including crookneck, pattypan, and zucchini–ripen during the hot months, have a thin, edible skin and seeds, and need to be eaten soon after picking. Winter squashes ripen during autumn and have a thick skin that makes them good for storing; examples include butternut, acorn, and Hubbard. Although summer and winter squashes look very different from one another, and certainly taste different, they have similar growing habits and are generally treated the same by gardeners.

BEST CONDITIONS Squashes need a great deal of room to grow, and full sun; plants grown in shady areas produce few fruits. Loose, loamy soils are best, but these plants can be grown in most soil types. Ideal pH is 6.0-7.0. The soil temperature at planting time must be 60° F. and higher for good seed germination.

PLANTING Generally, squash should be planted to allow 10-15 square feet per plant. Early planting can be done using transplants, but for good production, these should have true leaves when transplanted. Squash, like melon, does not

Above: The many shapes of summer squash

The beautiful squash blossoms that appear after about 3 weeks of growth play an important part in the development of the fruit. Male blossoms, which appear first, produce pollen. The female blossoms, which appear about a week later, have a tiny fruit on the base. Bees transfer pollen from the male to the female squash; a single bee can pollinate 100 flowers. The tiny fruit at the base of the female flower is actually an ovary; when pollinated, it grows to a full-sized fruit.

Edible squash blossoms are considered a delicacy. Usually, the larger male blossoms from long-flowering varieties make the best harvests. Be sure to leave a few male blossoms to ensure pollination. To harvest the tender *courgettes,* let the fruit at the base of the female flower develop a few days and pick the tiny fruit with the blossom still attached.

grow well when roots are disturbed. Squash should be planted in hills 3 feet apart in rows 5-6 feet apart. Early planting should be done from transplants, later plantings from seeds sown directly into the garden. Indoors, sow 2-3 seeds in a 2-inch container filled with light potting soil. Plant the seeds 1 inch deep. Seeds should germinate in 3-7 days, and seedlings should be ready to transplant into the garden in 2-3 weeks. Set out plants after all danger of frost has passed. Planting deeply, up to the first set of leaves, results in less wind damage to the hollow stems and will produce stockier plants. Sow later crops 3-4 weeks apart; sow seeds directly into garden, sowing 2-3 seeds to a hill. **CARE** Straw or a row cover can be used to protect the tender transplants from drying winds, sun, and late frosts.

Work a balanced (10-10-10) fertilizer into the soil 2-3 days before planting time. Continue to apply throughout the growing season once a month to keep blossoms and fruit production high.

These plants need 1 inch of water per week for even production. Drought conditions can damage the hollow stems, shutting down the plant's growth and slowing fruit production. Water early in the morning or with a drip irrigation system to prevent the spread of several foliage diseases.

The area around the plants should be kept weeded until the vines start

SUMMER SQUASH 'SENECA PROLIFIC' Hybrid. Short vines, 3 feet tall, 3-4 feet wide, produce straight bright-yellow squash with tender skin. Very productive; taste is good even when squash reach 8-10 inches in length. Prone to insect and disease damage in late summer. Days to harvest: 51.

SUMMER SQUASH 'SUNDROPS' Hybrid. Compact bush vines, 2 feet tall, 2 feet wide, yield 4-inch-long, 3-inch-diameter creamy yellow oval fruits. Best picked when 3 inches long. Space-saving habit. Very mild taste, quick producer. Days to harvest: 48.

ZUCCHINI 'ELITE' Hybrid. Open growth habit, 3 feet tall, 4 feet wide. Best harvested at 8 inches. Glossy dark green skin bruises easily. Yields 10-12 fruits per plant. Days to harvest: 48.

ZUCCHINI 'GOLDRUSH' Hybrid. Upright bush, 3-4 feet tall, 3-4 feet wide produces uniform yellow fruits. Best harvested at 8 inches long. Thin tender skin is easily damaged. Fast and prolific. Days to harvest: 52.

ZUCCHINI 'SENECA MILANO' Open-pollinated. Strong, upright vine, 3-4 feet tall, 3-4 feet wide, produces long, narrow fruit, best harvested at 10 inches long. Matures quickly. Crisp, firm flesh with good flavor. Less prone to leaf mildew, not easily damaged. Days to harvest: 52.

SCALLOP SQUASH 'PETER PAN' Hybrid. Vigorous, semi-bush plant produces 4-inch pale jade green deeply scalloped fruits that stay tender on the vine for several days. Yields 7-9 fruits per plant. Open habit, easy to harvest. Days to harvest: 52.

SCALLOP SQUASH 'SUNBURST' Hybrid. Compact bushy plants, 2 feet tall, 3 feet wide, produce disc-shaped yellow fruits, best harvested at 2-3 inches in diameter. Early producer, good butter flavor. Vivid gold flowers, dark green foliage. Days to harvest: 50.

ACORN WINTER SQUASH 'CREAM OF THE CROP' Hybrid. Semi-bush runner plants produce 2-pound fruits with ivory white skin. Nutty flavor. 4-6 fruits per plant. Days to harvest: 80.

running. Weeding after this can damage the stems. Care should be taken to prevent crushed leaves or nicked stems, which affect the plant's production.

PESTS AND DISEASES Vine borers and cucumber beetles often damage this vegetable. Remove and destroy any diseased foliage.

HARVEST Winter squash are best hand-picked when vines begin to wither and when the rind color changes to the expected final color. Harvest summer squash when fruits reach the desired size (usually smaller is better). The yield is variable depending on spacing and blossom set, which is affected by the presence of pollinators, whether the pollen got washed away by rain or sprinklers, day and nighttime temperatures, and other factors. They do very poorly where summers are very hot and humid, as in Houston, where daytime temperature averages 100° F. and nighttimes average 75° F. Summer squash must be kept harvested or future production will be reduced.

VARIETIES PUMPKINS: 'Autumn Gold' matures early, so there is less time for insect and disease problems to develop; most fruit are ready for harvest at the same time. Its handsome gold color, thick rind, and deep ridges make it a good jack-o-lantern pumpkin. AAS winner. 98 days to harvest.

'Connecticut Field' pumpkins are flattened on both ends and weigh up to 25 pounds.

'Ghostrider' pumpkins are medium to medium-large size and good for baking and carving.

'Jack Be Little' pumpkins can fit in a child's hand; they are best trellised. Used as decorations.

'Prize Winner' pumpkins can weigh over 100 pounds. If grown for competition, fruit thinning, extra water, and fertilization are required to grow huge fruits. To thin fruits: after first fruits appear, check fruits for good shape and remove

Above: Bottle gourds. *Left:* Ornamental gourds grown on a trellis take up less space.

Loofa gourds can be peeled to reveal a very useful sponge.

any that are misshapen. If plant stops blooming during the growing season, there are too many pumpkins per vine–cut off all but 2 or 3 of the best pumpkins.

'Spanish Pumpkin' is a medium-sized pumpkin, about 12 inches across, with a blue-gray exterior and orange blush on the exposed sun side. It tends to become more orange in hotter climates or with increased light exposure. Its bright orange to yellow-orange flesh is exceptionally sweet and has a smooth, creamy texture. (Fetzer Organic Gardens)

SUMMER SQUASH: 'Butterbar' a straightneck squash, grows on a space-saving bush-type vine.

'Early Golden Summer' must be harvested when neck is narrow. Best grown in hot weather. Seed is easy to find.

'Multipik' is a yellow straightneck squash that is best for late-summer or fall plantings. It produces high yields early. 55 days to harvest.

'Seneca Prolific', a yellow straightneck, has a very tender skin and is very prolific.

'Sundrops' is a heavy producer of oval-shaped fruit; harvest 2-3 times per week.

ZUCCHINI: 'Elite' has a distinctive, glossy skin. Harvest with care when fruit is 6-8 inches long to avoid pithiness in the seed cavity.

'Goldrush' has hard stems that must be cut when fruit is harvested and tender skins that must be handled carefully. Fruits produced late in the season sometimes are blotched or striped as a result of infestation of virus; yield will decrease but fruit will taste the same.

'Seneca Milano' needs to be kept harvested or fruit will become huge. Uneven watering causes uneven fruit shapes.

SCALLOP: 'Peter Pan' Excellent quality semi-bush variety, produces medium-green squash. Weather-resistant. AAS winner.

'Sunburst' produces disc-shaped yellow squash on compact vines. This AAS winner was the first yellow scallop squash.

WINTER SQUASH: ACORN 'Table King' is quick to mature and stores well. It is good for late plantings in midsummer and ripens easily for on-time harvest. It grows on short, bushy vines.

'Cream of the Crop' produces heavy yields on short bushy plants. The acorn-shaped fruits have a rich creamy, nutty flavor and store well.

BUTTERNUT: 'Early Butternut', a heavy-neck type, matures more quickly than most butternuts and stores well. Its hard rind helps it resist squash borers. AAS winner.

'Ponca', has a long, uniform neck, and a small seed cavity.

'Waltham', a butternut, has a small seed cavity and orange flesh. Stores well.

'Delicata' 8- to 9-inch ribbed squashes store well and have a bland, adaptable flavor.

'Elfrida' is a native variety that does well in dry climates. It is distributed by Native Seeds/SEARCH as well as through many seed catalogs. (Desert Botanical)

'Pink Banana' is a large winter squash with a thin, brittle green rind that turns pink at maturity.

BUTTERNUT WINTER SQUASH 'EARLY BUTTERNUT' Hybrid.
Semi-bushy 4-foot vines, 12-18 inches tall, produce tan fruit,
8-10 inches long. 3-6 squash per plant, 1-1½ pounds each.
Hard rind resists squash borers, stores well. Good for areas
with short seasons. Days to harvest: 85.

WINTER SQUASH 'DELICATA' Also called "Sweet Potato"
squash. Short vines produce 3 x 9-inch cylindrical yellow
fruits, 1-2 pounds each, with dark green ribbing, cream-colored flesh. Heavy yields. Stores well. Good for stuffing and
baking, needs no curing. Days to harvest: 100.

WINTER SQUASH 'ELFRIDA' Cushaw-type squash from the
irrigated fields of southern Arizona. Fast-growing vines
with large splotched leaves produce 2- to 5-pound fruits in
a variety of colors; pale yellow flesh is good for baking.
Days to harvest: 100-120.

WINTER SQUASH 'PINK BANANA' Extra-large squashes, 30
inches long and 12-14 pounds each, ripen to pale pink. Sweet
orange flesh is excellent for baking. Yields 2-3 fruits per
plant. Days to harvest: 105.

VEGETABLE SPAGHETTI: 'Orangetti' This space-spacing squash is much more productive than other varieties. It develops color before it is ready to harvest, so don't pick until vines begin to shrivel. When harvesting, clip, rather than twist, the stems. To prepare, cut the squash in half and remove the seeds before baking. **GOURDS** are rather bizarre-looking vegetables that are grown for fun rather than as food. Though they are edible when harvested small, gourds with hard, thin shells are grown for use as containers, dipping utensils, and even musical instruments. The oldest records of gourds dates back to Egyptian tombs of 2400 B.C. Gourds, particularly lagenaria gourds, are extremely invasive; they need a lot of space and are best for large gardens or trellises.

Most gourds are native to North and South America and have yellow blossoms and relatively soft but brightly colored shells. **Lagenaria** gourds are from Europe and have white blossoms and shells that dry quite hard. **Martin,** or **Birdhouse,** gourds produce a hard-shelled hourglass-shaped gourd on 8-foot vines; trellising them produces the best gourds. **Loofa** (*Loofa aegyptica*) gourds produce several cucumber-shaped gourds with thin skins that pull back to reveal the "sponge." **Mixed ornamental gourds** produce several oddly-shaped varicolored hard-skinned fruits that are often dried for harvest-time decorations.

STRAWBERRIES FRAGARIA x ANANASSA *Rosaceae*

FULL-SEASON PERENNIAL Today's strawberries are a cross between wild forms from North America and Chile. Strawberries are low-growing plants with rooting runners that produce cone-shaped fruit in spring and summer.

BEST CONDITIONS Strawberries like full sun, but can be grown in partial shade if they receive winter and morning sun. Strawberries grow in most climate zones, except very cold, dry, or tropical regions; they are not grown at the Desert Botanical Garden. They need rich, well-drained garden soil with a pH of 6.0-6.8.

PLANTING Because strawberry plants are usually purchased or shipped bare-root, be sure the garden space is ready when you get your plant. Buy transplants that are marked "certified virus-free root stock." Plant in early spring, or in warm climates in late fall. Space 12-18 inches apart in rows 2-3 feet apart. Cover the plants' roots, leaving the crown just above ground level. It is important not to cover the crown, as this often results in crown rot. Before planting, the roots can be trimmed back to a length of 6 inches. After the first year, the plant will probably need thinning.

One week before planting new plants, apply a balanced (10-10-10) fertilizer and till into the soil. When the plants put on new growth, fertilize again with a low-nitrogen balanced fertilizer. For mature plants, fertilize once with a balanced 10-10-10 fertilizer as soon as active growth begins in early spring.

CARE When the plants are in flower and fruit, they will need 1 inch of water per week, ideally applied with a soaker hose to prevent the fruit from getting wet. Mulch or a floating row cover protects the blossoms from light frost. Good mulches to use include wheat, straw or pinestraw, or black plastic. Mulch is important so that berries will not rest on the soil and rot quickly.

'Pink Panda', a new strawberry variety, is often grown as a compact border plant, good for edges of vegetable beds.

VEGETABLE SPAGHETTI SQUASH 'ORANGETTI' Hybrid. Short vines produce 3-4 bright orange oblong squash, 8-10 inches long, weighing up to 3 pounds each. Much more productive than most spaghetti squash. Space-saving habit. Days to harvest: 80-85.

GOURDS LOOFA Rapidly growing vines produce gourd that can be peeled to reveal a 6-inch sponge. Can be harvested at 2 inches for edible vegetable. North of Zone 6, start seeds indoors. Produces best on trellises. Pull skin when dry. Days to harvest for sponge: 90.

GOURDS BIRDHOUSE Hourglass-shaped fruits, mature in August, can be hollowed out to form birdhouses or used for other craft projects.

STRAWBERRY 'ALL STAR' Mid- to late-season plants bear large firm, flavorful berries in mid-June in Zone 6. Fruit is bright red, inside and out. Berries are borne on lateral shoots as well as in center of plant. Disease-resistant. Yields ½ pint per plant.

At Fetzer Organic Gardens, strawberries are "renovated" in the fall; leaves are cut back or mown, and the bed is redressed with a ¾-inch layer of screened or well-rotted compost. Results are excellent. At Callaway Gardens, strawberries are renovated in midwinter.

PESTS AND DISEASES To avoid problems, be careful to select disease-resistant varieties, to keep weeds under control, and to avoid crowding the plants.

In the South, it is best to select early-bearing plants to avoid small berries and fruit rot so prevalent in hot, humid weather.

HARVEST Hand-pick the berries, pinching off at the stem rather than pulling at the fruit, which often bruises it. Spring plantings produce a first harvest of fewer berries than plants put out in fall.

Strawberry plants usually bear for 2 years. Then, either pull up the plants and start over (which Callaway gardeners recommend because it will deter disease) or cut new runners from the mother plant; these runners will quickly mature and produce.

NOTE: Strawberries are a good rotation plant. If, after 2 years, the plants are pulled up and the mulch is tilled in, the loosened soil will be perfect for root crops such as carrots and potatoes.

VARIETIES Strawberries have been bred for different areas; check your local nursery for recommendations for your area. Specific varieties produce at different seasons; June-bearing varieties produce all their fruit at one time, usually in early June; everbearing varieties produce over a longer period, with most of the fruit ripening at the beginning; the total production for both June-bearing and everbearing berries is about the same. Callaway gardeners recommend growing several strawberry varieties to be sure that some will survive if frost hits the earliest bloomers.

'All Star' produces fruit at the center of the plant and along long, lateral shoots. The center of the fruit is bright red rather than white. June-bearing type.

'Cardinal' produces most of its fruit within a 3-week period, effectively cutting down on long-term problems with diseases and pests. Its thick, heavy foliage hides the berries from the birds. June-bearing type.

'Ozark Beauty' is a prolific, bright red everbearer that produces bright red, juicy berries.

'Sunrise' is grown for longer harvest. The fruit, which is red throughout, points upward, off the ground.

'Surecrop' has less foliage, which makes the berries easy to find (for birds as well as humans—protect with netting). Smaller leaf size also provides better air circulation, cutting down on fruit and foliage diseases. June-bearing type.

In the West, **day-neutral varieties** give fruit every 6 weeks except in midwinter. Some of the best varieties are **'Fern'**, **'Muir'**, and **'Selva'**.

Clump-forming **Alpine strawberries** (*Fragaria vesca*) produce red, yellow, or white elongated berries; they are very fragile and are rarely found in stores, but have great flavor. They are grown the same way as regular berries and can be seed-grown at home. It takes 2 seasons for the first harvest.

Opposite: 'Sunrise' strawberries

VIEWPOINT
ROTATING STRAWBERRIES

I rotate strawberries every 4 years; I find that diseases become rampant if we do it any less often, and the plants are less productive.
AVIVA TOPOROFF,
CHICAGO BOTANIC GARDEN

I have never rotated the strawberries in the vegetable garden. They continue to bear, but not as luxuriantly as they did at first.
JANET WHIPPO,
NEW YORK BOTANICAL GARDEN

We use the same bed for 3 years, but we renovate it each year by chopping off tops and dead leaves and covering it with ¾-1 inch of compost. Every 3 years, we start a new bed in the fall.
MICHAEL MALTAS,
FETZER ORGANIC GARDENS

Strawberries should be rotated at least every 3 years to minimize disease problems.
DR. LAURIE HODGES,
UNIVERSITY OF NEBRASKA

STRAWBERRY 'CARDINAL' Plant 12 inches wide (not including runners) produces 12- to 18-inch-tall upright foliage and firm, solid fruit that is bright red throughout. Cold-hardy and widely adaptable. June-bearing type. Yields 1 pint per plant.

STRAWBERRY 'SURECROP' June-bearing plant produces very large berries. Tolerant of drought; disease-resistant. Light foliage makes berries easy to find and harvest. Berries freeze well. Yields ½ pint per plant.

SUGAR CANE 8-foot-tall grass with woody stem grown for its sugar content. Grown in 3- to 4-foot clumps. Available in red (ribbon) and white forms. Can be eaten straight from the garden or cooked. Needs long, warm growing season. Days to harvest: 120-150.

SUNFLOWER 'SUNSPOT' Hybrid. 2-foot-tall dwarf variety produces a single 6- to 10-inch seedhead. A space-saver; especially good for birdseed. Days to harvest: 60-80.

SUGAR CANE SACCHARUM OFFICINARUM *Graminae*

WARM-SEASON PERENNIAL Sugar cane is a tall grass whose woody stem is used for its sugar content. This tropical native has a very long—120 days, at least—growing season.

BEST CONDITIONS Sugar cane can be grown only in a warm climate; it needs full sun as well. Rich, well-drained, loose soil with a pH of 6.0-6.8 is best. This plant needs 1 inch of water per week until stems start to color; dry conditions will cause crop failure of this shallow-planted crop.

PLANTING Sugar cane can be grown from commercial seed or root division, but planting stem cuttings yields the best results for the home gardener. These stem cuttings have joints that are visible as circular ridges on the stem. The joints have nodes that produce new growth. The nodes are about 8-12 inches apart on the stem.

Stem cuttings are sections of mature cane stems that have been harvested and kept from freezing over winter. Lay stem cuttings into the garden 3 weeks after the last frost; space 1 foot apart, with 3-4 feet between rows. Plant at least 6-8 inches deep; if sugar cane is planted too shallow, tender leaves will sprout and dry out. Nodes will sprout in about 2-3 weeks; roots develop before leaves appear. Plant 100 joints per 100-foot row.

A row of sunflowers dresses up any garden; they are available in both dwarf and towering varieties.

CARE Sugar cane is a heavy feeder. Apply 8-8-8 or 10-10-10 fertilizer 2-3 days before planting. Apply again when plants are 2 feet tall; no further fertilization is necessary after the canes reach that height. Mound soil around plants, as for corn, when they are 2 feet tall.

PESTS AND DISEASES None noted.

HARVEST When stems darken in the fall, usually 120-150 days after planting, cut stems at base of plant with a sharp knife. Discard bottom 12 inches; the next 2-3 feet of cane are sweet and can be eaten fresh after tough leaves and sheath are removed, or cooked to extract juices for syrup. Top of cane is grassy and should be discarded.

VARIETIES Two types are available—"white," which produces a green stem, and "red" or "ribbon," which is the type most often seen at roadside stands and county fairs. Red cane is best for fresh use, white is best for pressing for juice.

SUNFLOWER HELIANTHUS ANNUUS *Asteraceae*

WARM-SEASON ANNUAL Sunflowers are natives of the American prairie, grown for the beauty of their giant blossoms and for their seeds. Pioneers grew sunflowers as protection against malaria and used the leaves and stalks for fodder, the seeds for food, and ground the seed husks in a coffeelike drink.

BEST CONDITIONS Large-seeded sunflowers face east in the morning, and west in the afternoon, following the sun. They are held rigidly in that position; they need full sun to develop full seedheads. Because stem rot is common in wet soils, sunflowers do best in loose, well-drained soils of average fertility.

PLANTING Sunflowers produce large seeds that can easily be planted directly into garden soil. Prepare the ground by creating either rows or beds for the seed. If rows are used, space them at least 3 feet apart to allow room for cultivation. Plant 2-3 seeds 1½ inches deep, spacing 2 feet apart in the row or bed. If the growing season is long, plant successively until midsummer. It takes 60-90 frost-free days to get a mature seedhead.

CARE Water about 1 inch per week and treat the bed to an application of 8-8-8 or 10-10-10 fertilizer 2-3 days before sowing seeds.

VARIETIES 'Sunspot' is a dwarf plant growing only 2 feet tall and producing a single 6- to 10-inch seedhead. This is particularly good to grow for birdseed and is a good space saver.

'Italian White' is a beautiful white multibranching variety that grows 4-5 feet high and produces several 4-inch-wide flowers.

TOMATOES LYCOPERSICON LYCOPERSICUM, L. PIMPINELLIFOLIUM *Solanaceae*

WARM-SEASON ANNUAL Originally from the Andes Mountains, the tomato is probably our most popular homegrown vegetable. Because some members of its family are poisonous, the tomato was long considered unsafe to eat. From South America, tomatoes were sent to Central America and then to Europe, where they were popular long before they were accepted in the United States. Thomas Jefferson grew tomatoes and tried to convince people that they were

Because they are so popular, a wide range of tomatoes has been bred. They come in all sizes and shapes and in many colors—pink, yellow, orange, and the traditional red. Tomatoes have been bred for resistance to disease, for use in pastes and sauces, for slicing, and for extra-large fruit. Tomatoes are divided into three categories: cherries, paste, and slicers. Often, the name of the tomato will include a key letter indicating the diseases it resists—"A" for Alternaria, "F" for Fusarium Wilt, "N" for Nematodes, "T" for Tobacco mosaic, and "V" for Verticillium. Sometimes a number follows the letter; this indicates resistance to a particular strain of the disease.

CHERRY TOMATO 'SUN GOLD' Hybrid. Indeterminate. F. Tall vigorous vines produce grapelike clusters of small, tangerine-colored fruits, 1¼ inch long. Very sweet. Ripens very early. Days to harvest: 57.

CHERRY TOMATO 'SUPERSWEET 100' Hybrid. Indeterminate. F. Vines 6 feet long, 2-2½ feet wide when trellised, produce extremely sweet 1-inch fruits over an extended period. Resists cracking. Needs staking to keep fruit off soil. Days to harvest: 65.

CHERRY TOMATO 'YELLOW PEAR' Open-pollinated. Indeterminate. Vines 4 feet long, 2 feet wide, produce clusters of 2-inch bright yellow pear-shaped fruits with tender skins and true tomato flavor. Many fruit-bearing side shoots. Days to harvest: 75.

PASTE TOMATO 'ROMA' Open-pollinated. Determinate. Light foliage, 3-4 feet tall, 3 feet wide, produces thin-skinned, meaty tomatoes with few seeds. Harvest will extend to frost if kept picked. Days to harvest: 75.

TOMATO 'BETTER BOY' Hybrid. Indeterminate. Vines 6-8 feet long, 3 feet wide, produce large, flavorful fruit, with tender skins, averaging 1 pound in weight. Sets fruit throughout summer. Days to harvest: 80.

TOMATO 'CARO RICH' Hybrid. Indeterminate. Strong vines produce red-orange 4- to 6-ounce red-orange tomatoes, rich in vitamins A and C and beta carotene. Low acid, sweet flavor. Midseason. Days to harvest: 80.

TOMATO 'CELEBRITY VFN' Hybrid. Determinate. Bush 3-4 feet tall, 3 feet wide, produces medium-sized, 7- to 12-ounce fruits. Tolerates uneven weather. Less foliage than many bush tomatoes. Excellent flavor. Needs staking; don't prune heavily. Days to harvest: 70.

TOMATO 'EARLY CASCADE VF' Hybrid. Indeterminate. Produces clusters of 7-9 heart-shaped red fruits all season. Remains healthy from summer through frost. Heavy foliage affords protection. Needs modest fertilization. Days to harvest: 52-75.

delicious, but tomatoes did not become popular until the 1840s.

Tomato varieties are either determinate or indeterminate. In a determinate, or bush, variety, terminal buds set fruit and the stem is self-topping; these varieties require little or no support, and harvest period is generally short with most of the fruit maturing at the same time. Indeterminate, or climbing, tomatoes produce leaves and more stems from the growing tip, growing indefinitely. The blossoms and fruit develop progressively, so harvest continues over a long period of time. Indeterminate plants need support and pruning.

BEST CONDITIONS Tomatoes grow best in well-drained garden soil rich in organic matter. Soil pH should be 6.0-7.0; soil testing is essential to determine the pH. In the South, soils are often too acidic and need the addition of lime. Because lime may take several months to change the soil pH, it should be applied in the fall. For soil that is too alkaline, add sulfur. (See pages 172-77 for other information about improving soil.)

Tomatoes need 6-8 hours of sunshine daily. They should be transplanted into warm soils (70° F.) when temperatures are in the mid-70s by day and 60-65° by night. Tomatoes produce only when night temperatures are 55-75° F.; otherwise, flowers fall off and the fruit does not form.

PLANTING It is best not to plant seeds directly in the garden. Tomato seeds are expensive, and many are wasted in germination and thinning when planted outdoors. Also, tomatoes require warm growing conditions for long periods of time; seeding indoors extends their growing period. Another benefit of working with transplants is that they are easier to space properly.

Tomato transplants can be started from seed or bought at nurseries. Start seeds 6-8 weeks before last expected frost. Sow 2-3 seeds, about ½-inch apart in a seed-starting mix; cover with about ¼ inch of seed-starting mix and cover with plastic (but don't allow the plastic to touch the soil). Until the seeds germinate, they should be kept in an area where the temperature is 75-85° F. Fluorescent lights or strong sunlight is beneficial. When the second set of true

Tomatoes may be supported in a variety of ways–staking, wire cages, or trellises. At Callaway Gardens, a string-type trellis is supported by an overhead wire. Two strings are tied at the base of the plant and secured to the support wire to form a V. The new growth is continually trained around the string. To stake, drive 4- to 6-foot stakes about 1 foot into the soil, about 4-5 inches away from the plant. When the plant reaches the stake, tie cloth or coated wire to the stake and attach to the plants by tying loosely in figure-8 fashion. Cages are more expensive, but allow the plant to grow naturally and require less work.

Planting tomatoes in trenches protects them from drying wind and helps them develop strong root systems. Dig a shallow trench; remove the lower leaves from the plant, and place in the trench so that most of the stem is underground.

leaves appears, repot in larger containers and move to an area where daytime temperature is 65-80° F. and nighttime temperature is not above 55° F; tomatoes need cool nights or they will become spindly. Keep soil moist, but not wet. Fertilize weekly with a water-soluble fertilizer. Tomato transplants are fussy; too much fertilizer, too little light, warm nighttime temperatures, or too much water will cause leggy seedlings.

When buying transplants in nurseries, look for thick stems, good root systems, and dark green foliage. Avoid transplants that are very tall or that have blossoms or fruit.

Young transplants should be hardened off for 5-7 days because they are often hurt by hot sun, cool weather, or heavy winds and rain if moved outside too quickly.

Transplants should be spaced 3 feet apart; allow 4 feet between rows. Plant deeply–up to the first set of true leaves. Be sure to remove leaves that would be buried. Leggy transplants can be set in very deeply to keep the plant from being blown over; additional roots will form along the buried portion of the stem. Don't bury deeply in heavy soils.

Some gardeners plant tomatoes in trenches (see illustration at left).

CARE Two to 3 days before transplanting, treat the soil in the garden with 8-8-8 or 10-10-10 fertilizer. After the first blooms appear, side-dress with 12-4-8 or calcium nitrate to prevent blossom end rot.

After the soil warms and the plants have been in the ground for several weeks, apply a mulch 2-3 inches thick to maintain uniform soil and reduce weeds and soil compaction.

Tomato plants need to be pruned for best results. Indeterminate varieties may be grown on multiple or single stems; at Callaway Gardens, the multiple-stem method is used. The first sucker (leafy shoot at a stem junction) below the first flower cluster is allowed to grow and develop into the second main shoot. All other suckers are removed. When growing a single-stem plant, all suckers are removed. After mid-July, suckers may be left on the plant to help shade fruit and prevent sun scald. The single-stem method is rec-

Tomatoes planted along a driveway create an attractive, as well as delicious, border.

TOMATO 'EARLY GIRL' Hybrid. Indeterminate. Vines 5-6 feet long, produce 4- to 6-ounce slicing tomatoes with smooth, dark red skin. Can be set out early. Produces longer than most early tomatoes. Days to harvest: 60.

TOMATO 'GEORGIA STREAK' Hybrid. Indeterminate. Very large beefsteak variety with unusual marbled texture on both interior and exterior. A particularly good variety for the West. Low acid, very dense, excellent fresh, cooked, or dried. Days to harvest: 80.

TOMATO 'GOLDEN JUBILEE' Open-pollinated. Indeterminate. Vines 4-6 feet long, 3-4 feet wide, produce heavy yields of medium size (8-ounce) bright orange fruits with low acid levels. Resists blossom end rot. Days to harvest: 80.

TOMATO 'HUSKY GOLD' Hybrid. Indeterminate. Vines 4-4½ feet long with attractive dark green foliage produce medium-large, tasty golden yellow tomatoes with thick walls, 7-8 ounces each. Can be planted in containers. Days to harvest: 70.

TOMATO 'LEMON BOY VFN' Hybrid. Indeterminate. Heavy, early, producer of bright yellow fruits, 8-10 ounces each. Should be staked or caged. Mild flavor, low acid. Days to harvest: 72-95.

TOMATO 'OREGON SPRING VF' Hybrid. Determinate. Early, 4-inch red fruits, nearly seedless. Cold-tolerant, with short season; can be planted early and is therefore well-suited to northern climates. Days to harvest: 75-80.

TOMATO 'PARK'S WHOPPER' Hybrid. Indeterminate. Heavy yields of very large (1- to 2-pound) tomatoes, up to 4 inches across. Produces over a very long season. Days to harvest: 70-75.

TOMATO 'RED EXPRESS' Hybrid. Determinate. Bush 2-3 feet tall, 2-3 feet wide, produces 8- to 10-ounce fruits that ripen uniformly. Good for containers or small spaces. Needs staking or straw mulch to keep fruit off soil. Days to harvest: 74.

ommended when plants are spaced closely. When removing the suckers, you may wish to root them for a second crop of tomatoes (see page 182).

Tomatoes should be watered at least 1 inch per week. Uneven watering promotes foliage and fruit diseases and disorders. Cool, wet soil slows or stunts transplants. Tomatoes need protection if the temperature goes below 50° F. If unexpected cool weather comes after tomatoes are planted in the garden, protect from frost with one of the many products available on the market, such as "hot caps" or paper cones–but don't let the cover touch the plant.

PESTS AND DISEASES A number of diseases and pests affect tomatoes. Rotating crops cuts down on soil-borne diseases; it is best to leave at least a 1-year interval before planting tomatoes in the same spot. Select varieties designated by an "A" (Alternaria), "F" (Fusarium wilt), "N" (Nematodes), "T" (Tobacco mosaic), or "V" (Verticillium); these plants have been bred for resistance to the designated problem and will have fewer disease problems.

HARVEST Hand-pick vine-ripened tomatoes for best flavor. Read information from seed or plant sources to learn color and size expected at harvest time. Two plants per adult and one plant per child will usually yield enough tomatoes for general household use; adding an extra plant or two will provide tomatoes for preserving.

VARIETIES CHERRY TOMATOES: 'Chello Yello' produces unusually bright yellow cherry tomatoes, often used as a specialty tomato in restaurants.

'Sun Gold' produces clusters of very sweet orange fruit.

'Supersweet 100' has several side branches bearing fruit in long clusters. It will produce up to frost and is easy to harvest. This variety is easy to find as seeds and plants. Some gardens report that the fruit is prone to splitting.

'Texas Wild' is a prolific bearer of extremely sweet tiny fruits. One or two plants are usually sufficient, since they bear continuously and profusely until heavy frost.

'Yellow Pear' has extremely tender skins when fully ripe and needs a careful, timely harvest. Not as sweet as some cherries, it has a true tomato flavor and lots of seeds.

PASTE TOMATO: 'Roma' paste tomatoes can be picked early to ripen later and last a long time in the refrigerator. Good for cooling and grilling, fruits are smaller late in the season. Keep fruit picked to extend harvest until frost. It has a strong tomato flavor. Very susceptible to blossom end rot.

SLICING TOMATOES: 'Better Boy' needs occasional pruning of suckers to control bulk and weight of foliage. After harvest begins, discontinue pruning. Fruit will not usually crack if left on the vine until fully ripe. This variety is very susceptible to blossom end rot, especially if overfertilized, not pruned, and then subjected to drought.

'Bragger' produces large beefsteak tomatoes in 80 days. Vines are not hardy in cool weather. Plant at least 1 month after frost.

'Caro Rich' is very high in vitamins A and C and in beta carotene.

'Celebrity VFN' has less foliage than other bush varieties, making sunburn a problem on unstaked plants. This large-fruited variety resists cracking. It per-

TOMATO 'RUTGERS' Open pollinated. Determinate. Vines 4-6 feet long with side branches produce medium-size uniform fruit with excellent traditional tomato taste. Can be sown directly into garden. Days to harvest: 75.

TOMATO 'SUPERSONIC VF' Hybrid. Indeterminate. Vigorous vines produce large, 8- to 12-ounce red tomatoes in midseason. Solid and meaty, true tomato flavor. Disease-resistant. Days to harvest: 70-90.

TOMATILLO (Husk Cherry Tomato) Open-pollinated. Sprawling bush, 2-2½ feet tall, 2½ feet wide, produces novelty tomatolike edible fruit, in a unique "paper lantern" casing. Needs some staking, long growing season. Days to harvest: 90-100.

TURNIP 'TOKYO CROSS' Hybrid. Vigorous plants produce pure-white globe-shaped roots, up to 6 inches across, over a long period. Can be harvested at 2 inches. Resists disease. Yields 2 bushels of roots and 3 bushels of greens per 100-foot row. Days to harvest: 35 for greens, 55 for 2-inch roots.

forms well at the University of Nebraska as well as across the country.

'Early Cascade' is super early, and grows very tall.

'Early Girl' produces extra early, and fruits ripen evenly.

'Georgia Streak' is a very large beefsteak variety with a spectacular marbled red-orange-pink-yellow interior and exterior, often gently scalloped or convoluted. It has a full, meaty flavor with very little acid and is excellent for sauces, drying, or fresh eating.

'Golden Jubilee' and **'Jubilee'** bear heavily, then slow down on production. Fruit is gold or bright orange (not red) and low in acid.

'Husky Gold', 1993 AAS winner, produces thick-walled meaty fruits amid attractive green foliage.

'Lemon Boy' is an easy-to-find yellow variety; low in acid.

'Oregon Spring', released by Oregon State University, bears consistently early, very large, and exceptionally flavorful tomatoes.

'Park's Whopper' produces tomatoes up to 2 pounds over a long season.

'Red Express' has fruit that ripens at the same time, making it good for planning projects. Put in a second planting 8 weeks after the first crop, taking cuttings from the first.

'Rutgers' is best planted midsummer because it needs hot weather to get it growing. It presents even distribution of foliage and fruits rather than clusters that break off. It has an excellent flavor and produces until frost.

'Supersonic' is a reliable producer of large, meaty midseason fruits.

Tomatillos, also called husk tomatoes, are not true tomatoes; they produce small, tomatolike fruits in a papery casing.

Small tomatoes can be grown on arches; larger fruit are too heavy to do well this way.

TURNIP BRASSICA RAPA *Brassicaceae* (See also Turnip Greens, page 70)

COOL-SEASON ANNUAL OR BIENNIAL Turnips are grown for their white, purple, or yellow roots as well as for their tasty greens. Turnip roots need about 75 days to reach harvestable size; at that point, the greens will have a stronger flavor.

BEST CONDITIONS As for all root crops (see page 103), turnips grown to be used as roots need loose, well-cultivated soil; they can tolerate light shade. They do best as a spring or fall crop, and, if well-mulched, will survive until a hard frost. In cold climates, seeds can be sown in late summer for an autumn crop.

PLANTING Sow seeds directly into the garden 2 weeks before the last frost of spring and again in fall 4 weeks before the first expected frost. Sow seeds 1 inch apart in rows 1-3 feet apart (as opposed to 6-12 inches apart if grown for greens). Thin to 4 inches apart; the thinning can be eaten.

CARE Water thoroughly to ensure germination. When plants are small, keep soil loose by cultivating.

PESTS AND DISEASES Turnip roots are often affected by cabbage maggots.

HARVEST Pull up entire plant when ready.

VARIETIES **'Tokyo Cross'** is a white variety; can be used for roots and greens.

'Purple Top White Globe' produces the classic white base with a purple band around the top.

Amaranths have been grown by Native Americans for millennia. The leaves can be eaten raw or cooked, and the seeds can be ground for grain. As a bonus, amaranths produce highly decorative flowers. They thrive in warm climates and do not survive frost.

OTHER CROPS FOR THE VEGETABLE GARDEN

More unusual edibles are being cultivated today in North America than ever before, in part because we are learning to think of these practical plants as fair game for growing in pleasure gardens otherwise filled with "ornamentals." The major influence for this diversification has more profound implications: the European tastes that dominated our kitchen gardens for hundreds of years are being joined by an appreciation for the cuisines of the world, especially those of the Mexicans (including Southwestern "Tex-Mex") and the Asians. One indicator in the mass market is that domestic sales of salsa sauces now exceed those of ketchup.

Apart from working vegetables and herbs into the flower garden proper—or vice versa—there are certain perennial or woody crops that can play special roles in and around almost any home landscape, even one confined to containers. Bramble fruit such as raspberries and blackberries can be trained on fences and trellises. Grapevines or kiwis, the latter associated with Australia and New Zealand, can artfully and productively entwine an arbor at the edge of the garden. Fig trees make bold accents and can be trained variously as tree-form standards or multistemmed bushes; where deep freezes are a factor, bushel-size or larger containers facilitate wintering in a protected place. Blueberries, gooseberries, and currants all have the potential for being handsome shrubs or trained plants—espaliers or tree-form standards—as appropriate to a stylish front garden as to a farmer's orchard.

EXOTIC FOOD CROPS

Burdock Liberty Hyde Bailey referred to this plant as a "loathsome weed," but also said he would rather have it growing by his door than a pile of rubbish. The edible or great burdock is *Arctium lappa,* a Eurasian that has naturalized in North America. It grows to 12 feet and produces edible roots ready to harvest in autumn.

Chayote This member of the cucumber family, *Sechium edule,* native to tropical America, is a large, herbaceous vine that grows from a perennial tuberous root. The pear-shaped, pale green fruits are uniquely puckered across the tip; they and the roots are cooked as vegetables.

Jicama This root crop from tropical America is high in vitamin C and potassium. After peeling, slices can be slightly steamed or briefly grilled, but they are delicious raw, as crudites, dip sticks, or for crispy texture in a green salad.

Passionfruit The genus *Passiflora* is revered for incredibly complex and beautiful flowers on vines that vary from small, almost miniature, to great scrambling climbers. Some bear edible fruits, notably the tropical *P. edulis* (purple grandilla), the hardy *P. incarnata* (maypop, apricot), and the tropical *P. ligularis* (sweet grandilla).

Quinoa This cereal crop has gotten a boost in popularity as a means of diversifying one's dietary intake of whole grains. Pronounced KEEN-wah, the seeds resemble those of sesame and when cooked are soft-textured and sweet-tasting.

Sapodilla These golden-brown egg-shaped fruits glisten in sunlight, are pretty enough to decorate a tree (they grow on *Manilkara zapota,* a tropical that reaches 100 feet), but are also sweet-tasting. The original base of chewing gum came from the milky sap of the sapodilla tree.

Tamarind This is the breadlike fruit of *Tamarindus indica,* a tropical evergreen tree that grows to 80 feet. From Asia, it grows in Zone 11 gardens and in the warmest parts of Zone 10. The acid pulp of the fruit can be eaten fresh, but more likely candied or as an ingredient in chutneys and curries.

Blueberries require 3-4 years before they are ready for harvest, but will the produce abundantly for years. They need acidic soil, full sun, and protection when they are young. Prune them regularly.

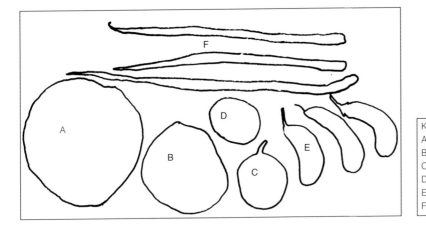

Key:
A=Jicama
B=Chayote
C=Tamarillo
D=Passionfruit
E=Tamarind
F=Burdock

SOUTHWESTERN INFLUENCE

Pepino melon is ovoid, a bit smaller than a grapefruit, and has creamy yellow skin with slight purple streaking. It is sweet and juicy when ripe, following a protracted warm season with moderately cool nights.

Peppers of the New World Species of *Capsicum*. Red and green 'Jalapeno' red and green 'Serrano', 'Holland Long Red', 'Scotch Bonnet', 'Habanero' (slightly larger than 'Scotch Bonnet'): these are most common in today's produce markets. Home gardeners can grow literally hundreds of different New World peppers. They vary in size, shape, and color, and in taste from mild to extremely hot, with a host of subtle variations that delight pepper afficionados. They grow best in warm weather and can be notably decorative. Smaller peppers are usually, but not always, hotter than larger ones.

Prickly pears (*Opuntia ficus-indica*) Cactus plants produce large green pads–technically flattened stems–that are harvested; after every trace of spine is removed, they are sliced and used in salads. The ripe fruits or prickly pears are cut open to reveal the bright red to purple flesh that is scooped out and eaten raw.

Tindora, a very small Mexican squash that is a member of the cucumber family grows on a tropical vine. It can be sliced and eaten raw as crudites or in salads; also lightly steamed or stir-fried.

Yucca roots (and flowers) Roots harvested when they are about 6 inches long by 2 inches in diameter are first peeled of their brown skin. The white flesh can be sliced and eaten raw–its taste is reminiscent of fresh coconut–or very thinly sliced and lightly toasted for a refreshing snack. The white bell flowers are also edible, crisp with a light freshness.

Grape vines require some care and pruning, but are immensely rewarding. They make a fine addition to the vegetable garden.

plant selector

3   **GARDEN DESIGN**

Raised beds work well for small gardens. A 4-foot-wide bed is easy to reach from all sides, making weeding and harvesting easy. Beds raised 8-12 inches high provide excellent drainage and speed up warming of the soil in the spring. The loose soil of raised beds is excellent for growing root crops and for growing lots of vegetables in a small space.

Planning a vegetable garden is perhaps the most exciting step of the process. During this stage, pests, diseases, and uncooperative weather are far away, and everything is still perfect in the unblemished vision in your mind.

A garden plan will allow you to make the most of the space that is available to you, planting crops in succession and interplanting vegetables that thrive as companions. If you plan your garden well, every available inch of your plot will be productive for 2, or in some regions 3, seasons.

THE FIRST STEP Start with some decisions:

• What do I expect from this garden? Food for the summer? Vegetables to can or freeze? Aesthetics? Fun?

• What specific vegetables do I want to grow?

• How important is it for the garden to look good as well as produce abundantly? Can I spare space for ornamentals or flowers for cutting?

• How important is productivity? Would I rather spend less time in labor-intensive preparation, even if that affects my yield?

• How much time can I devote to the garden? Will I–or someone else–be there through spring, summer, and fall to care for it?

• How much of an investment can I make in equipment, supplies, and seed? Can I afford an irrigation system, bamboo trellises, store-bought protection devices? Do I have the time and expertise to build the ones I want?

Keep the answers to these questions in mind as you read this chapter; choosing among the options presented here will depend on your decisions.

CHOOSING A SITE Before you act upon your decisions, you must take into account the factors that you cannot adjust. You can't decide how to plan your garden until you have chosen and analyzed your site.

Right: The plan for Callaway Garden's raised beds.

Bed A: spring harvest: Swiss chard, spinach; summer harvest: crenshaw melons, peanuts, peppers

Bed B: spring harvest: spinach, arugula; summer harvest: cherry tomatoes

Bed C: spring harvest: mizuna greens; summer harvest: tomatoes, parsley

Bed D: spring harvest: Swiss chard summer harvest: tomatoes, lemon thyme

Bed E: spring harvest: romaine lettuce, leaf lettuce; summer harvest: nasturtiums, watermelons, yellow squash

Bed F: spring harvest: lettuce; summer harvest: acorn squash, okra

Bed G: spring harvest: leaf lettuce; summer harvest: cinnamon basil, sweet potato, popcorn, sweet basil

Bed H: spring harvest: lettuce, dandelion greens; summer harvest: eggplant

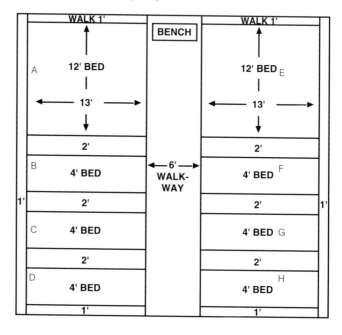

For most people, sunlight is the critical factor in choosing a site. Walk around your property to see where you have the greatest amount of open space and sunlight. Though most of us first think of putting a vegetable garden in the backyard, creative thinking can turn up other areas as well–attractively designed vegetable gardens make lovely frontyard gardens or borders; be sure to stay within the landscape guidelines for your neighborhood. Mark off a possible site with stakes and string and observe it over a few days. How many hours of full sun does it get? Is the sunlight blocked by a building or large tree?

If you have a site that receives 8 or more hours of sun in the summer, your options are wide. You can choose almost any vegetable and plan for long growth.

VEGETABLES IN THE SHADE If your sunlight is more limited, consider growing more shade-tolerant vegetables–cabbages and lettuces in the fall and spring, root crops such as carrots, parsnips, beets in the summer. Another option is to find several smaller spots where sunlight is better; you might be able to create a few postage-stamp-size gardens, using pockets of open space in an otherwise shaded area. Vegetable gardens do not have to be square or rectangular in shape; they can be any shape that fits. The shadier spots could be used to grow shade-loving herbs, shrubs, and flowers as well as the more shade-tolerant vegetables mentioned above. If you are gardening in a desert climate, you probably have more than enough sunlight; try to choose a site that affords some protection from the afternoon sun.

Before you make a final decision on your site, consider some other factors. You will need a source of water; all vegetables need to be watered at some time. Many vegetables need protection from wind, animals, and other elements; a wide open space might need a protective wall or enclosure. A site that is surrounded with deep-rooted trees or invasive weeds might require a great deal of work; if these are not removed, they will compete with your vegetables, robbing them of water and nutrients.

Once you have chosen your site, list the vegetables you want to plant. Divide them into cool- and warm-season crops; list the perennials–plants that will return year after year, like asparagus–separately.

Draw your site on a sheet of graph paper; mark all structures, water sources, areas of most shade and sun. Mark off the best places for sun-loving vegetables and for those more shade-tolerant. Decide whether new structures such as outside walls are necessary (and be sure they don't block sunlight!). Now proceed to fill in the blanks.

RAISED BEDS One major decision that must be made is whether to use rows or raised beds. If new beds are being created in poor soil, or in areas where there is little soil, raised beds often offer the best possible planting areas, for the soil is easily amended and drainage is usually excellent. There are several advantages to raised beds (see list of pros and cons at right); however, they do require time, effort, and some money to start.

The size of the beds or rows varies depending on the needs and resources of

Raised beds are elevated soil beds that are used because they improve drainage and allow the gardener to import soil that is better than his garden holds. Beds can be simple mounds of earth just a few inches higher than the ground; or, their sides can be held in by timbers, stones, or some other edging. These edgings discourage run-off and are decorative.

Pros:
• Locates good soil in a small area and keeps it confined.
• Provides good drainage.
• Provides terracing on slopes.
• Size allows for easy maintenance by hand.
• Pathways are permanently delineated and become compacted, less prone to weeds, and easier to maintain.
• Has lots of loose soil for good root systems.
• Weeds don't thrive in raised beds.
• Production per square foot is greater than in row gardening.
• Introduces a landscape element into the home garden.

Cons:
• Assembling a bed requires time and expense (the extra soil has to come from somewhere).
• Dries out quickly.
• Difficult to use equipment in small area.
• Because total space is limited, pest damage or crop loss is felt more severely.

COOL-SEASON CROPS
Artichokes
Asparagus
Beets
Broccoli
Brussels Sprouts
Cabbage
Cauliflower
Greens and Spinach
Horseradish
Kohlrabi
Lettuce, Salad Greens
Parsnips
Peas
Radishes

WARM-SEASON CROPS
Beans
Corn
Cucumber
Eggplant
Jerusalem Artichoke
Melons
Okra
Peanuts
Southern Peas
Peppers
Potatoes
Sweet Potatoes
Squash
Sugar Cane
Sunflowers
Tomatoes

FULL-SEASON CROPS
(those that stay in the garden over
more than one season)
Celery
Onions
Strawberries

the gardener and on the kinds of vegetables grown. Not only plant width, but height should be considered, as taller plants such as corn or pole beans will shade other plants. Ample space is a necessity because crowding produces inferior plants and reduces yield. A good width for a raised bed is 4-6 feet; remember that you have to be able to reach into the middle of the bed–the wider it is, the harder that will be.

It is important to space plants so that they can be reached easily for maintenance and harvest; if there is enough room to manipulate a small tiller, a lot of hand-weeding can be avoided. To make access as easy as possible, vegetables are most often planted in long rows or squares; however, curved shapes or beds can take advantage of oddly-shaped sites and be attractive as well.

INTENSIVE GARDENING A more elaborate plan is necessary if you intend to garden intensively. Intensive gardening–often called French intensive gardening–is a way to get the most out of your plot. It is a series of methods for using every inch of your garden to its greatest effect. Among the practices involved:

• Planting crops more closely than usual; the theory is that the plants' foliage will form a dense cover or canopy, shading out weeds and keeping the soil cool while providing fruits from more individual plants. Smaller seeds are often planted in bands of several plants spaced horizontally rather than in rows of single plants.

• Providing the most fertile soil by using compost and other soil additives (see pages 172-77 for information on soil improvements).

• Interplanting crops so that small, fast-growing crops such as lettuce or radishes take advantage of the space between crops that take longer to produce, such as peppers or tomatoes. Shade-tolerant crops such as lettuce can be planted in the shade created by taller plants such as corn. When harvesting early spring vegetables that have been interplanted among others, take care not to rip them out of the soil, thus disturbing the roots of the maturing plants. You may want to cut the stalks at the surface of the soil, leaving the roots to rot and enrich the soil.

• Starting seeds indoors, often under fluorescent lights, so that the space in the garden is not used until absolutely necessary.

• Planting crops in succession; close planning is required to keep track of when a crop is ready to be harvested and to be sure that seedlings for the next crop are ready to be planted outside immediately.

• Using raised beds, trellises, and other structures to take advantage of vertical space as well as garden soil.

• Planting earlier than usual by warming soil with mulches (including black plastic mulch) and by protecting plants with blankets, cold frames, cloches, and row covers.

Good planning is essential for effective intensive gardening. As soon as one crop is through and ready to be pulled from the garden, transplants or seeds for the next should be ready to go in. Timing is crucial to success, and it helps to keep records of the length of time from planting to harvest.

There is no question that intensive gardening practices lead to greater yields; there is also no question that they are time-consuming and labor-intensive. If you do not like rigid planning and careful attention to detail, you may not enjoy intensive gardening.

SUCCESSION PLANTING Even if you do not follow all the methods of intensive gardening, some of them may be attractive to you. Succession planting, for example, is a practice that has many advantages. Planting early, midseason, and late varieties of the same vegetable will yield harvests for a long period of time. Staggered plantings (sowing seed or transplanting at 2-week intervals throughout the planting season) will also yield a longer harvest. If several varieties of the same vegetable are planted in succession, a crop failure in a particular variety will be offset by success with a variety more tolerant to the condition that caused the failure.

When planning for a succession, start with the vegetables that stay in the ground the longest, including all vegetables that take 70 days or longer to mature. Around these, plan to put cool-season or short-term warm-season plants. For example, tomatoes will go into the ground as soon as the soil warms in spring. Because most tomato varieties produce until frost, they will take up space nearly the entire growing season. Next to the tomatoes, however, you could plant lettuce that will be large by the time the small tomato plants go in. When the tomatoes begin to need more room, harvest the lettuce and put in quick-growing bush beans. After the last bean harvest in late summer, pull up the old bean plants and put in a fall crop of broccoli.

COMPANION PLANTING Many myths surround the practice of planting different crops in the same bed or even right next to each other in the same row. Some of these—such as the idea that radishes repel pests from squash if they are planted together or that onions inhibit the growth of beans—are pure folklore and have never been scientifically proven. However, there are good reasons to mix plants in some cases.

INTERPLANTING SUGGESTIONS

Bush beans with corn or beets; never with onions.

Pole beans with corn or radishes; never beets or onions.

Brassicas such as broccoli, cabbage, and cauliflower with savory herbs (celery, dill, sage, rosemary) and potatoes, beets, and onions; hyssop, thyme, wormwood, and southernwood repel some pests. Never with tomatoes, pole beans, or strawberries.

Carrots with onions, leeks, and savory herbs.

Corn with potatoes, peas, beans, cucumbers, pumpkins, and squash; never with tomatoes.

Cucumbers with beans, peas, radishes, and sunflowers.

Eggplant with peas; never with potatoes.

Greens with cabbages and potatoes.

Lettuce with strawberries, cucumbers, carrots, radishes.

Melons with corn and cucumbers; never with potatoes.

Peas with carrots, turnips, radishes, cucumbers, corn, beans, and tomatoes; never with onions.

Tomatoes with onions, parsley, and carrots; never with members of the brassica family.

Adapted from *Carrots Love Tomatoes,* by Louise Riotte, which contains more information about companion planting

Left: An intensively planted area of The Cook's Garden, in Londonderry, Vermont. Intensively managed gardens take advantage of vertical space, providing space-saving trellises or stakes for vining plants. Careful spacing allows adequate growing room for large plants, and interplanting produces a diversity of crops for early and late harvests.

'Lingue de Canarino' lettuce has interesting color, shape, and texture.

One reason to mix plants is to take advantage of the spaces created between slow-growing plants–the practice of interplanting as described.

Most plant combinations are beneficial because they make good use of space, shade each other, or look attractive. But research has shown that some plants do help each other even more directly: tomatoes repel diamondback moths from cabbages; beans will set nitrogen into soil, which enhances the growth of corn; and peanuts planted with corn or squash increase yields.

Many flowers and herbs, when grown among the vegetables, not only beautify the area, but also serve to help keep away unwanted garden pests. French marigolds and catharanthus (annual vinca; periwinkle) not only add floral color, but also serve to suppress nematodes in the soil. Herbs are reported to help repel certain pests: mint keeps away ants, basil keeps away bean beetles, rosemary repels slugs and snails, and horseradish keeps away potato beetles.

CROP ROTATION Moving vegetables to different sites in successive years will help to deter many problems from pests and disease and over time is the most effective way to control pests and disease. Pests generally attack one kind of plant family–such as cabbage maggots, which prey not only on cabbage but also on broccoli, Brussels sprouts, and cauliflower, all of which are relatives of cabbage.

Insects and disease cycles generally activate in the spring, and if their host plant is gone from that spot, the pest and disease cycles are interrupted. If the same crops are planted there again and again, the cycle is never broken. Rotate beds as far as possible; at least 60 feet in large gardens.

Many crops are heavy feeders and quickly deplete the soil of nutrients. However, different species will use large amounts of different nutrients. For example, cabbage uses a great deal of nitrogen, while corn needs more potas-

Even the tiniest of raised beds can produce a wealth of vegetables. These beds at Old Westbury Gardens, in New York, with soil held firmly in place by edgers, require less water than open-sided beds.

Above: Dolichos lablab (hyacinth bean) produces bright purple pods and fragrant lavender flowers. Although it is used more for its looks than for its beans, the beans are very tasty as well. *Left:* Planting the garden in rows and blocks makes cultivation for weeds easier. Including flowers in the vegetable garden attracts important pollinating insects and dresses up the garden with color.

sium. By rotating crops, the soil will have a chance to recover from nutrient loss.

To most effectively rotate crops, plant varieties from the same family in the same bed, and then the following year rotate the beds where they are grown. For example, you might plant the following vegetables in the same beds in succession.

- potatoes, tomatoes, peppers, eggplant
- peas and beans
- spinach, lettuce, endive, beets, carrots

Divide your garden into quadrants. If you plant melon in the southeast quadrant this summer, next year plant tomatoes and peppers there. Keep the soil fresh and healthy by rotation. The few vegetables grown as perennials—such as asparagus and rhubarb—do not need to be rotated. Strawberries, though perennial, benefit from rotation every 2-3 years.

BEAUTIFUL BEDS There are truly few things more beautiful than a healthy plant producing plump, ripe fruit. Vegetable gardens are usually grown for the edible produce rather than their aesthetic value; but that does not stop them from being beautiful in their own right. To make your garden as aesthetically pleasing as possible, pay attention to details.

Shape Beds need not be square or rectangular. Vegetables can be grown in diamond shapes, ovals, crescents, or any other shape that is pleasing to you and blends well with the landscape. Although it makes maintenance a bit more difficult, vegetables can also be grown in swaths or clumped together in gentle curves. Try planting vegetables in a large circle that has been intersected with lines of dwarf hedges. Each "piece of the pie" can hold a different kind of vegetable. Herbs have been grown this way traditionally. Just remember that you will have to be able to reach the center of the bed.

These scarecrows are modern variations of the traditional scarecrow (opposite bottom). *Above:* Longwood Gardens. *Opposite top left:* The New York Botanical Garden. *Opposite top right:* Callaway Gardens

Edges The edge of the vegetable border can be as simple as mounded soil or as ornate as old-fashioned edging stones. Edging serves to separate the bed from the surrounding areas and can be created from stone, wood, or brick. Small plants are also often used as edging. Staying true to the edible theme of the vegetable garden, use everbearing strawberries, curly-leaved parsley, or small light-green lettuce varieties to edge your beds.

Ornamentals Mixing flowers or ornamental vegetable and herb varieties among your vegetables adds color and vertical shapes. Flowers attract pollinating insects and can be cut for indoor use. At Callaway Gardens, quick-growing annuals like cosmos, pansies, petunias, and marigolds are planted around vegetable beds. At The New York Botanical Garden, blue pansies are planted in early spring, mums and ornamental cabbages in the fall. Perennial daylilies are very easy to care for and can be eaten as well. Frilly herbs such as basil and parsley work well in many vegetable beds. And small shrubs, such as conifers, can supply a neat anchor in a corner of the bed–just be sure not to plant a shrub that will become invasive and need to be pruned constantly.

Pretty vegetables Many of the most delicious and hardy vegetables are attractive as well–white eggplants are lovely, as are purple beans. Tomatoes can be yellow, orange, or red, and peppers come in just about every color of the rainbow. Janet Whippo uses the following vegetables to add aesthetic value to the vegetable beds at the The New York Botanical Garden.

Peas and beans have lovely, delicate white, lavender, and purple flowers, and trellising their vines is an effective way to show off flowers and fruit. Pole beans can be trained over a trellis or arbor, and by midsummer they will cover it with leaves. Combined with other flowering vines such as morning glory, pole beans can be truly stunning.

Lettuces come in a fabulous array of shapes and colors. Leaf lettuces make excellent edging plants and can be arranged in complex patterns. 'Lingue de Canarino' is a yellow green cultivar with spiky leaves, and 'Lolla Rosa' has deeply ruffled red leaves; both of these are European varieties and are slow to bolt. 'Oak Leaf' lettuce can be found in both red and green. Romaine, iceberg, and cos lettuces give variety in form and texture. Radicchio, which looks something like a small red cabbage, is another striking plant.

Both alpine and garden strawberries have attractive dark green foliage that looks good as ground cover. The white flowers and red fruits add to the beauty of the plant and make it a good specimen to use in containers. Small alpine strawberries can be grown in rock walls or other places suitable for ground cover.

Cabbages have a beautiful form similar to that of an enormous rose. Their heads can be pointed, rounded, or flattened, their leaves rippled or smooth, and their colors include yellow green, soft blue green, and reddish purple. Other members of the cabbage family have bold shapes–the bell-like bok choi, the strong, upright Brussels sprouts, and sturdy but ruffled Chinese cabbage. Broccoli and cauliflower come into their own with the formation of massive white, green, and purple flowers. Broccoli 'Romanesco' has an unusu-

al geometric form and sharp chartreuse color.

Bush types of cucumbers, squash, and melons are included in the garden for aesthetic reasons. Vining types that produce plants 12 feet long or longer can be beautiful if grown along a wall or fence or on a trellis. The dark green leaves and bright yellow flowers of squashes are pretty additions to any garden.

Okra, a member of the hollyhock and hibiscus family, produces a large creamy yellow blossom usually marked with red at the throat. The seed pods are long and deeply ridged. The variety 'Red Okra' is particularly atttractive because of its red stems, yellow and red flowers, and red pods.

Few people believe that scarecrows ever accomplish the goal stated in their name, but that has not stopped their use by many different cultures over the last 3,000 years. In 1000 B.C. Egyptian farmers covered themselves in white scarves and chased quail away from their crops. About 500 years later, Greek farmers built statues of a homely god named Priapus whose ugly face frightened birds from the vineyards where he played; Roman armies carried this custom with them when they conquered the rest of Europe. Meanwhile, in Japan, farmers built another kind of scarecrow, called a *kakashi,* by hanging old rags and smelly fishbones on sticks and then igniting them; eventually they began hanging streamers and noisemakers from the sticks, and then to build human shapes.

During the Middle Ages, peasants attached all sorts of legends and superstitions to their scarecrows. In Italy, skulls were placed on top of the scarecrows in the hope that evil spirits would drive away birds. In Britain, children were paid to act as human scarecrows, running through fields and shouting, clapping, and banging wooden boards to scare away birds. Many Native American tribes had their own scarecrows. Zunis in the Southwest built complicated models in both male and female forms; some of them had elaborate contraptions that rattled and clattered when the wind blew. Pennsylvania Dutch farmers called their scarecrows bootzamon , or boogeyman, and often built bootzafraus alongside them to help defend the corn.

Adapted from *The Scarecrow Book* by James Giblin and Dale Ferguson

This vegetable garden, part of a famous New England nursery, is organized around a central axis with four square parterres from which leaves and fruits can be picked without disrupting the design. Around the four main beds, the gardeners plant linear rows of annuals that can be harvested and replanted as needed. Morning glories, annual flowers, and a prized red salvia add color and shape while the edibles grow; at the corner of each bed stands a carefully shaped dwarf Alberta spruce, lending both height and formality. Repeating patterns of herbs line the walkways, which are uncovered, but assiduously scratched after rain or watering.

This garden, which is over 75 square feet in area, contains a multitude of vegetables: dark and white eggplants, squash, beans, carrots, corn, green and red lettuces, bell peppers, tomatoes and potatoes. The patterns in the garden are revised each year.

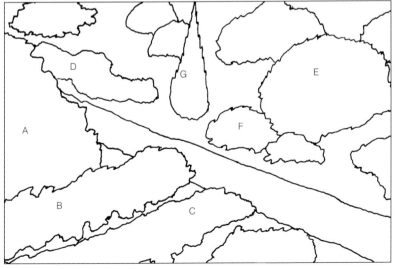

KEY:
A=Corn
B=Carrots
C=Bush Beans
D=Curly Kale
E=Purple Cabbage
F=Yellow Squash
G=Topiary Rosemary

At The New York Botanical Garden Vegetable Demonstration Garden, gardener Janet Whippo shows how a small plot can grow a wide range of vegetables. Whippo grows almost everything in wood-enclosed raised beds; some exceptions are strawberries, rhubarb, and fennel. A simple trellis takes advantage of vertical space. Peas climb up the trellis in early summer; it supports tomatoes later in the season. Carefully designed interplanting takes advantage of every inch of space. Grape vines and espaliered crabapples have been trained along the back wall.

KEY:
A='Showbor' Kale
B=Purple Pansies
C=Broccoli Raab
D=Interplanted Lettuces

In most cases, seedlings are grown indoors and then transplanted; this saves valuable garden space. Shown here in late spring, the garden includes cabbages, lettuces, broccoli, broccoli raab, and greens; beet and cabbage foliage add to the display. Whippo planted a border of pansies (*Viola* x *wittrockiana*); the bright color provides interest until the vegetables begin to take over.

The spring vegetable garden, full of neatly formed lettuces and cabbages, is always more orderly than that of late summer, when dense foliage of tomatoes, peppers, and eggplants overshadows the smaller vegetables.

The vegetable garden at Mount Vernon includes vegetables that George Washington grew. Turf pathways between planting beds make excellent permanent walkways. Herb plantings around the beds define the spaces around the beds where the vegetables are grouped; they provide an attractive as well as edible edging.

Herbs are a valuable addition to any vegetable garden. They are less demanding than most vegetables and can be grown in shadier spots. They require less fertilization, and many people believe that some of them repel insects from the vegetables. And, of course, many of them are used in the same recipes as the vegetables. Some unusual herbs you might want to try:

Lemon basil has smaller leaves than sweet basil and a delicate lemon fragrance and taste.

Cinnamon basil is a very sturdy plant with green leaves, purple flowers, and a spicy scent; it is delicious in tomato sauces.

Coriander ('Slow Bolting' or 'Leaf'), also known as cilantro and Chinese parsley, is used in Chinese and Mexican cooking. The leaves and seeds are both used—the ground seeds are coriander, the leaves are cilantro.

'Fernleaf' is a slow-bolting variety of dill that is attractive in the garden, self-sows, and can be used fresh or dry.

Perilla frutescens, also known as Shiso, readily self-sows. The green form has cinnamon-scented leaves; the purple form is used to color pickled vegetables. Both types are used in Japanese cooking and are very ornamental—they are often found in flower beds.

Flowers not only dress up the garden, they can dress up a salad too—and they attract pollinating insects to the garden. Nasturtiums from this small backyard garden have a pleasant, peppery flavor. Some gardeners reserve a portion of their vegetable gardens for edible flowers; others mix them right in with the vegetables.

When choosing flowers that will be served as food, be careful to avoid those that have toxic properties. The plant world is full of species that are very dangerous. Even some vegetables contain elements that would be dangerous in large quantities—for example, spinach contains oxalic acid. In some cases, only one part of the plant is poisonous—the leaves of rhubarb, for example—and in some cases plants that do not harm animals are quite dangerous for humans. And often the ingredient that makes a plant harmful also makes it useful when made into a medication, such as digitalis. Oleander, lily-of-the-valley, crocus, sweet pea, daffodil, clematis, and buttercups are only a few examples of flowers that should never be included in recipes.

Among the safe flowers, in addition to the widely-accepted nasturtiums:
Violets and **pansies** come in many colors, and taste a bit like lettuce. They are also used as decorations.
Rose petals can be candied and used in jams and jellies.
Scented geraniums come in many different flavors, including peppermint, apple, and cinnamon.
Daylilies are crunchy and delicious, raw or stir-fried.
Squash, pea, garlic, and **runner beans** blossoms are quite tasty.

KEY:
A=Buxus (Boxwood) shrub
B=Cabbages
C=Lettuces

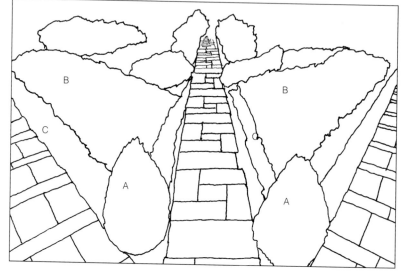

The strong geometric lines of this formally planted space, part of a large British estate, prove that vegetable gardens don't have to be countrified. The paved walkways form the backbone of the bed design and provide a handsome contrast to the fresh green of the garden.

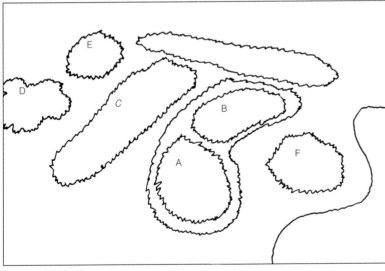

KEY:
A=Greens
B=Carrots
C=Bush Beans
D=Summer Squash
E=Tomatoes
F=Herbs and Flowers

This unique design incorporates curved, circular, and rectangular raised beds, all tied together with a thick straw mulch, which becomes the gardeners' path. The garden, photographed in July, is completely organic; no chemical fertilizers or pesticides are used in it.

At Callaway Gardens, one gardener waters newly transplanted seedlings with a "special" cup that has a hole punched at the bottom. He has found that this cup supplies just the right amount of water to the seedlings. Experienced gardeners try and invent new techniques and tools all the time; when they work, they retain them.

Aviva Toporoff, who is now director of the vegetable island at Chicago Botanic Garden, spent a year in a third world country as a Peace Corps volunteer. She remembers that the villagers she worked with used only one gardening technique: they would cast whatever seeds they had on the earth–and something always grew. Today, practicing such advanced techniques as raised beds and intensive gardening, she knows that the extra labor she expends is what makes the difference between getting the vegetables that happen to grow, and enjoying a high percentage of successful and abundant crops.

There is no technique that will guarantee success; the weather plays too great a part in gardening for people to be infallible. Even the most assiduous and experienced gardeners often experience crop failures–you will notice that seed catalogs are occasionally unable to provide seeds for a particular variety because they–huge, commercial organizations–had crop failures.

But knowing the proper techniques does make a difference. This chapter covers accepted methods that are used in every phase of gardening. You will, no doubt, have your own ways of accomplishing some of them, and many of your own techniques will work as well or better than the ones described here. Some of the practices described here are time-consuming and labor-intensive; you might decide that you want to expend less time and energy even if that brings lower yields. There is no need to follow every standard practice–but it is useful to understand how and why they have become standard.

ANALYZING YOUR SITE By now, you will have chosen the site on which you will place your vegetable garden; as discussed in Chapter 3, choosing a welcoming site will avoid much toil and grief. There are many things about the site that you cannot change–the shade it receives from buildings or unmovable trees, the weather in your area. But some things can be improved. Though making

Right: After years of careful soil management, the soil at Callaway is rich and crumbly–friable.

Previous pages: Lucinda Mays interplants lettuce with potatoes at Callaway Gardens.

these improvements is not easy, they will save time and effort in the long run.
UNDERSTANDING YOUR SOIL Gardeners and farmers learn to understand soil; some
can smell when something is wrong with it–they often use terms like *sweet*
and *sour* to describe their soil. In fact, soil is probably the single most important determining factor in the success of most gardening ventures. It is from
the soil that the plant derives almost all the mineral nutrients it needs to grow
and produce fruit. The soil provides the home for the most critical part of the
plant, its roots.

Soil is made up sand, clay, and silt particles (about 45 percent); air (about
30 percent); water (about 20 percent); and organic matter (about 5 percent).
The spaces between the particles in soil allow water and nutrients to travel to
a plant's roots; the soil must have enough water and nutrients to supply the
plants, and enough space between its own particles to allow water and nutrients to make their way to the roots. Organic matter–a black, crumbly sub-
stance also called humus–is the product of decomposing living things; it is the
"glue" that holds the particles together. Organic matter is also where most of
the nutrients that the plant needs are held.

There are 3 basic types of soil: clay, sandy, and loam.

In clay soil, there is a large percentage of clay (the smallest particles), as
opposed to sand and silt–water and nutrients have a hard time moving
through it. Extremely clayey soils are almost impermeable to water and air;
they usually have a high concentration of organic matter. Clay soils are sticky
when wet.

Sandy soil has the greatest percentage of sand (the largest particles); water
will travel through the soil easily, but the soil will not be able to hold onto the
organic matter that the plant requires. Sandy soils are coarse-grained and do
not stick together.

Loam is a combination of the two–the best mix of sand and clay to allow
the soil to hold organic matter and still leave room for nutrient-laden water to
travel to the roots of the plant. The term *friable*, which means easily crushed
or pulverized, is often applied to loamy soil; it is the most fertile and easiest-
to-work soil type.

You can determine which type of soil is in your garden by looking at it and
touching it; if it does not stick together in your hand, and is light brown, it is
probably sand. If it is sticky, it is probably clay. Another way of judging soil
type is by checking drainage.
DRAINAGE You will note that almost all vegetables require good drainage.
Drainage is the ability of the soil to move water so that the roots of the plant
do not get waterlogged; if water can't move around in the soil, neither can
nutrients. To check drainage, dig a hole the size of a 1-gallon pot; fill it with
water, and see how long it takes to drain. If it drains immediately–in less than
2 hours–you have sandy soil and will probably need to add organic matter to
help the soil hold water. If the water drains between 2 and 4 hours, you are
blessed with loam. If the water is still standing after 4 hours, you probably
have clay soil–and poor drainage.

To determine whether your
drainage is adequate, dig a
hole large enough to hold a
gallon pot. Fill the hole with
water, and see how long it
takes to drain.

In a single handful of earth live millions of microorganisms, invisible to the naked eye and yet essential to our existence. The pyramid of life above the earth's surface is supported by the base of microscopic life below. Our civilization and survival depend on those unseen specks of organic matter. They are the beginning of our food supply, the air we breathe, the clothing we wear, our art and science, the thoughts we think, the dreams we dream. Is that not miracle enough for anyone?

That, after all, is the real business of gardening: miracles.
FROM *VOICES FROM THE EARTH* BY WILLIAM LONGGOOD

There are several ways to correct poor drainage:

1. Add sand and organic matter to the soil. Sand plus clay results in cement; but sand, clay, and organic matter will give you friable soil.

2. Use raised beds, which always provide better drainage and also allow you to mix better soil from elsewhere into your site.

3. Insert a drainage pipe. These pipes, usually plastic, can be purchased at most garden supply or hardware stores and move water to a place where it will do less harm. Dig a trench, about 1 foot deep and 1 foot wide that is the length of the pipe; at the end where you wish the water to go, dig a dry well. Cover the end of the pipe that starts in your garden with porous material so that it is not clogged by rocks and soil. Place the pipe in the trench, and cover it with gravel. Replace the soil over it. Water will be conducted through the pipe to the dry well.

4. If your problem is serious, or if you think it is worth the investment, talk to a professional landscaper about inserting a drainage system, such as tile, gravel beds, or more elaborate pipe network.

SOIL IMPROVEMENT Good drainage allows water to travel through your soil. This water must carry nutrients with it; if they are not present in the soil, they must be added.

To identify exactly what the soil in your garden needs, there is no substitute for a soil test. A small but representative amount of garden soil is analyzed for nutrient deficiencies and excesses. To get an accurate reading for your entire garden area, take small amounts from several different spots in your garden, mixing them to make a total of about ½ cup of soil; mix topsoil and soil one-spade-deep. For a small fee, a full laboratory analysis can be done by a County Extension Office (listed under "government" in your phone book), an agricultural university, or perhaps even a local garden center. The

XYZ AGRICULTURAL LABORATORIES   **prepared for:**

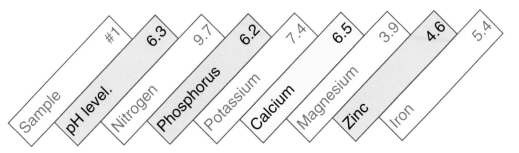

Sample	pH level	Nitrogen	Phosphorus	Potassium	Calcium	Magnesium	Zinc	Iron
#1	6.3	9.7	6.2	7.4	6.5	3.9	4.6	5.4

Results from laboratories can be mystifying at first glance. Here are the items you should look for. Most labs assign their own number values to express levels and acceptable ranges. Look for the range level chart to see if the level in your tested sample is normal.

1. pH: 6.0-7.0 is the acceptable range.

If your soil has a low pH reading, it is too acidic.

Quick fix: Add calcium in plant sprays or fast-acting pellets, available in bags.

Soil-building fix: Add inexpensive agricultural lime; it takes 2-3 months before the lime has any effect, and 4-6 months before it works fully.

2. Nitrogen (N; sometimes listed as "organic matter" on lab reports): If your nitrogen level is below the accepted range, your soil is low in organic matter.

Quick fix: Add chemical nitrogen fertilizers to crops when planted and as they grow. Even for a quick fix, there is no need to add chemical fertilizers until the plants are in the ground. It is best to use a balanced 8-8-8 fertilzer.

Soil-building fix: Add well-composted organic matter; grow and till in cover crops (especially nitrogen-fixers like clover, peas, and alfalfa) or add "cold" composted animal manures.

3. Phosphorus (P): In most gardens where fertilizers have been used over several years, phosphorus levels tend to be high rather than low. If your level is low:

Quick fix: Apply fertilizer with a high middle number (8-12-8); the middle number refers to phosphorus. For an organic option, add bonemeal (which also contains nitrogen) or powdered rock phosphate.

Soil-building fix: Rotate crops regularly. Different plants pull different nutrients from the soil.

4. Potassium (K): If your level is low:

Quick fix: Apply chemical fertilizers with a high third number (8-8-12); the third number refers to potassium.

Soil-building fix: Add small amounts of clean wood ashes to soil. New Jersey "Greensand," available at garden centers, has a high organic potassium level.

5. Trace elements: Laboratories will provide analysis of recommended fertilizer mixture, including trace elements in the mix.

If you have questions about the report, call the lab and ask them to explain fully; that's what the professional gardeners at Callaway and other botanic gardens do!

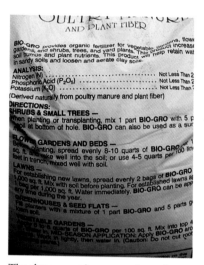

The three most important ingredients in chemical fertilizers are nitrogen (N), phosphorus (P), and potassium (K). The percentages of these three elements are listed in that order; for example, a 15-10-10 fertilizer is 15 percent nitrogen, 10 percent phosphorus, and 10 percent potassium.

analysis will often be accompanied by recommendations for needed nutrients and their application rates. It usually takes about 3 weeks to receive a full report; this wait is longer in the spring, when most people get around to testing their soil.

One item that is almost always tested is pH–the level of acidity or alkalinity of your soil. The pH level is measured on a scale of 1-14, with 1 representing pure acid, 14 representing pure alkaline, and 7 being neutral. The pH level indicates the level of negative charges in your soil, and that level greatly affects how the soil can transport nutrients to the plant. For most vegetables, a pH level of 6.0-7.0 is best. You can also measure pH level with a simple home kit that can be purchased in garden centers.

In addition to pH, your soil test will tell you whether you need to add organic matter, lime, and/or fertilizer. It will also tell you what not to add. Soil sampling and testing is, over time, a money saver. By knowing exactly which additives are needed, you can save quite a bit by not using unneeded or excessive additives.

Soil building is not an overnight process; significant improvements usually take 3-4 years. Once nutrient and pH levels reach normal range, soil will need only minor adjustments. Although there are many ways to fix soil quickly (see "quick fixes" on the preceding page), these are generally more expensive than soil-building practices and are sometimes harmful to the environment. Take your soil tests in the fall, so you will have time to employ a soil-building fix; take them regularly, year after year, until your soil stabilizes at an acceptable level.

Horticulturists have established the following principles of soil management:

1. Match the crop to the soil; planting the wrong crop can result in not only a crop failure, but also damage to the soil.

2. Use organic matter generously; planting cover crops and adding compost and other fertilizers will keep your soil rich in organic matter.

3. Rotate crops so that soil can replenish materials used by a particular plant.

4. Keep a layer of topsoil in place.

5. Adjust soil that is too acidic with lime only when indicated by a soil test.

6. Use fertilizers that add missing ingredients, including trace elements.

If you manage your soil properly, it will increase in fertility after several years of cultivation and provide the best possible home for your plants.

SOIL ADDITIVES Organic matter: If your soil is low in organic matter it will often have a high pH level. Organic matter can be added with any of several products that are on the market, including bark chips, peat moss, packaged manure, or commercial composted manure, available in bulk either in bags or bales, ready for immediate use and usually "weed-free." Compost is one of the safest and most effective ways to improve the pH and general condition of your soil and help the environment at the same time. Compost is decomposed plant material that adds nutrients to the soil while improving its overall composition. It is safer and usually less expensive than chemical fertilizers, but not as fast-acting or as efficient in correcting specific nutrient deficiencies. See page 189 for information on how to make your own compost.

Agricultural lime: Lime is an essential additive to acidic soils, as it will help raise the pH to levels that many vegetable plants require. It is slow-acting and should be tilled into the soil 60-90 days before planting. Agricultural lime is available as dust or pellets; pellets are preferable because they are easier to measure and apply, though lime dust is less expensive. If your soil has a high magnesium level, be sure to avoid dolomitic limestone; get calcareous limestone ($CaCo_3$) instead.

Fertilizers: Granular or pelletized fertilizers are generally used as "starter" fertilizers for your plants and seedlings. These are applied 2 days to 1 week prior to setting out plants or sowing seeds.

Different kinds of fertilizers are available for different growing needs. The nutrient content is identified by a series of three numbers. The first number represents the percentage of nitrogen in the mixture. The second tells the percentage of phosphorus, and the third the percentage of potassium, or potash.

Nitrogen is the fastest-reacting part of the fertilizer mix and promotes rapid growth of foliage and stems. Phosphorus promotes root growth; it does not move around within the soil, so it should be mixed deeply or it will not reach the roots. Potassium releases relatively slowly and is most useful to root crops such as beets, carrots, and potatoes and to plants that blossom and set fruit, such as squash and tomatoes.

A good general starter mix for a wide range of plants is 8-8-8 or 10-10-10. Higher mixtures such as 13-13-13 or 20-20-20 could burn young plants and seedlings.

Fertilizers also contain trace elements, such as copper and zinc. Plants need only minute amounts of these elements, and they ususally do not have to be added; but they are important to your plants' development, and if your soil test indicates that they are lacking, they are easy to add. A soil analysis should tell which nutrients you do not need to add, as well as those you need to amend. For example, if your soil already has high amounts of phosphorus present due to years of adding a general fertilizer mix, or native soil fertility, you should now add a mixture without phosphorus in it such as a 15-0-15 mix. In much of the Great Plains region, soils are very high in P and K; only N needs to be added each year. The goal is to have a balance of nutrients in your gardening site.

PREPARING THE GARDEN PLOT The first step in preparing a garden site is general clean up–removal of rocks, sticks, stumps, or other debris. Once the area is relatively clean, lay out the boundaries of your site using string, garden hose, or spray paint.

If the site is a grassy area, skin the turf off using a shovel or spade. Take the top 2 inches off, grass and roots, and knock the soil loose from the roots. The turf can be used to start a compost pile. If the area is covered with brush or weeds, mow first and then skin off the vegetation.

One of the first steps in preparing the garden plot is skinning off the top layer of turf.

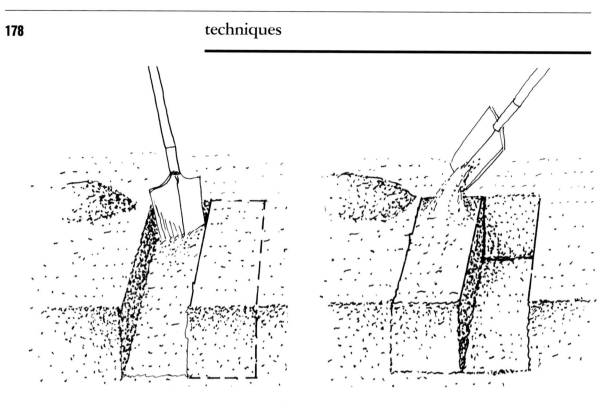

Double digging is a method of creating a loose, well-tilled bed; it requires digging two shovels deep, breaking up clods as you dig. Soil from the first digging is used to fill the adjacent rows.

PREPARING THE SOIL If you have decided to garden on a standard, single-dug plot, loosen soil to a depth of 4-6 inches. If there is tender vegetation growing on the site, turn it into the top part of the soil. Pull out any woody stems or thick roots.

Wait at least 2 weeks after tilling to allow the tilled plants to decompose and again turn the soil under to a depth of 4-6 inches to ensure the breaking up of dead plants and to further loosen the soil. If perennial grasses were growing on the plot before, be sure they are gone–either through decomposition or by killing them with a herbicide–or you will be plagued with weeds for years to come. Frequently, this stage is completed in the fall and a cover crop (see page 62) is planted.

After the second tilling, or the spring following fall preparation, apply soil amendments such as fertilizer, lime, compost, or sand. Till once again, this time to a depth of 8-10 inches with a tiller, or 12-18 inches by hand with a spading fork.

Many gardeners don't stop with a standard plot. On the following pages, 2 other methods for preparing beds are illustrated. Both are ways to achieve loose, well-drained soil.

1. Double digging is done in many home garden sites to assure a deep, well mixed soil. Double digging is time consuming, but is greatly beneficial to the future health and yield of a vegetable garden. Although it seems complicated, the procedure simply requires digging down a second shovel-depth. As you dig, place the soil you've removed alongside the trench; fill in each trench

with the soil from the trench before it; break up all clods in the soil and amend as necessary. Double digging is back-breaking work; very few people have the stamina to do large areas. Soil in large sites can be tilled, then amended with compost. If your site is very large, you might consider renting a tractor filler to prepare the soil.

2. Raised beds have many advantages, as well as some drawbacks. If you decide to take the time to double dig or raise beds, refer to the illustrations on the following pages.

Now your bed is ready. Depending on the season, there may be a waiting period before planting can be done. Most garden seeds will germinate better in warm soils. Frequent tilling of the soil in cool weather can help soils to warm faster. But beware of overtilling, which can also be disastrous. Be sure not to till wet soils, as this will destroy the soil's structure and lead to compacted soil; wait until the soil is no longer saturated with water before you begin. Soils are just right to till when a handful of soil can be squeezed to make a lump that easily breaks apart in the palm. Soil that makes a sticky ball is far too wet; soil that won't form any ball is too dry. Tilling very wet or dry soils destroys soil structure and contributes to erosion.

A raised bed at Callaway Gardens.

1. Loosen the soil with a spade and throw a shovel-depth of soil off to the side of the row.

2. Redig the same location, turning the soil in place.

3. Use a gardening fork to break up the turned soil.

4. Break clods so that no clods larger than the size of an apple remain. At this point, coarse organic soil amendments should be added.

5. Begin the next row by turning the first layer of soil in the previous row.

6. After the entire bed is dug, complete the process by raking the beds to remove any remaining clods.

1. Start with level ground that has been double-dug (see opposite).

2. Lay out strings to delineate beds and walkways. Scoop soil from walkways into beds.

3. The edges of raised beds may be left open or shored up with soil or other materials. In this case, slate roofing tiles were used. Walkways are mulched with pine bark.

AMENDING THE SOIL

1. Add chemical fertilizers and other soil additives while preparing the bed or after breaking up the clods in double-dug rows.

2. Amend soil generously with compost, peat moss, or other organic matter.

3. Water generously and deeply.

When buying transplants, avoid those with yellow leaves or pot-bound roots. The top transplant is healthy; the bottom one will require more care if it is to thrive.

GETTING PLANTS Most home gardeners start vegetables from seeds (which can be started indoors or sown directly into the garden) or from transplants or seedlings purchased from nurseries or garden centers. In Chapter 2, recommendations have been listed for which to use for each vegetable, and for which type of seeds to use. In general, vegetables that are started from tiny, expensive, or hard-to-germinate seeds are grown from transplants.

BUYING TRANSPLANTS When buying transplants or seedlings, look for young, healthy plants that have not outgrown their pots. If the root systems have been confined too long, the stressed plants will mature too quickly and may not grow and produce properly. Look for bright, white roots; their color indicates active root development. Watch out for:

• heavy flowering of small pot plants.

• reddish or yellow leaves at the base of the plant, indicating the plant is root-bound.

• any plant whose roots have grown into heavy mats or have densely spiraled in the pot.

After buying plants from the nursery, allow them to harden off for a few days at home before you plant them. Set them in a shady spot with protection from the wind.

STARTING FROM SEED Starting seeds indoors for early growth is a necessity for some vegetables, particularly those with a long growth period, or for people working in regions where there is a short growing season. There are many containers suitable for holding seeds started indoors. Some of the best include small 2- to 3-inch pots or a 3-inch-deep corrugated fiberboard or plastic tray; make sure that your container provides good drainage. The potting mixture should be lightweight and sterile to prevent seedlings from damping off (a fungal disease that attacks the seedling stems at soil level) and to avoid weed seeds. Several "soilless" mixtures are available commercially, containing perlite, vermiculite, and peat moss. See page 81 for a discussion of different potting mixtures.

Seeds should be sown as deep as their vertical dimension; a ¼-inch-long lettuce seed should be planted ¼ inch deep, and a ½-inch-long lima bean seed should be planted ½ inch deep. Some seeds need light in order to germinate; if they are planted too deeply, light will not reach them.

Seeds need three elements in order to germinate: light, moisture, and heat. The ideal temperature for most vegetable seeds is 60-70° F. If room temperature is below that, keep seedlings in a sunny window, and turn them every few days. Fluorescent lights hasten germination, as do "greenhouse" enclosures. These items are expensive, but will often improve the rate of seed germination. The growing medium should be kept moist and never allowed to dry out; but it should not become waterlogged. Water seedlings gently to avoid battering them. Seedlings usually do not need extra fertilizer if they are grown in the proper soil mixture.

Two to 3 weeks after the seeds have been sown, examine the seedlings for signs of the first "true" leaves. After these leaves appear, thin to one plant per

1. Fill the container almost full with the potting mixture.

2. Space seeds the correct distance apart and cover with the recommended depth of soil.

3. Water well. The soil must be kept moist, but care should be taken not to batter the tender seedlings. Overwatering promotes disease problems.

4. When the first two leaves appear, thin or transplant the seedlings to the correct distance. Seedlings grown too close together can develop damping off (a soil-borne fungal disease that attacks the seedling stems at soil level). When the next set of leaves appear, transplant

into individual pots and a slightly heavier soil mixture. **5.** When transplanting, hold the plant by the leaves rather than the stem. (New leaves will grow back, but if the stem is damaged, the entire plant suffers.)

6. Gently and thoroughly water the transplants to settle soil around roots.

1. Select a healthy side branch, 8-10 inches long, making a slanted cut at the base of the cutting.

2. Remove (cut) all but the top 2-3 small leaves.

3. For large-leaved plants, like this eggplant, cut most of the leaf surface away; this keeps rootless cutting from drying out.

4. Insert the cutting, at a slant, into a container of potting soil or in the shade of the mother plant. Keep carefully watered until roots form. Transplant when new leaves appear in 3-4 weeks.

2-inch pot. Use a slightly heavier soil mixture; a good homemade mixture would be 3 parts well-composted soil to 1 part sand, or a commercially available potting soil. If seeds are sown in a larger container (such as a flat), thin to 2 inches apart. (Seedlings that have been thinned out can be re-potted for extra plants.) Particularly for cool-season crops, early thinning is recommended because it discourages damping off and encourages stocky stems, good foliage color, and the even growth of root systems. It is important to water before thinning seedlings to avoid tearing at their root systems or stressing the remaining plants. The next time the seedlings are watered, do it very gently for the remaining plants will not have the support they had while they were crowded together.

At Fetzer Gardens, watering is done after seedlings are pricked off; gardeners find it easier to separate the seedlings when the soil is not soggy, and that the seedlings in the original pot need a watering to resettle the soil.

Some vegetables can be propagated from stem cuttings. Tomatoes, in particular, are easy to do this way. Wait until the mother plant blooms, then choose a healthy side branch, and follow directions on the opposite page.

GOING OUTDOORS

SOWING SEEDS DIRECTLY IN THE GARDEN When sowing seeds directly into the garden, begin soil fertilization 2-5 days before planting time. Add compost or fertilizer at this time as recommended in the plant selector section.

Sow seeds according to the recommended spacing. Plants sown either too thickly or too thinly will not produce as well as those planted uniformly and evenly.

Mechanical seeders are better at spacing seeds uniformly, but hand-seeding is fine, too. To keep very fine seeds from being sown too deeply, it is best to firm the soil by gently pressing it with the flat blade of a hoe before sowing seeds. Water gently and well after planting and then wait until after the seeds germinate to water again. At the University of Nebraska, horticulturists water very lightly and then keep soil slightly moist until plants emerge. This reduces crusting and keeps seeds from germinating and then drying out if there is no rain for 2 weeks. Depending on the vegetable, watering can be done either with a drip hose or an overhead sprinkler (preferably set for a fine spray or fog-mist).

PLANTING SEEDLINGS AND TRANSPLANTS Before transplanting indoor seedlings outside, it is necessary to harden them off, a process that gradually accustoms the transplant to outdoor conditions. To do this move the transplants outside in an open, shady area, making sure to protect against drying winds. Keep them well watered and leave them there for 2-3 days before planting in the garden. In colder areas, cold frames are sometimes used. Cold frames are boxes that rest on the ground, but are enclosed on four sides and have a light-permeable (glass or plastic) cover. This cover can be lifted to allow outdoor elements to reach the plant; in the event of a frost or high wind, the cover is closed to protect the plant.

Cold frames like the one above are used in cold climates to help transplants gradually adjust to the outdoors. By opening and closing windows, gardeners can control the amount of cold air reaching the plant. In the event of a sudden frost, the cold frame can be sealed–some models even come with heating units. In warmer climates, transplants should be placed in a protected environment for a few days before being planted in the garden.

Some seeds have extremely hard coats; soaking them overnight improves germination rates. Soaking beans loosens their flexible seed coat, softening flesh and enouraging rot. At Callaway Gardens, okra, squash, and melon seeds are soaked.

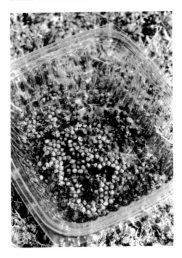

1. At Callaway Gardens, furrows are made with the aid of a simple machine.

2. Plant big seeds, like beans, in deep furrows. Space big seeds 2-3 inches apart.

2. Use a rake to cover the seeds thoroughly with soil (1-2 inches of loose soil), and tamp down lightly over the seed row.

4. To plant in hills, gather 3-4 inches of soil to form a mound about 12-18 inches across. Make a hole 2-3 inches deep in the center of the mound.

5. Drop a few seeds into the hole and cover with soil. Firm the loosened soil to ensure good soil-to-seed contact.

6. After seeding, water gently but thoroughly.

1. Lay plants in location where they are to be transplanted.

2. Dig a generous hole, at least twice as wide as the plant's rootball.

3. Set plant in hole and press soil gently around rootball.

4. Water thoroughly but gently.

5. Cover for 2-3 days to protect from drying wind and strong sun.

Spacing transplants is important; if they are planted too closely they will not develop properly. Spacing boards like the one shown above can be purchased or created at home from a piece of wood. Notches indicate standard distances.

When planting in early spring, plant during the warmest part of the day. If planting during the hot summer months, wait until late in the day to transplant, allowing temperatures to cool off a bit.

Although plants that grow from small and expensive seeds are best started as transplants, there are many garden vegetables that can be grown from seeds sown either early in the season indoors, or directly in the garden outdoors.

When to Plant The gardeners at Callaway Gardens always push the season a little, planting out while there is still a slight chance of frost, with the full knowledge that they might have to replant if frost does hit.

Once in the garden, protect the tender young plants from sun, wind, and frosts. They can be temporarily protected by a movable A-frame covered with plastic or newspaper, or any temporary, portable cover, even an old sheet. In early spring tender transplants might benefit from being covered with agricultural netting, a light fabric net that helps keep moisture in and also protects the plants from cold and frost. This can be used in late summer as well to help protect young cool-season crops from the heat. Lightweight spun (not woven) netting also offers protection from insects.

Place store-bought or homegrown transplants in prepared outdoor beds at the recommended distance apart. When putting in these young plants, get them in deeply, close to the first set of leaves for most vegetables. Firm loose soil around the stem, providing better support and to reduce the threat of disease and pests.

After planting, rake out any tracks you may have left to reduce compaction and poor drainage.

When watering transplants, water around the plant rather than on top of

Spaces between large vegetables can be put to use by planting smaller, faster-growing vegetables in them; this process is known as interplanting Don't interplant too closely; be sure to leave enough space for cultivation and for both plants to reach their proper size.

COMPOST

In forests and prairies, swamps and backyards, an amazing process is continuously taking place. Plant parts and animal leavings rot or decompose with the help of fungi, bacteria, and other microorganisms. Earthworms and an assortment of insects do their part digesting and mixing the plant and animal matter together. The result is a marvelous, rich, and crumbly layer of organic matter we call compost.

BENEFITS OF COMPOST Compost encourages the growth of earthworms and other beneficial organisms whose activities help plants grow strong and healthy. It provides nutrients and improves the soil. Wet clay soils drain better and sandy soils hold more moisture if amended with compost.

HOW TO MAKE COMPOST A compost pile keeps organic matter handy for garden use and, as an added advantage, keeps the material from filling up overburdened landfills. To make your own compost, start with a layer of chopped leaves, grass clippings, and kitchen waste like banana peels, eggshells, old lettuce leaves, apple cores, coffee grounds, and whatever else is available. Keep adding materials until you have a 6-inch layer, then cover it with a 3- to 6-inch layer of soil, manure, or finished compost.

Alternate 6-inch layers of organic matter and 2- to 3-inch layers of soil or manure until the pile is about 3 feet tall. A pile that is 3 feet tall by 3 feet square will generate enough heat during decomposition to sterilize the compost. This makes it useful as potting soil, topdressing for lawns, or soil-improving additives.

COMPOST CARE Keep your compost pile in a semishaded area to keep it from drying out too much. But if your compost pile is near a tree, turn it frequently to make sure tree roots don't grow into it. Make an indentation in the top of the pile to hold water and sprinkle the pile with a garden hose when it looks dry. Keep the compost moist, but not wet. Beneficial organisms cannot survive in soggy conditions.

USING COMPOST When your compost is ready, it can be mixed into the soil before planting, or applied to the surface of the soil as a soil-enriching mulch.

QUICK COMPOST If you need compost in a hurry, speed up the process by turning the pile with a pitchfork once a week for a month. Mixing the compost allows oxygen into the center of the pile, where it encourages the growth of bacteria and fungi. A pile that is turned regularly will become finished compost in 4-8 months.

MAKING A COMPOST BIN As illustrated below, many elaborate compost bins are sold. Some of these have devices for turning the compost and for removing it from the bin. Although these store-bought bins don't do the compost pile any harm, they are really not necessary. An enclosure made from chicken wire or from 5 wood pallets (one on the bottom, and four wired together for the sides) does the job just as well.

WHAT TO COMPOST
- kitchen waste
- lawn clippings (in thin layers so they do not mat down)
- chopped leaves (large leaves take a long time to break down)
- shredded branches
- garden plants
- shredded paper
- weeds (but be sure to use before they go to seed or weeds may sprout in the garden)
- straw or hay

WHAT NOT TO COMPOST
- orange and other citrus peels
- meat scraps, fatty trash (to avoid rodents and animals)
- excessive wood ashes

TOOLS

Every gardener has favorite tools that fit his or her needs; sometimes it pays to buy the finest, most expensive tool that will last a lifetime. In other cases, a homemade tool does the job just as well. These basic tools are needed by every gardener:

A **spading fork** has four tines made of heavy-gauge forged metal. It is best used in soils that contain big roots and rocks and is effective in loosening the soil, particularly in clay soils where a motorized tiller might slice through the clay and form a watertight wall.

A **rigid-tined rake** has 14-20 rigid tines mounted on a long handle. It is useful for smoothing and leveling soils, incorporating ferilizers, and applying small amounts of compost into the top 1-2 inches of soil. It is also used to pull soil over seeds at planting time.

A **spade** has a heavy metal square blade mounted on a long handle and is used to dig uncultivated soils, to dig trenches, or to create planting holes. It is also useful for cutting straight edges but is not intended to lift any amount of soil.

A **shovel** is made of a curved pointed metal blade mounted on a long handle. It is used to scoop and move soil, lift and turn soils. It is not useful for very deep digging or to work in rocky soils.

Other tools most gardeners use are tillers, which turn the soil for cultivation; and, for pruning, small garden scissors, propagator's snips, pocket knife, and garden clippers.

Whenever possible, borrow or rent a tool and see how it works for you before investing in it.

Tools need to be maintained if they are to remain useful. They should be cleaned with water or a brush after every use, and cleaned and oiled every winter. Repairs should be made whenever necessary.

it. A drip system or soaker hose works better for this than an overhead sprinkler that could damage the transplants.

ROUTINE CARE

Cultivation Cultivating around the plants is done to break up hard-packed soils, to get applied fertilizer into the soil, and to get rid of competitive weeds. It is best done at least every 3-4 weeks, beginning when the plants are small. As the crops mature, cultivate further away from developing plants to keep from damaging the roots. Cultivate with a tiller or by hand to a depth of only 1-2 inches. Cultivate each time you apply fertilizer or as needed for weeds or compacted soils.

Mulches A variety of materials can be used as mulch, but the purpose of each is to suppress weed growth and retain moisture by slowing evaporation. Other benefits include helping to keep the soil temperature even and the prevention of soil compaction.

Inorganic mulches include black plastic, clear plastic, and paper-backed aluminum foil. These are particularly effective when used on raised beds, to warm the soil quickly in early spring. The edges of plastic mulches need to be held down with bricks, stones, or soil. Plastic or fabric mulches need to be removed at the end of the growing season. Plastics will probably need to be discarded and replaced each year.

Organic mulches include leaves, compost, sawdust, pine bark, grass clippings, straw, and hay (if it is free of weed seeds). Locally available agricultural by-products such as cocoa or peanut hulls can also be used. Organic mulches should be spread and kept at a depth of at least 2 inches to help reduce the need for watering and inhibit weeds throughout the growing season.

Mulch should be used on any plant that grows for 3 months or longer or that produces fruits that are likely to rot when in contact with the soil, such as squash and melons.

Most plants are mulched when they are 4-8 inches tall, making it easier to get the materials up underneath the plants. Organic mulches have the additional advantage of contributing nutrients to the soil after the growing season, when they are tilled under. At Callaway Gardens, the mulch is left in place to help hold the soil during the winter months and is then tilled under in early spring before planting.

Pinching and pruning Cutting back plants during the active growing season helps keep the plants in good condition. Pinching (snipping back new growth) is used for young plants or tender growth. This is often begun when the plants are still in the greenhouse or under lights. Usually the top tender growth is pinched back to keep the plant from getting leggy. DO THIS ONLY FOR PLANTS THAT PRODUCE MULTIPLE BRANCHES, SUCH AS TOMATOES. After the transplants are put in the garden, pinching back is continued to keep the plants compact and to encourage side branching on melons, cucumbers, squash, and other vining plants.

Pruning is continued as the plants get larger to keep the vegetables in con-

1. Crowded spinach seedlings need thinning if they are to produce large healthy plants.

2. If thinned when seedlings have just produced their second set of leaves, the thinnings can be transplanted to an empty bed. Use a pointed stake or knife to lift the tender roots from the soil.

3. Leave enough space between remaining plants to allow them to develop fully. Gently press soil around remaining plants to discourage rapid drying.

ROUTINE CARE

Weeding is a tedious but necessary part of vegetable gardening. If used carefully, long-handled scuffle hoes or other weeding devices can remove weeds with less toil than hand-pulling.

When applying mulch or fertilizer, be sure to lift plants and fruits and place the material directly on or in the soil. Fertilizer should not come into contact with foliage or fruit, because it can burn them.

Plant protection methods, from top: Agricultural netting keeps birds and chipmunks away from plants; a permanent row cover blocks out sun and wind; a floating row cover provides protection from sun and some pests.

tinual production. Tomatoes need to be pruned up till the first harvests begin by removing small suckers that grow in the junctions between the stems and leaves. This allows the plant to grow faster and lets more sunlight to the fruit. (These suckers can be rooted and used for late-season tomatoes.) Pruning is not necessary for indeterminate varieties, or for caged tomatoes.

Pruning is also done to take out old or diseased parts of the plant, and to top off the plant late in the season once it has reached the top of a support stake. Note: particularly after cutting out diseased stems or leaves, clean the cutting tool with a disinfectant mix (10 parts water to 1 part household bleach), or with alcohol, which helps avoid corrosion.

Vines that get out of control should be trimmed back. Some fruit may be lost, but the remaining vines will produce fuller, better-quality vegetables. Removing surplus or undersized fruits on squash or melons will result in a superior harvest.

Thinning When seeds have been sown thickly (owing to the small size of the seed or predictable low germination rate) removing extra seedlings is necessary to avoid overcrowding.

The space left between seedlings in hand-seeded row crops will depend on the ultimate size and needs of the vegetable. Out in the garden, early spring crops need to be thinned when they start to show the second set of leaves on the stem. Waiting until later disrupts the root systems of the remaining plants because the roots begin to intertwine. Ideally, thinning should be done when the plants are healthy, actively growing, and there is plenty of moisture in the soil. If the soil is dry, water before thinning. If there is a threat of frost, delay thinning because the crowded plants will protect each other.

Left: David Chambers harvests from a trellis at Callaway Gardens. *Above and opposite bottom:* Devices for supporting tomatoes.

The best thinning tools are small hand tools. For small plants, a table knife works well, removing the plant but leaving other roots undisturbed. For crops that need to grow closer than 6 inches apart (such as carrots) simply hand-thin by pulling to the desired spacing. Some thinnings–tiny lettuce leaves, small carrots, or radishes–can be used as a first harvest.

At Fetzer Organic Gardens, many greens and salad greens are NOT thinned. They are sown normally or thickly, then harvested in "cut and come again" fashion by clipping with normal household scissors. So long as they are not cut too low, they regrow. This method works with leaf lettuce, spinach, chard, kale, mustard greens, collards, and mizuna.

Trellising, staking, caging Some plants–including peas, beans, and some cucumbers–need support in order to grow properly. A trellis, homemade or store-bought, will provide support and, at the same time, allow you to make use of valuable vertical space. See page 33 for information on how to make a simple trellis.

Indeterminate varieties of tomatoes require staking or caging. See page 141 for more information on providing support for tomatoes.

Above: A drip irrigation system saves water because it can be set at adjustable rates.

WATERING Once the plants are established, they need 1 inch of water per week, either from rain or sprinklers. Winter or early spring crops need less water because there is less evaporation in cool weather and young plants do not use as much water. To determine if a plant needs water, look for these signs of drought stress:

1. wilting of stem tops
2. leaves that begin to turn, fold, or wilt (flagging)
3. yellow or brown leaves generally appearing on the lower third of the plant
4. dusty soil around the root zone
5. fruit drops prematurely
6. plant does not set blossoms or fruit

Young plants do not need as much water as mature fruit-bearing plants. Daily watering at the immature phase encourages shallow root systems, making the plant water-dependent and more difficult to maintain at maturity. Many signs of overwatering are identical to those signs of drought stress. These include:

1. wilting of stem tops
2. leaves that turn, fold, or wilt (flagging)
3. yellow or brown leaves on lower part of the plant
4. fruit drop
5. plant doesn't set blossoms or fruit

Serious overwatering causes the roots to quit growing or to rot. An indication of this is a dark stem incapable of supporting the plant.

If you have plants that have been overwatered, rake back mulch to allow sunlight and air to reach the soil. Prune back the wilted stems, and cultivate lightly (1-2 inches deep).

Methods of watering Overhead watering systems spray water on the plants and soil. These include oscillating, rotary, or fan sprinklers. These are easy to find and inexpensive to buy but can take 4 times longer to apply an inch of water than a drip system.

A drip system can simply be rigid hoses with emitters or a sophisticated permanently installed underground system. These are water savers, as they emit water only where they are set at rates that can be adjusted so run off and evaporation are not a problem.

Soaker hoses "leak" water along the length of the hose. "Sweaty" hoses or "leaky" pipe soakers that ooze water slowly are excellent waterers. They're made of recycled rubber tires. Plastic flat hoses have a series of holes where the water leaks or sprays. A spaghetti system is made up of small flexible tubes that plug into a feeder hose. These emit water to the root zone.

Hand-held systems are good for watering young transplants where it is necessary to make sure the young plants are not being battered by the water. Adjustable nozzles are easily found that vary water pressure from a fine mist to a heavy stream. Water wands are a 12- to 48-inch pipe with a water breaker on one end. These allow watering in hard-to-reach spots. Special heads are also available for misting or fogging to produce a very fine spray.

Above: A soaker hose emits water close to the plants' roots. *Top left:* An overhead watering system is a good choice for most home gardeners. *Bottom left:* A standard watering system with an adjustable nozzle.

HARVEST

To gather the greatest amount of produce possible, it is generally necessary to harvest vegetables as soon as they are ready. Fruits that are left to overripen on the vine are a signal to the plant to shut down production and the plant's productivity drops drastically. Continuous harvesting is particularly beneficial for those vegetables, such as pole beans, cucumbers, and summer squash, that produce fruit over a long time period.

In planning your garden, schedule planting as well as harvesting. For example, if you are going to be gone on summer vacation at the time your tomatoes ripen, you might want to try an early or late variety instead.

Generally, the best harvest comes during the first few weeks of the plant's production. After this time, the fruit tends to be smaller and take longer to reach maturity.

Some plants, such as lettuce, mustard greens, and broccoli, need to be checked daily for harvest, as the fruit can overripen quickly.

Cucumbers, squash, beans, strawberries, okra, blueberries, and sweet corn should be checked for harvest every other day.

Tomatoes, peppers, eggplant, lima beans, English peas, carrots, onions, beets, and Southern peas should be checked every third day.

Melons, winter squash, pumpkin, potatoes, peanuts, and gourds have a one-time harvest. As they begin to mature, check weekly (daily in hot western climates; the University of Nebraska recommends checking cantaloupes every 2-3 days) and look for a yellowing or withering of the stem, and a mature size and color in the fruit. After harvest, vines should be destroyed.

Storage crops (winter squash, pumpkins, potatoes) store best if they are not washed. Knock off big chunks of soil and store in a cool dry place. Check often for spoilage.

Harvest is best done early in the morning before the heat of the day, or late in the evening after the sun goes down.

CALLAWAY GARDENS
MID-WINTER (DECEMBER 15-FEBRUARY 15)
Prune and fertilize muscadines, fruit trees, blueberries,
kiwi; start seeding transplants in greenhouse
FEBRUARY 15-MARCH 15
Set out cool-season transplants and seeds
MARCH 15-APRIL 15
Till in cover crops
APRIL 15-MAY 15
Set out summer transplants and seeds
MAY 15-OCTOBER 15
Succession planting
Mulching, trellising, thinning, pruning,
watering, weeding, fertilizing, de-bugging
Harvesting
OCTOBER 15-DECEMBER 1
Plant cover crops
Test soil and add compost
Prepare soil for winter
DECEMBER-JANUARY
Planning for upcoming year
Ordering seed
Look for new varieties, as well as proven ones
Repair and maintain tools
Order equipment

CHICAGO BOTANIC GARDEN
MID-WINTER (DECEMBER 15-FEBRUARY 15)
Start seeding transplants in greenhouse
SECOND WEEK OF APRIL
Set out cool-season transplants and seeds
MARCH 15-APRIL 15
Till in cover crops
JUNE
Summer crops (tomatoes, corn, etc.) planted
MAY 15-OCTOBER 15
Succession planting
Mulching, trellising, thinning, pruning,
watering, weeding, fertilizing, de-bugging
Harvesting
AUGUST
Fall crops planted (cool-season vegetables like peas and
lettuce)
OCTOBER 15-DECEMBER 1
Plant cover crops
Test soil and add compost
Prepare soil for winter
DECEMBER-JANUARY
Planning for upcoming year
Ordering seed
Look for new varieties, as well as proven ones
Repair and maintain tools
Order equipment

THE NEW YORK BOTANICAL GARDEN
FEBRUARY 15-MARCH 15
Start seeding transplants in greenhouse
MARCH 15-APRIL 1
Set out cool-season transplants and seeds
APRIL 15-MAY 15
Set out summer transplants and seeds
MAY 15-OCTOBER 15
Succession planting
Mulching, trellising, thinning, pruning
watering, weeding, fertilizing, de-bugging
Harvesting
OCTOBER 15-DECEMBER 1
Test soil and add compost
Prepare soil for winter
DECEMBER-JANUARY
Planning for upcoming year
Ordering seed
Look for new varieties, as well as proven ones
Repair and maintain tools
Order equipment

UNIVERSITY OF NEBRASKA
MID-WINTER (FEBRUARY 15-MARCH 15)
Start seeding transplants in greenhouse
MARCH 15-APRIL 30
Set out cool-season transplants and seeds; till in cover
crops
MARCH 15-APRIL 15
Till in cover crops
APRIL 30-JUNE 6
Set out summer transplants and seeds
APRIL 30-AUGUST 15
Succession planting
Mulching, trellising, thinning, pruning,
watering, weeding, fertilizing, de-bugging
Harvesting
AUGUST 1-NOVEMBER 15
Plant cover crops
Test soil and add compost
Prepare soil for winter
NOVEMBER 15-FEBRUARY 15
Planning for upcoming year
Ordering seed
Look for new varieties, as well as proven ones
Repair and maintain tools
Order equipment

HOME REMEDIES

Horticulturists in botanic gardens have the same insect problems as home gardeners. Here are some remedies used at the Chicago Botanic Garden. These are home remedies; many are not scientifically proven and are certainly not foolproof. But they work for our gardeners, and they might work for you.

1. Plant garlic, onions, and hot peppers around vegetable crops; these plants deter insects.

2. Plant marigolds or aromatic herbs around vegetable beds; many pests are deterred by the scent of marigolds and do not venture farther into the bed.

3. Blend hot peppers, garlic, and onion; dilute in a gallon of water and leave for 24 hours. Spraying this concoction on crops deters mites, aphids, and vine borers.

4. Place a slice of melon or cucumber near squash, melon, or cucumber plants. Cucumber beetles that feed on the leaves of the crops will be attracted to the fruit; remove the fruit once it is covered with beetles.

5. Remove the silks from corn after pollination, so that earworms do not lay eggs on the silks.

6. Protect plants from cutworms by placing a metal or paper collar around transplants. Bury the lip of the collar under the soil.

7. Place a shallow container of beer in the garden. Slugs and snails are attracted to the beer and drown in it.

8. A drop of vegetable oil placed on cornsilks will discourage earworms from attack.

9. Plastic bird netting (¼ inch) also keeps out cabbage looper butterflies.

BY AVIVA TOPOROFF,
CHICAGO BOTANIC GARDEN

PESTS AND DISEASES

We share our gardens with millions of other living things, ranging from microscopic bacteria to full-grown deer. Just about every crop is connected with a particular pest, such as cabbage loopers, Mexican bean beetles, or squash bugs, in addition to the whiteflies, slugs, and mites that are less particular. It is impossible to eradicate them all.

Nor would we want to. We actually need the tiny creatures that live off our vegetables; our plants would not grow without them. They are an integral part of the soil, enriching it with organic matter and speeding up decomposition. Some insects perform the critical task of pollination. And other insects are prey for more beneficial creatures; if we eliminate the prey, the "good" insects will leave our gardens.

For these reasons—and because we understand that all organisms play a part in the ecology of the universe, and because we know that many of the chemicals previously used to control pests are dangerous in both the long and short run—we deal with garden pests very differently today than we did in recent generations past. Very few gardeners still spray regularly. Many safer and still quite effective methods have been found to control pests. (See page 213 for more information on organic gardening.)

1. The first and easiest way to control pests is to rotate location of crops each growing season. A separation of at least 10 feet from the site used the previous year will slow down insects that overwinter. It's a good idea to rotate compost and mulch locations, too.

2. Spacing. Plants given lots of room and good air circulation will have lower foliage-damaging insect populations. Insecticidal soaps and water sprays work best on amply-spaced plants because the gardener can reach the problem areas.

3. Include trap crops to lure insects away from your preferred plant. For example, plant a border of inexpensive bush bean seed to lure bean beetles away from pole beans, which have a much longer growing season than the bush beans. Plant the bush beans 3-4 weeks earlier than the pole beans (they tolerate cold better). When the trap crop is mostly eaten, or when you notice that the insects have moved to the preferred plant, remove the trap crop, eliminating whatever insects are on the plants. Be sure to move it a good distance away from the preferred plants. Pulling trap crops interrupts and slows insect reproduction cycles. The trap plants will be sacrificed, but insects will be controlled early in the season. This method is less effective in mid-season when insect populations are already high.

4. Plant "lures" to attract beneficial ("good") insects. Nectar-producing flowers (which are also ornamental, an added bonus) and early cover crops planted to enrich and protect the soil (clover, wheat, rye, Austrian winter pea) also attract ladybugs, which, along with their larvae, are a good control for aphids.

5. If a particular pest or disease is rampant in your area, choose a cultivar that is resistant to it.

6. Sanitation in mid- to late-season is one of the best controls when insect populations are high. Always remove
- dead, yellow, or damaged leaves
- ripe or overripe fruit
- stems that are through producing fruit
- leaves and plant debris at soil level where insects hide

When pulling yellowed leaves, examine their undersides (where most insects hide) and hand-pick insects. If insect populations are discovered early, they can be controlled by hand-picking before they build up. It is important to find the first one or two beetles. It is too late to control them by hand when they are all over the top sides of the leaves.

Don't wait until your plants die—pull plants from the garden when they've reached their production peak to benefit second plantings and next year's garden. Insect levels continue to build on unproductive plants, and production levels are too low to be worth the extra bugs. Fruits from plants beyond their production peak are generally tough-skinned and small.

After pulling mature plants, till or spade the soil to interrupt the life cycle of soil-level active insects.

7. Water sprays work very well when water pressure of at least 60 pounds is available. Use a brass-nozzled garden hose to spray the underside of the foliage. This knocks the insects off, temporarily relocating populations and damaging a few insects. This control is fairly effective for 2-3 days. It works well on plants that have some tolerance for insect damage, such as beans. Water sprays are most effective on small insects—whiteflies, red spider mites, aphids.

8. Soap sprays. Insecticidal soaps (store-bought or homemade) are most effective when the plant is actively growing and producing new leaves. Sprays applied 3 days in a row provide the best control of soft-bodied insects; multiple applications are more effective than one application of a stronger soap mix. When more time is left between spraying, the control is much less effective. Apply spray directly to insects, generally to the underside of leaves. Spray until drip point (when moisture drips off leaves). Spraying early in the morning serves to catch the earliest insect activity, reduce sunburning of plants, and allow plants time to dry off before sunset. Soap spray is ineffective if it evaporates immediately, so avoid spraying on hot, windy days.

9. Beneficial bugs can be purchased through mail-order garden supply catalogs. Look for non-wild-collected sources; buy only those that are labeled "nursery propagated."

10. Use netting or floating row covers to shield crops from insect and animal pests.

Realistic gardeners understand that yield will be somewhat reduced when plants are spaced more widely and pulled earlier in the season; allowing some insect damage means that there will be a little less for the humans. For most of us, because we understand the alternatives, this is a completely acceptable compromise.

Powdery mildew

Diatomaceous earth is a nonharmful-control for slugs.

It is much easier to control an insect infestation when you recognize it before it is fully established. Constant inspection of plants–flowers, leaves, fruit, and especially the undersides of leaves–will alert you to the existence of a problem while it can still be controlled with benign measures such as hand-picking, water sprays and insecticidal soaps. Some common pest and disease problems to look for:

PEST	DESCRIPTION OF PEST AND DAMAGE	REMEDIES
Aphids	Tiny, pear-shaped sucking insects cause stunted, deformed plants and leaf drop	1. Prune to remove infected parts 2. Soap sprays 3. Plant trap crop of clover
Beetles	Varieties include aparagus, Mexican bean, cucumber, Colorado potato, flea; they range in size from ¼-¾ inch and eat small holes in leaves, flowers, and fruit; damage can be extensive.	1. Hand-picking early in the day (higher temperatures encourage active flight) 2. Plant trap crop of bush beans nearby
Cabbage loopers	Large gray caterpillars eat large holes in leaves, often destroying plants	1. Apply Bt 2. Place netting over plants
Cutworms	Brown, black, or gray caterpillars, 2 inches long, eat stems at soil level, especially on young transplants	Place a cardboard or plastic collar around the stem, pushing the collar 1 inch into the soil
Corn earworms	Striped caterpillars, 1-2 inches long, eat kernels inside husks; also damage tomatoes	1. Place 2-3 drops of vegetable oil on cornsilks 2. Plant early varieties 3. Plant tight-shuck varieties such as 'Silver Queen'
Leaf miners	Larvae of flies or beetles; eat area between leaf surfaces, causing yellowing and leaf drop	1. Rotate crops to interrupt cycle of miners. Most leaf-miner damage doesn't affect fruit production
Nematodes	Microscopic organisms cause plants to wilt, with poor yield and stunted fruit	1. Rotate crops 2. Plant nematode-resistant varieties 3. Solarize soils by covering with clear plastic for 3 weeks in mid summer. 4. Plant and till in French marigolds, annual vinca, or winter rye
Plant bugs	Including squash bugs and potato bugs; ¼-inch oblong winged greenish-yellow bugs that suck plant juices, causing spots and sometimes deformed roots and fruits	1. Hand-pick potato bugs 2. Apply sabadilla dust to squash bugs
Slugs and snails	Slimy, short, worm-shaped creatures, some with hard shells, often leave silver streaks on plants; eat holes in leaves	Trap with small saucers filled with beer, soft drinks, or juice
Spider mites	Tiny sucking mites, red, yellow or brown, cause leaves to become pale and dry and stunted	1. Prune and remove affected parts 2. Clean area beneath affected plants

PEST	DESCRIPTION OF PEST AND DAMAGE	REMEDIES
Vine borers	White caterpillar, 1 inch long, inside stems; identified when yellowish substance appears on stems. Causes wilting of vine leaves	1. Remove and replant young affected plants 2. Prune and remove affected vines on large plants
Whiteflies	Tiny, $\frac{1}{16}$-inch flies; often look like a cloud of smoke; suck juices and weaken plants	1. Apply high-pressure water spray to affected plants 2. Prune and remove affected parts

DISEASE	SYMPTOMS	REMEDIES
Blight	Irregular dark brown spots appear on leaves, spreading to fruit, such as tomatoes and potatoes; includes alternaria and phytophtora. Early blight occurs in spring, late blight in fall	1. Plant resistant varieties 2. Prune and remove affected parts 3. Use soaker or drip systems 4. Remove all affected young plants 5. Rotate crops 6. Clean garden space before tilling after growing an affected crop
Anthracnose	Fungus disease causes brown pockmarks on beans and tomatoes	Same as for blight
Damping off	Fungus disease that causes seeds and seedlings to rot and die	Prevent by providing adequate light and good air circulation; by watering in midday so plants dry quickly; by not overwatering; by sowing seeds in sterile soil mix; by removing affected plants promptly
Powdery mildew	Fungus disease, identified by white dust on leaves, causing stunted fruit	1. For young plants, prune affected parts; remove mature affected plants 2. Prevent by watering in early morning; use drip or soaker systems so water doesn't splash foliage 3. Wait until foliage is dry before moving through rows.
Mosaic	Virus disease causes mottled, yellow, curled leaves and discolored fruit	Same as for blight
Root rot	Fungus or bacterial disease, usually soilborne, turns roots dark and mushy	1. Provide good air circulation and adequate sunlight (pruning can help) 2. Remove affected plants or parts 3. Pull back any mulch
Wilt	Can be caused by virus or by fusarium or Verticillium fungus. Causes leaves to turn brown and often causes sudden death of plant	Same as for blight

GARDENING IN SMALL SPACES

For many gardeners, the sight of a field bursting with vegetables evokes a pang of envy. They know they will never have the kind of garden that requires large, open spaces. But for some gardeners who garden on small–even tiny–plots, working in a small space is a blessing. In all probability, enough produce can be grown in a small area to feed your family, and with much less work than required by a larger area. Caring for each plant individually is easier in a small area.

The process of intensive gardening–sometimes called French intensive gardening–was developed to get the most out of a small area. The practice of intensive gardening calls for placing plants closer together than usually recommended and leaving much less room between rows. Such quick-growing crops as leaf lettuces or annual herbs such as dill or cilantro can be interplanted between slower-growing crops so that the surface space is used until the slow-growing crops need it. Foliage forms a tight canopy that keeps roots cool and cuts down on weeds. Intensive gardens are planned to allow several successive crops in each space. For example, beans and melons are planted after beets and cabbages are harvested, and the harvesting of a second planting of cabbages and radishes follows the harvesting of the melons and beans. Start plants indoors and do not transplant until they outgrow their 4-inch pots; this saves space in the garden for ear-

A small backyard patch can produce an abundance of vegetables; this 10 x 12-foot plot between a garage and a fence yields corn, beans, lettuce, tomatoes, zucchini, cabbage, and potatoes, as well as basil and other herbs. It even boasts a small fig tree.

lier crops. Intensive gardening practices are popular in many larger gardens as well as in tiny ones (see page 156 for further information on intensive gardening practices).

Many people who garden in small spaces use containers or raised beds (see pages 155 and 181 for information on how and why to set up a raised bed). These allow good soil to be brought into previously unusable corners and to make use of every inch. Using a bed instead of a row also eliminates the need for space between rows if the bed is small enough that you can reach all sides.

One of the advantages of a small space is the feasibility of acquiring excellent soil by creating a raised bed or by adding liberal amounts of organic matter to the soil. This will make the small space more productive, inch by inch, than a larger space with poorer soil. Moreover, every inch of the garden can be watered easily, using a soaker hose, drip irrigation, or direct watering.

Many small-plot gardeners make up in quality for what they lack in quantity. A small plot can be intricately designed, with annual flowers and herbs mixed in to make attractive patterns without the monotony of rows. When selecting the site for a small garden, it is critical to find a spot that will get plenty of sunshine. A slightly shaded area can be used for root crops, but as noted throughout this book, most vegetables need at least 6-8 hours of sunshine each day. Many beginning gardeners make the mistake of planting in an area shaded by a building; they allow tall plants to shade lower ones completely. Although they are using every inch of soil, their yields are invariably poor and their fruits small.

Not every vegetable can be adapted to a small plot. Pumpkins, for example, need at least a 4-foot-square area for each plant. Many vegetables do well in small spaces, and many varieties have been bred specifically for that use. Bush beans grow on stocky compact plants that fit into tight spaces; they need only 3-4 inches between plants and can be planted every 2 or 3 weeks all summer. Pole beans climb up a structure and do not use a lot of surface space, but make sure the structure you provide does not shade the entire garden. Lettuces and other salad greens are compact and grow quickly; cabbages take up a bit more room but are still useful. Choose small dwarf varieties of tomatoes, peppers, squash, cucumber, and eggplants.

Another way of saving space in a garden is to plant in patterns rather than in rows. The most common of these is the square grid—rows without spacing between them. Some gardeners also create hexagonal patterns, as shown below, with seeds or transplants positioned so that every inch of space is used.

SPACE-SAVINGS TIPS

1. Grow only what you need and want. How many people are you feeding? Which vegetables are most expensive at the grocery store? What do you eat the most? How many loaves of zucchini bread is necessary?

2. Grow vertically. Ground space is always at a premium; air space is rarely used. Trellises can be created from inexpensive materials. Let your vines grow over your head; create a pleasant shaded place to sit.

3. Plant containers. If you don't have a permanent place to garden, create one. Anything can be grown in containers; this is essentially what raised beds are.

4. Do not plant in rows. Most seed packets list the optimum space between plants and between rows. A great deal of space can be gained by eliminating row spacing.

5. Interplant. Grow fast-maturing, shallow-rooted plants around crops that are slow to mature. Leafy greens work particularly well for this.

6. Use transplants. Whether starting seeds at home or buying vegetable plants at a nursery, they give you a jump on growing time. They do not have to be thinned and mature faster.

7. Plant in succession. This allows you to harvest as you need to. Plan ahead so that there is never any bare space in your garden; as one crop comes out, the next is planted.

8. Harvest early. Don't allow fruit to get too large and tough; harvest when young and tender. This will give you a constant supply as you need it.

9. Choose compact plants. Most catalogs point out those plants bred for home gardeners who have limited space. Look for small cabbages, bush beans, determinate tomatoes, short-vine melons.

10. Select for minimum days to maturity. Many breeders have begun to develop plants for faster harvest. Scrutinize your catalogs; they contain a wealth of information.

BY JANET WHIPPO,
THE NEW YORK BOTANICAL GARDEN

GARDENING IN CONTAINERS

Containers are a good choice:
- When garden space is limited or unavailable
- When garden soils are contaminated or pest-infested
- When the gardener's physical abilities or time are limited
- When growing varieties developed for containers

In addition, containers can be used to start plants early in the season indoors.

When selecting containers, look for those that are wider than they are tall, for these hold water better. Plastic containers retain water better than wood or clay. Drainage holes are necessary. A 3-gallon pot is large enough for 1 pepper or 1 tomato; or it can be used to grow several leafy vegetables (2-3 lettuces, 2-3 collards).

Use an artificial soil mix that drains well and holds moisture; such soils are usually better than garden soils, which tend to be compact and are not sterile. Purchase a good mix of sand, perlite, or vermiculite, peat moss, and ground bark. Such mixes are sold in bags as "soilless potting soil" (true soilless mixtures do not contain sand or bark). Bags that are heavy to pick up are generally not good. Since many mixes can legally be called potting soil, the best way to decide on a mix is to lift the bag. If it's surprisingly light for its size, it is probably a good mix.

Since such soil mixes usually do not include nutrients, plant nutrients must be added to plants in containers. Time-release mixes are excellent for this purpose. These are pellets of fertilizer that are mixed into the soil; the nutrients in the pellets gradually leach out as the soil gets warmer and water is applied. (Pellets can be applied to the soil surface for a second application and work best when cultivated in the top inch of soil.) They come in 3-, 6-, and 9-month strengths. We recommend the 3-month formulation. When purchasing release pellets, look for those that supply trace elements (like zinc and molybdenum) to give your plants balanced nutrients. Purchase 10-10-10 or 13-13-13 mix. Compost is also a good soil amendment.

Also recommended are water-soluble fertilizers. Apply these when plants require additional feeding (when flowering or fruiting).

Avoid overcrowding containers; plants grown in containers need the same amount of space as garden-grown vegetables.

Gardening with containers also requires small hand tools, including a trowel for planting and a small-pronged handheld cultivator to keep crust from forming. Also useful is a watering wand: container-grown plants require frequent watering, as containers dry out far more rapidly than garden beds. Plan to water or check watering needs daily. Mature plants will use more water than young plants just getting established.

Above: Many varieties of tomatoes have been bred for container growing, including 'Jet Star' above. *Left:* Two arrangements of lettuces in containers, with annual flowers and herbs.

Sunken beds, as pictured above, are used to conserve water in dry climates; this practice was first used by Native Americans.

DESERT GARDENING

Vegetable gardeners new to the desert find themselves facing some startling truths. Many traditional gardening methods are useless in the desert, and the methods used can seem upside down. Eccentric seasons, impoverished soils, and sparse rainfall conspire to unravel traditional gardening methods. The most important difference in desert vegetable gardening is the near reversal of the nature and meaning of the seasons. Spring does not have the same meaning in the desert as elsewhere. Although it is a beautiful time of awakening, spring is not the beginning of the gardening calendar; instead, it is harvest time, reaping the delicious rewards of the late-winter garden.

Late summer and fall, the planting seasons for the desert gardener, take place at the beginning of the cycle. Starting in mid-July, plantings of corn, squashes, melons, pumpkins, beans, peppers, tomatoes, eggplant, okra, and cucumber will germinate to thrive in the humid warmth of the monsoon season. Fruit ripens through the fall.

Take advantage of the fall. September and October are the time to prepare and plant the winter garden. Vegetables familiar as early spring crops elsewhere grow throughout the winter in the desert, reaching their peak in late winter. With a benevolent spring, crops of lettuce, spinach, greens, cole crops, green onions, leeks, many herbs, and Swiss chard will continue through the end of March.

A short, tightly scheduled period of spring vegetable gardening is possible but dicey. Peppers, cucumbers, and tomatoes have to be put in by mid-March to exploit the short spring warm-up. One must also hope for good weather. The pollen of tomatoes and peppers loses its viability at temperatures over 95° F. The real heat-seekers—eggplant and okra—get a strong beginning at this time.

The great rest period, which temperate-climate gardeners equate with winter, begins in mid to late April in the desert and ends with the monsoon. These hot, dry months are a good time to renew beds, pour on compost, collect seed, and make certain irrigation systems are in good working order. The monsoon months of increasingly spectacular skies and powerful, unsettling storms close the circle of the desert gardener's year. Each cloud rising in the southeast signals movement along the cycle of planting, cultivation, and harvest.

Certain tricks and techniques can enhance a desert vegetable garden's success. Think shade, beds, drip, and mulch. Most vegetables, especially warm-season plants, are expected to grow in full sun. But once again in the topsy-turvy world of desert gardening, some of these plants improve with shade, particularly peppers and tomaotes. Shade cloth makes better shading for vegetable beds than do trees and can be manipulated more readily. Attached with a frame over a bed, such shade is a valuable addition to the garden.

Raised beds are routine in areas with tough, tight clay soils that resist tillage, so they work wonderfully here. Most vegetables will not grow well in the poor soils of the desert without significant additions of organic matter. Raised beds make controlling soil composition easy. Many desert gardeners prefer to sink their beds, making small pondlike areas—vegetable ponds. This technique helps use water efficiently, especially if you water only with a hose.

Most vegetables grow best with even moisture and therefore require more water than desert ornamental plants. At the Desert Botanical Garden, a grid of drip irrigation with intermittent emitters provides the water directly to the root zone. Such a system can be automated with a timer or simply hooked up to a garden hose. It is easy, efficient, and inexpensive. Confined beds can be watered by laying down a hose with slowly running water.

Mulch offers countless benefits and cannot be overpraised or overused. It conserves water by retaining soil moisture; it eliminates weeds that compete with the vegetables; and it slowly breaks down over the seasons to renew the soil. When used with a drip system, mulch eliminates water evaporation in the air—and keeps the drip line from rotting in the sun.

The final step in successful vegetable gardening in the desert is the selection of appropriate varieties. Look for those known to be successful in warm weather or those that were developed for arid parts of the world. Ironically, many varieties developed for short growing seasons do well here; although the overall desert growing season is not short, optimum conditions are short for some vegetables such as tomatoes.

Experiment with vegetables. Open-pollinated varieties, those that set seed true to what was planted, are wonderful ways to find the outstanding squash or the successful tomato. Save the seed of plants that do well in your garden, plant them next year, and see if you get the same results. If so, pass it around. Native Seeds/SEARCH (see source list) distributes many native varieties that do well in the Southwest and were developed by generations of Native American, Mexican, and Anglo farmers.

BY MARY IRISH, DESERT BOTANICAL GARDEN

The following vegetables are grown in Native Crop and Hispanic Vegetable gardens at Desert Botanical Garden (pictured below left); this list includes winter and summer crops:
O'odham flour corn
O'odham brown tepary bean
O'odham bottle gourd
Striped cushaw gourd
O'odham mottled limas
Devil's claw
Satacon aboriginal cotton
Amaranth
Sonoran wheat
Black-eyed peas
Tohono O'odham shallots
Careless-weed
Purslane
Black mission figs
Tohono O'odham pomegranate
O'odham yellow watermelon
Tomatillos
O'odham sugar cane
Fava beans
Mayo melon
Lentils
Chiles

GROWING VEGETABLES ON THE GREAT PLAINS

The weather of the Great Plans region is characterized by rapid changes and wind. Following a day of warmth, a cold front will blow through, and the temperature will plunge 40 or more degrees within a few hours. Wide swings in temperature occur most often in spring and fall. Summers are often hot and dry, with widely scattered thunderstorms; daytime temperatures may reach 100° F., but the nights are cool, rarely above 80° F. Winters are cold, with weeks when the temperature rarely goes above zero.

Wind is almost constant in the Great Plains. It can be only a mild 2-5 m.p.h. breeze, but occasionally it blows 25-40 m.p.h. for a week or more. These high winds tend to be dry, causing great stress to succulent plants.

Although largely classified as USDA Zone 5—comparable to Boston, New York, or Madison, Wisconsin—the Great Plains region faces conditions of plant growth that are quite different because of the changeable climate and the wind.

The vegetable gardener must attempt to control both factors to produce a good crop. Since daytime temperatures are erratic in the spring, many gardeners find soil temperatures a better gauge than specific dates for determining when to plant a specific crop. Soil gains heat more slowly than air and retains it longer, thereby moderating the extremes. Many vegetables can tolerate a chill in the air as long as their roots are warm. Setting out transplants or planting seeds before the soil has warmed to an appropriate level can cause root rot and poor germination. This is especially true of cantaloupe, watermelon, tomatoes, and peppers. A regular outdoor thermometer inserted 4 inches in the garden soil for a few minutes will give a good indication of soil temperature. The tendency for soil to retain heat allows low-growing fall vegetables to continue producing even after a few leaves are damaged by an early frost. Heavy clay soils retain more heat than sandy soils, but sandy soils warm more rapidly in the spring. Using raised beds and tilling the soil also promote earlier soil warming in the spring.

Gardeners can use tall plants or buildings to break the wind and protect the vegetable garden. A hedge of lilac or several rows of corn will work well, as will a screen erected on the side of the garden toward the prevailing wind (usually south-north or northwest). The general rule of thumb is that a barrier will protect plants from wind for a distance of 10-15 times the barrier's height; so a 6-foot-high row of lilacs will protect the garden behind it from strong winds for a distance of up to 90 feet.

High daytime temperatures and low relative humidity can rapidly subject plants to drought stress. Plants should be watered before they show signs of wilting. Light misting of the foliage of especially tender plants such as lettuce can temporarily reduce the air temperature around the plant and increase the air moisture (relative humidity). Mist plants only when enough time remains for the leaves to dry before nightfall to minimize the potential for disease. If the soil is moist, many plants can recover from high daytime temperatures during the cooler nights.

Cool nights combined with warm days and lots of sunshine can produce high-quality vegetables, especially peppers, tomatoes, watermelons, and cantaloupes. The sun and warmth help produce good color and high sugar levels. Plants recover best and give the highest yields when nights are cool.

Since the first occurrence of frost in the fall is unpredictable, gardeners should plant early maturing varieties and use sequential plantings to stretch the harvest as long as possible. Many members of the cabbage family and the more hardy greens such as kale, collards, and turnips can continue to produce for several weeks after the arrival of cool weather and even after having frost on their leaves. Root crops also do well since many weeks may pass after the first frost before the ground freezes.

Fall on the Great Plains is often a longer season than spring, with many weeks of Indian summer—ideal for a "second" garden harvest of many of the same vegetables usually planted during the spring, such as lettuce, radishes, broccoli, peas, turnips, cabbages, and snap beans.

The winds are especially strong in the spring, making protection of the young, tender vegetables of prime importance. Taller plants can be used as wind barriers; a second row of winter cover crops can be left to protect new seedlings along the windward edge of the garden. This cover crop can be turned under later in the year after the taller vegetables such as the corn have grown high enough to provide protection.

BY DR. LAURIE HODGES,
UNIVERSITY OF NEBRASKA DEPARTMENT OF HORTICULTURE

Left: The vegetable garden at the Minnesota Landscape Arboretum is planted near a wall, creating a slightly warmer and more protected environment.

COLD-CLIMATE VEGETABLE GARDENS

Since most vegetables are annuals, the issue of overwinter survival is not as important for northern vegetable gardeners as it is for those growing perennial flowers, shrubs, or trees. Most vegetable crops can be grown in Zones 2 and 3 simply by making sure they are not planted in the garden until the soil is sufficiently warm and all danger of frost has passed. Not even the most coldhardy cultivars (except for some greens and root crops) will survive a frost that occurs during the growing season. In some cases, this means that long-season crops will not have time to mature; northern gardeners do not always have the 100 or more warm days required for crops such as celery and artichokes. Many varieties have been bred for shorter-season growth, and northern gardeners should look for these. Day-length is an important factor to consider; shorter days signal a plant to begin its period of dormancy, even if the weather remains warm. Onions are available in short-day varieties specifically adapted to northern climates. When choosing plants for cold, and particularly for very cold, areas, it is best to buy your plants in that region, or to swap with friends; local sources naturally breed more cold-hardy versions of most vegetables. Take advantage of the many crops, like broccoli and cabbage that actually do better in cooler climates.

Starting seeds indoors is a useful, and often necessary practice for cold climates. It extends the growing season by allowing crops to spend some of their time indoors. Cold frames are used to allow vegetables the chance to acclimate themselves to the outdoors before being placed in the garden.

Locating the vegetable garden in a sheltered area will help some marginally hardy plants survive. Of course, the sunniest spot should be chosen, but try to find an area that is protected by a wall or large trees, creating a microclimate that is warmer and less exposed than the rest of the garden. If your property is large, you will note that there are several microclimates within it—hilltops, valleys, and open areas will usually be the coldest, areas protected by trees and walls will be the warmest. But don't allow your protective device to block out sunlight. Exposure to southern currents is advantageous.

A plant will have less trouble adapting to cold if it is well-nourished in other respects; northern gardeners should pay particular attention to soil maintenance, supply sufficient water, and monitor diseases and pests. A plant that is already weak because of moisture or nutrient deficiencies or infestations will be the first to die in the event of a cold spell.

A variety of devices has been developed to help the cold-climate gardener. Black plastic mulch is very effective at warming the soil at the beginning of the season and will reduce weeds if left on all summer. But if you find it unsightly—and it is—other mulches will work almost as well. Protective devices—floating and permanent row covers, hot caps, cloches, and shades—protect new seedlings in the event of a cold snap.

Perennial plants that survive northern winters—such as hardy strawberries, asparagus, and horseradish—can be protected by a winter mulch of bark chips, straw, or Christmas tree branches; remove as soon as threat of frost is over. Fertilize only lightly, if at all, at the season's end, as tender new growth is easily killed by early frost.

ORGANIC GARDENING

Few gardeners today are unaware of the devastating effect pesticides and other chemicals used in the past have had on our environment. Rachel Carson's searing exploration of the subject, *Silent Spring* (1962), exposed the "needless havoc" wrought by products designed to promote healthy plants. Not only were the chemicals poisoning our environment, they were also killing the natural predators of the pests we were seeking to destroy, making it impossible for nature to come to its own defense.

In the past few decades a vast and successful effort has been made to find new ways to garden without using harmful chemicals. The approach is directed at the soil and at the measures taken to control pests.

The soil is built up through the addition of organic materials, especially compost. The addition of compost, homemade or store-bought, and other organic material such as peat moss, green cover crops, and bone meal makes the soil so fertile and productive that petrochemicals are not needed.

Pest problems are handled through a practice called Integrated Pest Management (IPM), developed by the Council on Environmental Quality. IPM is defined as "maximum use of naturally occurring pest controls, including weather, disease agents, predators, and parasitoids. In addition, IPM utilizes various biological, physical, chemical controls and habitat modification techniques. Artificial controls are imposed only as required to keep a pest from surpassing tolerable population as determined from accurate assessments of the pest damage potential and the ecological, sociological, and economic costs of the control measures." In other words, gardeners must make reasonable assessments of how much damage a particular pest will do. If the pest is just munching on foliage, let it be. If controls must be taken, nonharmful ones should be tried first. Only in extreme cases is chemical warfare waged—and then in the most nonharmful ways possible.

The weapons in the IPM arsenal include:

•Careful monitoring to identify problems before they become widespread.

•Beneficial insects, such as ladybugs, praying mantises, and some nematodes, which feed on garden pests. Some of these reside naturally in your garden; others can be bought and placed there.

•Bacteria such as Bt (*Bacillus thuringiensis*) that attack garden pests. These bacteria can be bought by the pound and dusted on the plants; strains have been discovered that breed and attack many common pests.

•Insecticides such as rotenone, pyrethrum, and sabadilla and insecticidal soaps.

•Pest-repellent plants such as marigolds, which repel bean beetles and nematodes, and garlic, which repels whitefly.

•Hand-picking pests off foliage wherever they are seen in small numbers.

See pages 196-201 for more information about pest control.

SOME SOURCES

American Horticultural Therapy
Association
 362A Christopher Avenue,
Gaithersburg, Maryland 20879
800-634-1603

Canadian Horticultural Therapy
Association
c/o Royal Botanical Garden
PO Box 399, Hamilton, Ontario,
Canada, L8N 3H8
416-529-7618

ENABLING GARDENS

Being forced to stop gardening is one of the worst fates that can befall a gardener, but the inability to get down on one's hands and knees owing to arthritis, a bad back, a heart problem, the need to use a wheelchair—or the normal aches, pains, and fatigues of advancing age—is no reason to stop gardening. By using a few different gardening techniques, modifying tools, following new criteria in the selection of plants, and tapping into the many resources available for information and help, no one should ever have to stop gardening.

Begin by thoroughly and frankly assessing your situation.
•How much time can you devote to gardening?
•Do you need crutches, a cane, or wheelchair to get around?
•Can you get up and down from the ground without assistance?
•How much sun or heat is wise for you?
•Can you bend at the waist easily?
•Is your coordination impaired? balance? vision? ability to hold tools?

Consult your doctor, occupational or physical therapist, and most importantly speak to a horticultural therapist.

Horticultural therapists are specially trained in applying horticulture in therapeutic programs for people with disabilities and older adults. They have developed specialized gardening tools and techniques that make gardening easier for every situation.

Once you've decided how much you can and want to do, the garden can be planned. For example, people with relatively severe mobility impairments should have firm, level surfaces an easy distance from the house and should use containers or raised beds to bring soil up to a comfortable working height—usually somewhere around 2 feet high with a maximum width of 30 inches if worked from one side and 60 inches if both sides of the container or bed are accessible. People with more mobility can work with easily worked, light soils mounded to 8-10 inches above grade and should use lightweight, long-handled tools. Smaller containers can be hung within easy reach on poles or fences, and an overhead structure can be used to support hanging baskets on ropes and pulleys so the baskets can be lowered for care and then replaced to an out-of-reach position.

Important considerations when planning the garden layout include:
•Start small: keep it manageable
•Use or create light, easily worked soils so less force is required to work them either by hand or with tools
•Keep all equipment and tools in accessible places
•Arrange for a nearby water source—soaker hose or drip irrigation, perhaps—to minimize the difficulties in watering
•Use mulches to cut down on weeding

Vining plants allow wheelchair users to harvest without bending and stretching. Avoid plants like corn or taller varieties of pole beans, for they can be hard to reach. Look for plants described as easy to harvest.

GROWING HEIRLOOM VEGETABLES

The gardeners who worked on this book have divergent opinions on just about every subject except one: all of them advocate the use of heirloom varieties of vegetables. Heirloom vegetables are those that existed in the 19th and early 20th century, before advances in hybridization led to the proliferation of new, disease-resistant cultivars. Many are even older, dating back to colonial—or even ancient—times. In the past few decades, these varieties were dropped by some major seed companies and were facing extinction until a group of dedicated seed savers began collecting them and spreading the word these endangered varieties should be cherished.

There are several reasons to grow heirloom vegetables. The first is their own intrinsic value; most people agree that some of the old varieties taste as good or better than new versions bred for their colors, disease-resistance, transportability, or hardiness. Tiny 'Yellow Pear' tomatoes have a unique taste and shape, 'Cherries Jubilee' potatoes are usually included in every list of desirable varieties, heirloom and current. These vegetables also have a history that should not be forgotten and add another dimension to the vegetable garden: 'Jenny Lind' was named for the famous opera singer; 'Scarlet Runner' beans were grown by Thomas Jefferson. Another important consideration is the maintenance of these vegetables in the gene pool. The newer varieties were developed from the older ones; if the older ones die out, they will not be available for future improvements. By growing heirloom vegetables, you can do your part in ensuring biodiversity.

Many seed companies specialize in heirloom varieties, and even the major companies are now promoting historical seeds. Some of these companies specialize in specific regions, particularly the Southwest and Native American seeds. In addition, seed-saver organizations strive to collect seeds of endangered varieties from homegrowers; many of the unnamed varieties that were handed down from generation to generation have an incomparable flavor.

Although many heirloom varieties are available from seed companies, one of the best ways to acquire seeds it to save them yourself and exchange with friends. Seed saving can be done with open-pollinated new varieties (though not for hybrids). It is an easy and uncomplicated process. First, choose a particularly healthy and vigorous plant; observe the foliage, size of fruit, productivity, resistance to insects and disease. Allow the plant to ripen fully, and remove the seeds. Seeds from fleshy vegetables should be separated and allowed to dry on paper towels; seeds from pods can be allowed to dry in their pods. Seeds should be cleaned by "winnowing," tossing the seeds in a shallow basin with holes that are big enough for dust particles, but not seeds, to pass through. Dry, clean seeds should be kept in airtight storage containers. Keep accurate records of what you've saved.

If you are interested in preserving a specific variety, it is important to prevent cross-pollination with other varieties that might overwhelm it. Some gardeners find it useful to segregate plants that they are raising for seed so that they can control cross-pollination.

Above: An heirloom tomato.
Some sources of information and seeds:
• Seed Savers Exchange, Route 3, Box 239, Decorah, Iowa 52101
• Native Seeds/SEARCH, 2509 N. Campbell Avenue, #325, Tucson, Arizona 85719
• Heritage Seed Program, RR3, Uxbridge, ONT Canada L9P 1R3
• Mount Vernon, Mount Vernon, Virginia 22121
• Abundant Life Seed Foundation, PO Box 772, Port Townsend, Washington 98368
• D. Landreth Seed Company, Leadenhall and Ostend Streets, Baltimore, Maryland 21230
• Seeds of Change, 1364 Rufina Circle, #5, Santa Fe, New Mexico 87501

acidic soil: Soil with a pH below 7.0; most vegetables do best in a slightly acid soil, around 6.5.

alkaline soil: Soil with a pH above 7.0.

annual: A plant that lives for only one year or one growing season.

biennial: A plant that lives for two years or growing seasons, producing leaves the first season and flowers and seeds the second.

blanching: Process of whitening a plant's leaves, stem, or shoots by excluding light—e.g., by covering with soil.

bolting: Going to seed, especially prematurely.

bonemeal: Ground and crushed bones used as an organic fertilizer; high in phosphorus.

broadcasting: Scattering seed, fertilizer, or other materials over a large area instead of placing in specific rows or planting holes.

Bt: *Bacillus thuringiensis,* a bacteria that attacks and kills many common garden pests; can be bought by the pound.

bulb: Encased leaf or flower bud, as an onion or tulip.

chlorophyll: Green coloring matter in plants, essential to photosynthesis.

clay soil: Soil composed of many very fine particles, sticky when wet but hard when dry; water and air have a hard time moving through clay soil.

cloche: Portable plastic cover used to protect plants from cold.

cold frame: A low frame or box on the ground with a light-transmitting cover that protects young plants from frost and helps transplants harden off.

companion planting: Practice of planting different plants near each other for their helpful effects, such as shading or repelling insects.

compost: Decomposed plant material that adds nutrients to the soil and improves soil composition.

cover crops: Shallow-rooted plants grown close together to cover the soil and prevent erosion when the garden would otherwise be empty; tilled under, they add nutrients to the soil.

crop rotation: Moving vegetables to different garden sites in successive years, to help deter pests and disease.

crown: The section of a plant where stem and root meet; the topmost part of a root system, from which the leaves and shoots emerge.

cultivar: A variety of a plant that has been created by human intervention rather than naturally.

cultivation: Stirring of the soil surface to eliminate the weeds, aerate the soil, and promote water absorption.

cutting: Part of a plant (stem, leaf, root) cut off and then rooted to form a new plant.

direct seeding: Sowing seed directly into the garden rather than starting seeds indoors.

drainage: The ability of the soil to move water so the roots of the plant don't become waterlogged, and so nutrients move through the soil.

fertilizer: Any material that supplies nutrients to plants.

flat: A shallow container in which seedlings are started.

floating row covers: Commercially available covers, in many sizes, used to protect young plants from frost, sun, and wind and maturing plants from insects and birds; the covers can be easily removed and folded for storage.

floret: One of the individual, closely growing small flowers that make up a dense flower cluster, as a broccoli head.

friable: Term for soil that easily breaks apart or crumbles when handled.

fungicide: A product that kills disease-causing fungi.

germination: The beginning of plant growth from a seed.

greensand: Sea deposits used as an organic fertilizer, a good source of potassium.

harden off: The process of gradually accustoming a young, indoor-started plant to the outdoors.

hilling: Growing plants in raised mounds, as squash; the process of pulling soil up around stems or roots of a plant, as potatoes or corn.

humus: Decayed organic matter, black and crumbly, that improves soil texture and moisture retention.

hybrid: A plant created by crossbreeding two or more different plants.

insecticide: A product that kills insects.

intensive gardening: A method of gardening that uses every inch of the garden to the greatest extent possible.

interplanting: The practice of planting small, quick-growing plants like lettuce in the space between larger, slower-maturing plants like corn.

leaching: The loss of nutrients as water drains down through the soil.

loam: The best garden soil, a balanced mix of silt, sand, and clay.

manure: Livestock dung used as an organic fertilizer, rich in nitrogen.

mulch: Any material spread on the soil surface to conserve moisture, check weed growth, and protect the plant from excessive heat or cold.

nitrogen: One of the three most important plant nutrients, needed for production of leaves and stems

nutrients: Elements in the soil absorbed by plants for growth.

open-pollinated: Pollinated by the wind or animals, not by human manipulation.

organic gardening: Practice of gardening without the use of synthetic chemicals.

organic matter: Part of the soil that consists of decayed or decaying plant and animal matter (humus).

ornamental: A plant grown mainly for its attractive appearance.

peat: Decayed remains of ancient plants, added to soil to increase the soil's ability to absorb and hold moisture.

peat pot: A small molded pot made of peat, used to start seeds; plant and pot are transplanted together into the garden.

perennial: A plant that lives for more than two years.

pesticide: A product that kills garden pests.

petiole: Leaf stem or stalk.

pH: A measure of the acidity or alkalinity of the soil, on a scale of 1 (extremely acid) to 14 (extremely alkaline), with 7.0 being neutral. Vegetables grow best at a pH between 6.5 and 7.0.

phosphorus: One of the three most important plant nutrients; good organic sources are bonemeal and powdered rock phosphate.

photosynthesis: Process by which plants capture energy from the sun and convert it into compounds that fuel growth and life.

pinching: Snipping back of new growth, to keep plants compact and encourage bushiness.

pollination: The movement of pollen from one flower to another, necessary for fertilization and therefore fruit production.

potassium: One of the three most important plant nutrients; good organic sources are greensand and small amounts of wood ashes.

pruning: Removal of dead or living plant parts, to improve the plant's form or increase fruit or flower production.

pyrethrum: A biological insecticide, made from dried plants.

raised bed: Elevated soil bed used to improve drainage and create a garden from imported soil.

rootbound (also **potbound**): Condition of a pot-grown seedling or plant whose root ball is thickly matted and contains little soil.

rotenone: A biological insecticide, made from ground roots of tropical plants.

sandy soil: Soil with a high percentage of sand, or large soil particles; water travels through sandy soil very easily, so nutrients leach out quickly.

seedling: A young plant, especially one grown from seed.

set (fruit): develop fruit or seeds after pollination.

set out: Plant a seedling in the garden.

side-dress: Apply fertilizer along a seed row or around a plant or hill.

soil test: Analysis of the soil to determine its pH and available nutrients.

succession planting: Process of planting a new crop as soon as the earlier one is harvested.

sucker: Leafy shoot at a stem junction.

thinning: Pulling up or pinching out young plants so remaining plants have room to grow and mature.

till: Cultivate the soil, especially with a mechanical tiller.

topsoil: Dark surface layer of the soil that contains organic matter and supports plant life.

trace elements: Soil compounds essential to plant growth and development but present and needed in only very small amounts.

transplant: Move a plant to another location; also, the plant so moved.

trellis: Latticework frame that supports vining or climbing plants.

true leaves: The leaves that appear after the first, or seed, set of leaves.

tuber: A short, naturally swollen underground stem, as a potato.

vegetable: As commonly understood, the edible portion of a plant, or a plant grown for its edible parts.

virus: A ultramicroscopic disease-causing organism.

SEED COMPANIES

Abundant Life Seed Foundation
PO Box 772
Port Townsend, WA 98368
206-385-5660

Agway, Inc. Seed Division
PO Box 4933
Syracuse, NY 13221

Bountiful Gardens
18001 Shafer Ranch Road
Willits, CA 95490
707-459-6410

Bonanza Seed International
PO Box V
Gilroy, CA 95020

Burgess Seed and Plant Company
905 Four Seasons Road
Bloomington, IL 61701
309-663-9551

W. Atlee Burpee & Co.
300 Park Avenue
Warminster, PA 18974
215-674-4915

D.V. Burrell Seed Growers
PO Box 150
Rocky Ford, CO 81067
719-254-3318

Companion Plants
PO Box 88
Athens, Ohio 47501
614-592-4643

The Cook's Garden
PO Box 535
Londonderry, Vermont 05148
802-824-3400

Crockett Seed Company
PO Box 237
Metamora, OH 43540

Cruickshank's, Inc.
1015 Mount Pleasant Road
Toronto, Ontario, Canada
M4P 2M1
416-488-8292

DeGiorgi Seed Co.
6011 N Street
Omaha, NE 68117
402-731-3901

Earl May Seed and Nursery
Shenandoah, IA 51603
800-432-5858 (Iowa)
800-831-4193

Ecology Action
5798 Ridgewood Road

G.S. Grimes Seeds
201 West Main Street
Smethport, PA 16749

Gurney's Seed & Nursery
110 Capitol
Yankton, SD 57079
605-665-1930

Harris Moran Seed Co.
60-A Saginaw Drive
Rochester, New York 14623
716-442-6910

Harris Moran Seed Co.
1155 Harkins Road
Salinas, CA 93901

C.C. Hart Seed Company
304 Main Street
Box 9169
Wethersfield, CT 06109
203-529-2537

H.G. Hastings Company
1036 White Street SW
PO Box 115535
Atlanta, Georgia 30310
404-755-6580

Henry Field's Seed and Nursery Co.
415 N. Burnett Street
Shenandoah, IA 51602
605-665-9391

High Altitude Gardens
PO Box 1048
Hailey, ID 83333

Horticultural Enterprises
PO Box 810082
Dallas, TX 75381

Ed Hume Seeds
PO Box 1450
Kent WA 98035
206-859-1110

J.L. Hudson, Seedsman
PO Box 1058
Redwood, CA 94064

Jackson & Perkins
1 Rose Lane
Medford, OR 97501
503-776-2000

Johnny's Selected Seed
305 Foss Hill Road
Albion, Maine 04910
207-437-4301

Jung Seeds and Nursery
335 S. High Street
Randolph, WI 53957
414-326-3121

N.K. Lawn and Gardens
7500 Olson Memorial Highway
Golden Valley, Minnesota 55427
800-328-2402

Orol Ledden & Sons
Centre and Atlantic Avenues
PO Box 7
Sewell, New Jersey 08080
609-468-1000

Le Jardin du Gourmet
PO Box 275G
St. Johnsbury Center, Vermont 05863
802-748-1446

Le Marche Seeds International
PO Box 190
Dixon, CA 95620
916-678-9244

Liberty Seed Company
PO Box 806
New Philadelphia, OH 44663
216-364-1611

The Meyer Seed Co.
600 S. Carolina Street
Baltimore, MD 21231
410-342-4224

Midwest Seed Growers
10559 Lackman Street
Lenexa, Kansas 66219
913-894-0050

J.E. Miller Nurseries
5060 W. Lake Street
Canandaiugua, NY 14424
716-396-2647

Native Seeds/SEARCH
2509 N. Campbell, #325
Tucson, AZ 95719

Nichols Garden Nursery
1190 North Pacific Highway
Albany, OR 97321
503-928-9280

North Star Gardens
19060 Manning Trail N.
Marine-on-St. Croix, MN 55047
612-433-5850

Nourse Farms
41 River Road
South Deerfield, MA 01373
413-665-2658

Park Seed Company
Cokesbury Road
Greenwood, SC 29467
803-223-7333

The Pepper Gal
10536 119th Avenue
Largo, FL 34643

Peter Pepper Seeds
PO Box 415
Knoxville, TN 37901

Piedmont Plant Co.
PO Box 424
Albany, GA 31702
912-883-7029

Pinetree Garden Seeds
PO Box 300
New Gloucester, ME 04260
207-926-3400

Plants of the Southwest
Agua Fria Road
Route 6
PO Box 11A
Santa Fe, NM 87501

Redwood City Seed Co.
PO Box 361
Redwood City, CA 94064
415-325-7333

Ronniger's Seed Potatoes
Star Route
Moyie Springs, ID 83845

Sandy Mush Herb Nursery
316 Surrett Cove Road
Leicester, NC 28748
704-683-2014

Seeds Blum
Idaho City Stage
Boise, ID 83706
208-342-0858

Seeds of Change
621 Old Santa Fe Trail
Suite 10
Santa Fe, NM 88038
505-983-8956

Seed Savers Exchange
Box 239
Decorah, IA 52101

Sheperd's Garden Seeds
7389 West Zayante Road
Felton CA 95018
408-335-5400
30 Irene Street
Torrington, CT 06790

Southern Exposure Seed Exchange
PO Box 158
North Garden, VA 22959
804-973-4703

Southmeadow Fruit Gardens
2363 Tilbury Place
Birmingham, MI 48009

Stark Bros.
Highway 54
Louisiana, MO 63353

Stokes Seed Co.
183-185 E. Main Street
PO Box 180
Fredonia, NY 14063
716-672-8844

Sunrise Enterprises
PO Box 330058
W. Hartford, CT 06133
203-666-8071

Talavaya Seeds
Po Box 707
Santa Cruz Station
Santa Cruz, NM 87507

Territorial Seed Co.
PO Box 157
Cottage Grove, OR 97424
503-942-9547

Thompson & Morgan
PO Box 1308
Jackson, NY 08527
201-363-2225

The Tomato Seed Company, Inc.
PO Box 323
Metuchen, NJ 08840

Twilley Seeds
PO Box 65
Trevose, PA 19053

Vermont Bean Seed Co.
Garden Lane
Fair Haven, VT 05743
802-273-3400

Wilhite Seed Company
PO Box 23
Poolville, TX 76487
817-599-8646

Wyatt-Quarles Seed Co.
PO Box 739
Garner, NC 27529
919-772-4243

MAGAZINES

The Avant Gardener
PO Box 489
NY, NY 10028
(newsletter, bimonthly)

Fine Gardening
Taunton Press
PO Box 5509
Newton, CT 06470
(monthly magazine)

Flower and Garden Magazine
4251 Pennsylvania Avenue
Kansas City, MO 64111
(monthly magazine)

Horticulture
300 Massachusetts Avenue
Boston, MA 02115
(monthly magazine)

National Gardening
National Gardening Association
180 Flynn Avenue
Burlington, VT 05401

Organic Gardening and Farming
Organic Park
Emmaus, PA 18049
(monthly magazine)

LEAF SHAPES

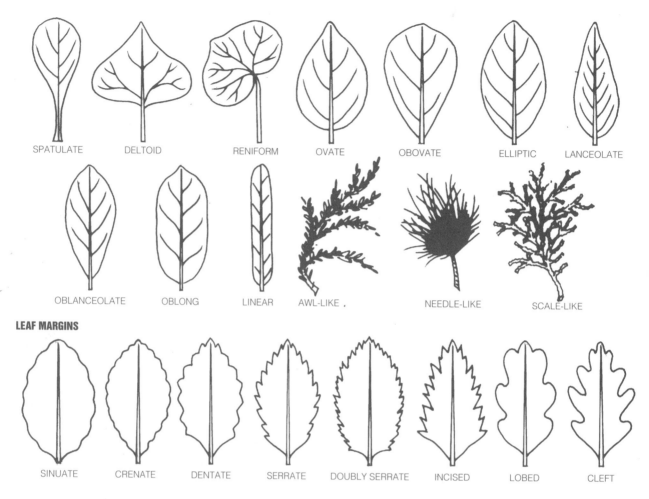

SPATULATE   DELTOID   RENIFORM   OVATE   OBOVATE   ELLIPTIC   LANCEOLATE

OBLANCEOLATE   OBLONG   LINEAR   AWL-LIKE   NEEDLE-LIKE   SCALE-LIKE

LEAF MARGINS

SINUATE   CRENATE   DENTATE   SERRATE   DOUBLY SERRATE   INCISED   LOBED   CLEFT

LEAF ARRANGEMENTS AND STRUCTURES

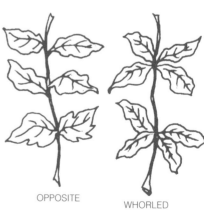

SIMPLE   PALMATE   COMPOUND BIPINNATE   ALTERNATE   OPPOSITE   WHORLED